THE
GENTLEMANLY SERPENT

The New *Island Packet* Building,
Hilton Head Island, South Carolina

The Gentlemanly
Serpent *and Other Columns*
from a Newspaperman in Paradise

BY JONATHAN DANIELS

From the Pages of the Hilton Head
Island Packet, 1970–73

Edited by RALPH HILTON

With a Foreword by
Elizabeth Boatwright Coker

UNIVERSITY OF SOUTH CAROLINA PRESS
COLUMBIA, SOUTH CAROLINA

Copyright © University of South Carolina Press 1974

First Edition

Published in Columbia, S.C., by the University of South Carolina Press, 1974

Manufactured in the United States of America

Marylyn Maxham (Mermade) graciously consented to the use in this book of many of her editorial cartoons, which have delighted readers of *The Island Packet* since its second issue (July 16, 1970).

Library of Congress Cataloging in Publication Data

Daniels, Jonathan, 1902–
The gentlemanly serpent and other columns from a
newspaperman in paradise.

Includes index.
1. Hilton Head Island—Description and travel—
Addresses, essays, lectures. 2. Hilton Head Island—
History—Addresses, essays, lectures. I. Title.
F277.B3D36   917.57'99   74–22077
ISBN 0–87249–319–9

Contents

Contents   vii

Contents ix

Foreword

It is not easy to discover when Jonathan Daniels first became aware of Hilton Head Island or when Hilton Head Island became aware of Jonathan Daniels. The certainty is that the combination of old Jonathan and the recently awakened island will not soon be forgotten in the story of the interlaced land and water of the golden shores of South Carolina and Georgia.

With few of the attributes of the hermit, Daniels, as a less-solemn philosopher than Thoreau, has never quite regarded Broad Creek, Calibogue Sound, or even the Atlantic Ocean as his Walden Pond. He has built no hut, planted no herbs. No Crusoe either, the black men and women Fridays he requires wear neat uniforms at the bars and tables where they serve incandescently clothed ladies and gentlemen of this manicured wilderness. The general opinion is that Jonathan communes with nature through the plate-glass windows of air-conditioned rooms. Some of his readers were both dubious and delighted when he described a sunrise. He takes his exercise by watching others at play. An ardent ecologist, the environment he chiefly guards is his own happy situation. Though he is devoted to the magic isle he has found, the multiplying neighbors around him are not sure whether his role upon it is that of Prospero or Caliban.

Strangely, research into the life of the man discloses early distaste for the shore to which he is now devoted. He first set foot on the island in the autumn of 1961. A quarter of a century before that he had traversed the region as self-described discoverer. Although he already considered himself middle-aged at that time, Daniels was only at the beginning of a crowded career. In the following years he became a widely quoted newspaper editor, the author of a score of well-received books, a Democratic national committeeman, Press Secretary to President Franklin Delano Roosevelt, and an adviser who traveled with President Harry S. Truman in the 1948 campaign.

His friend Vermont Royster, former editor of *The Wall Street Journal*, once described Jonathan as "a journalist by trade, a novelist by dream, an iconoclast by habit, and a philosopher in spite of himself." Jonathan wrote Vermont that he would accept that statement as his epitaph if he might add "a politician by accident." Now above all he is an islander by determination, despite his insistent pretense that he is only a "sojourner" on Hilton Head Island.

The distaste for this southern shore which he expressed on the earlier journey along it was written in a younger man's mood which combined sociology, pity, applause, hilarity, and exuberance. Together they made an American travel classic, recently reprinted with a new preface in mellow retrospect. *A Southerner Discovers the South* (1938) he called it. Hereabouts, as he moved discovering, he regarded "the winter islands of the millionaires" as irrelevant to the picture of the South. He was more concerned with the terrible disease of "coastalitis" which made the shore behind the islands "in all reality a land without hope" for both the black and the white poor. Hope there remains strictly limited still. But seaward from a still too stagnant mainland the "winter islands" and summer ones, too, now have flourished, with Hilton Head leading the procession. There seems no limit to "millionaires" in settlement—or at least to those who nowadays, often by compact to condominium, make a reasonable facsimile thereof.

With his conscience still acutely aware of such contrasts, it seems strange that Jonathan joined the stream to this island which was suddenly developed in the 1950s after a century of somnolence with no bridge and rarely a ferry connecting it to the South Carolina shore. Indeed, he might have seemed the last to be expected to cross the bridge when it was belatedly opened to make the island in reality a part of the poor but proud South Carolina Low Country. As a man from North Carolina, where few great plantations ever rang with slave song in the moonlit Southern past, Jonathan was known to cherish the impertinent epigram that his state was a vale of humility between two mountains of conceit. Not absolutely humble himself, Jonathan elaborated on that jibe at the pretensions of Virginia by describing the Old Dominion as "the cradle and the grave of democracy."

South Carolina he characterized in more personal terms. After his marriage to a lady of South Carolina antecedents, he was taken

to the Palmetto State to be presented to her kin. Legend in the
Cathcart family to which his lovely Lucy belonged had it that her
grandfather as a lad too young for arms still performed dramatic
service. As a messenger in the infancy of the telegraph, he carried
communications between militant Confederates and the besieged
Yankees in Fort Sumter. Though that seemed an odd pre-radio
arrangement, Daniels allowed himself to be properly impressed.
But when he was safely back in North Carolina he expressed his
sentiments.

"Lucy," he said, "I have discovered that there are only two kinds
of South Carolinians. One kind never has worn shoes and the other
kind makes you feel like you've never worn shoes."

His next return to the state after that episode in enlightenment
was a movement more in research than geography. In a book called
Prince of Carpetbaggers, he went vicariously to Hilton Head for the first
time in the biography of a notorious Yankee "Bummer." This
charming and predatory rogue, General Milton S. Littlefield, was
first sent to the area by President Lincoln to organize regiments of
black soldiers on this island, which was the depot for supplying the
great Union blockade fleet. Littlefield well performed that congenial enterprise, which included picking up bounties for black soldiers
as substitutes for some whites in the North who had no hankering
to go to war. Then he stayed in the South in the fetid politics of
Reconstruction. He picked up some Southern State bonds and some
pieces of railroads at larcenously low rates. He and several thousand
other Yankees, however, also took North with them from Hilton
Head honestly acquired precious memories of the magic isles.

Their magic remained. Beginning at the end of the 1950s other
definitely less hostile Yankees began to make a beachhead on Hilton
Head Island. They made a third kind of South Carolinian in addition to the two kinds Daniels had found years before. In their delight
with the island to which they moved, they became almost instant
aborigines. The first happy troop of them had already settled
around golf courses where drill fields had once been when Daniels
came to the island for the first time almost by accident and for a
weekend which has now stretched into more than a dozen years.

Then not quite sixty, Daniels eagerly confronted the terrain which
had underlain the documents he had studied. While he went around
inquiring about the scene of history of which he had written, Lucy

was buying building lots. As a slightly startled antiquarian, he pointed out to her that the land she purchased was located within the bounds of a former plantation called Old Woman's Folly. Not disturbed, Lucy built first on Piping Plover Road. Then she purchased the place on Calibogue Cay. She bought it from a lady whose building plans had been changed by the death of her husband, for a sum which as land prices fabulously rose left Lucy open to the charge that she had stolen it from a little widow woman. Imperturbed, Lucy built again.

So beginning in 1961 the Danielses came regularly to the island. But Jonathan still had his job as editor of *The News and Observer* in Raleigh. He was, he said, "sneaking into senility." He continued to write of matters far from the island. However, never one to overlook imperfections in paradise, about 1963 he lightly turned his indignation into verses about sticky asphalt walkways to the beach which, melting in the subtropic sun, resulted in footprints, as visible as Friday's in the sand, on rugs and carpeting in the houses. Possibly victory for concrete in this crusade aroused the old editor to other causes. Seeing early the dangers of sylvan sprawl, he wrote his now much mimeographed poem, "Condominium, the Gem of the Ocean." It must be said candidly that that was a sort of King Canute enterprise. The villas, cabanas, condominiums, cluster homes, even Sealofts for tree-tall dwelling multiplied around him. Unintimidated, he turned to prose in *The Island Bulletin,* a weekly mimeographed sheet produced by the island's women's association. This time he inveighed against the sudden appearance of many gleaming white portable latrines on building sites where once luxuriant flora had sufficed. Recognizing the necessity of such necessaries, he only proposed that aesthetics be served as well as sanitation by altering the color of these roadside marble-like monuments to human need—maybe changing them to cypress or perhaps avocado. The power of the pen failed again. The bucktoothed backhouses sat in greater and greater numbers before the multiplying condominiums.

In the face of such discouragements any other man might have become mute. But suddenly circumstances intervened. The amateur journalists of the women's association were wearying of their task in the publication of *The Island Bulletin.* And Ralph Hilton, former newspaperman and foreign service officer, was restless in retirement. He sought backers for a weekly newspaper. But a first

fairly large group to whom Hilton outlined his plan was skeptical
to a point which Hilton regarded as insulting. He found one man
ready to help back the enterprise in Thomas Wamsley, a real estate
salesman, innocent of journalistic experience but young, energetic,
and sanguine. Then one day at the Port Royal Inn, Hilton ran into
Lucy and Jonathan, who were having lunch there. By this time
Jonathan had become "editor emeritus" in Raleigh, but he still had
books in process on Calibogue Cay, where he and Lucy keep two
electric typewriters going. The Danielses listened to Hilton's hopes.
Lucy had money to invest (a pittance in the parlance of most modern publishers). And Jonathan said suddenly, perhaps inspired by
his martini, "I'll be glad to write a column every week." The wonder
is that Lucy did not lose her enthusiasm then. One of her discoveries
in a long married life is that Jonathan will promise to meet any
deadline as much as a week away.

The upshot was that the women's association happily presented
its *Bulletin* as a free gift to the entrepreneurs. It had four hundred
paid subscribers and a broken-down mimeograph machine. Hilton
not only came up with the paper's name, *The Island Packet,* but he
found a silhouette of such a vessel with smoke billowing behind it,
for its masthead. Jonathan wrote the paper's salute to its expectant
readers. The first issue, ready for the printshop up the road in
Walterboro, was produced in a single room 8 X 11. That issue,
replete with typographical errors and words hyphenated at wild
random, was loaded with the welcoming advertisements of island
business firms. It is a collector's item now. The subscriptions rolled
in. Today the paper with over 5,000 paid readers has its own building on the island's main avenue on a site between a golf green and
a lagoon. And Jonathan, despite Lucy's forebodings, has met his
deadline every week.

His pieces have ranged from the sentimental to the hilarious, and
also from the wise to the occasionally wrathful. His neighbors appear as characters in them and as characters who would be recogniz-
able in all developing island resorts. Hilton Head's first developers,
Charles Fraser and Fred Hack, wiser and more ecology-minded than
many other developers, are still figures who could fit into other
scenes from the isles of Casco Bay to the keys of Florida—and in
California and on the ski slopes too. Wilbert Roller the liquor dealer
and Louis McKibben the grocer, Norris Richardson, who still per-

sonally runs his Laundromat despite the soaring value of his shopping center, are personages who would fit into the cast of characters of any other island. And as condominiums might be shifted—like pieces in a Monopoly game—without much changing the scene from island to island, so might their occupants. Jonathan has written not merely about his neighbors, rich and poor, black and white, on Hilton Head but about islanders everywhere.

As one who has read all of his pieces, from the launching of *The Island Packet* to the present, I can speak for hundreds of others who have been delighted by them. They go weekly like letters from a well-loved island to those enamored of this one and all islands in every part of the United States and to many places overseas. With other readers of *The Island Packet* I am delighted that the pieces will now be available in permanent form.

The hope is that Jonathan will be long available. Certainly, at this point, he seems a durable septuagenarian. Maybe American daily journalism and American politics lost much when a few years ago he took, as he says, an oath on the altar of God never to cross the Potomac River again. Now sometimes he says he is ready to modify that oath to Skull Creek, which divides this island from the mainland. Oddly enough, after a crowded career he finds this island world enough for any man. Certainly he seems to me to have found the proper potation for a senior citizen (a term at which he snarls): salt water and printer's ink with enough bourbon added to provide eternal insurance against snakebite. Reading these pieces is like sharing such a draught with him in the hours before sunset on his terrace overlooking the orchestrated changes in the green and gold marshes along Broad Creek and Calibogue Sound.

Finally I salute old, forever young Jonathan with lines which another light essayist, Joseph Addison, translated from the Latin or pretended that he did:

> In all thy humours, whether grave or mellow,
> Thou'rt such a touchy, testy, pleasant fellow,
> Hast so much wit and mirth and spleen about thee,
> There is no living with thee, nor without thee.

Elizabeth Boatwright Coker
Hartsville, South Carolina

THE
GENTLEMANLY SERPENT

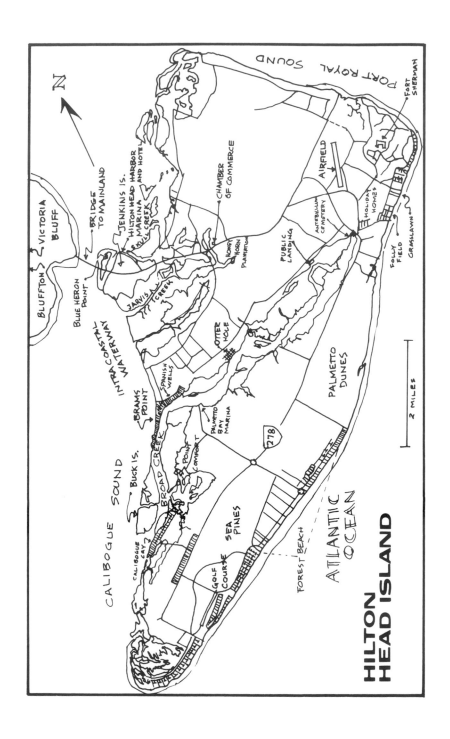

HILTON HEAD ISLAND

The Launching of *The Packet*

They went to sea in a sieve, they did;
   In a sieve they went to sea. . . .
And when the sieve turned round and round,
And everyone cried, "You'll all be drowned!"
They called aloud, "Our sieve ain't big,
But we don't care a button; we don't care a fig—
   In a sieve we'll go to sea!"

That verse about the Jumblies by Edward Lear may be a proper anthem for this occasion. Few, even of those who have his bird prints hanging on their walls in congenial company with those of Audubon and Catesby, realize that Lear was noted not only for his nonsense verse but also for his beautiful and scientifically accurate paintings of birds, sometimes in collaboration with the famous naturalist John Gould. So, as serious reporter of plumed loveliness, who still possessed the comic touch, his spirit seems one meriting evocation now. The verse above is more appropriate to this island-faring newspaper enterprise today than another oceanic lyric which he wrote:

3

> The Owl and the Pussy-Cat went to sea
> In a beautiful pea-green boat;
> They took some honey, and plenty of money
> Wrapped up in a five-pound note.

The crew of *The Packet* hopes to bring honey, but money is exactly what they haven't got. *The Packet* breasts the seas with a shoestring for a sail. Still, as Mr. Lear's Jumblies did in their voyage by sieve, we hope to take our readers "to a land all covered with trees" and bring them "an owl, and a useful cart, and a pound of rice, and a cranberry-tart." We may bring them "a pig, and some green jackdaws, And a lovely monkey with lollipop paws, and forty bottles of ring-bo-ree, and no end of Stilton cheese."

That at least suggests the variety we hope to put into our weekly cargo. We are, however, not addicted to the fantastic. We hope to give the Hilton Head colony and colonies of island-minded people everywhere the news this island needs in a paper which, while first concerned with this neighborhood, will have a flavor appealing to all people to whom islands are dreams as well as real estate.

Out model reader on this island, where many of us have passed puberty, is certainly not going to be Whistler's mother. We mean to be no organ of barely breathing Senior Citizens. Let those who will celebrate the "golden years." We prefer mermaids or merladies who know the tragedy of the Rhine and other rivers, who study with the Coast Guard and respect the sailfish and the amberjack, but who also know how to wear Park Avenue clothes as if they were the garb of fishermen's sweethearts. We hope to caddy for mermen who are getting out of the gray flannel suits in belated understanding that men can join the birds in emulation of the male's more brilliant plumage. We are passionately for ecology but sometimes appalled by its vocabulary.

We certainly do not mean to be concerned merely with those decorative people who constitute the chorus of rising decibels on what has been impertinently called Cirrhosis Shores. If there be, as some have sharply said, "fat cats" on this island, there are lean ones, too, many of whom have a better right to be called Hilton Headers. The cocktail circuit deserves no more attention than the run-around in which too many have too long been only invited to participate. Happiness on Hilton Head is something to be eternally sought not merely up the landscaped drive but down the most weed-grown, unpaved road. A land of milk and honey cannot be one of cocktails and canapes for some and 'pone and popskull for the rest. A magic isle must be concerned with the cockleburr as well as the camellia, the serpent as well as the apple.

To speak solemnly once as to our editorial position: Our purpose will not be so much to save the world as to guard its islands, not all of which have to be surrounded by water. As to politics, our position will be much like that of the girl who said she had only been kissed by two parties—the Democrats and the Republicans. We honor all those whose imagination and hazard, too, have parted the jungle here to let us in where sleeping beauty lay so long behind the briars. We can best help them and all those whom they piped to pleasure by being tied to nobody's apron strings. We hope to write colloquially, as members of the family, and we trust not too often with the tartness which sometimes accompanies family conversations. But we reserve the family right of uproar when required.

Finally, this voyage in a sieve or a beautiful pea-green boat is going to require not only careful navigation by the crew but also some aid and encouragement from the shore. We welcome—we are going to need—comments, contributions, even complaints. Also charity!

We hope that like the Owl and the Pussy-cat of our drafted patron Mr. Lear, if not like his more adventurous Jumblies in the sieve, we can: "hand in hand, on the edge of the sand . . . dance by the light of the moon, the moon, the moon, we can dance by the light of the moon." Or at least by the phosphorescent glow we hope to provide in lieu of any lighthouse, real or architectural.

Cast off!

July 9, 1970

Sojourner's Entrance

The grapevine groweth.

And I am pleased that Ralph Hilton and Tom Wamsley have invited me, as frequent and enamored visitor to Hilton Head, to swing upon it every now and then.

Like everything else, communications have moved fast and forward on this magic island. Certainly the grapevine did not suffice as a means of spreading the news back in the old, old days. In the great hurricane of 1893, hundreds in the island's environs were drowned who had not dreamed they were in danger. It has never been quite that bad in the memory of present islanders. Radio and TV make it possible for them to know everything that is happening in the world but practically nothing about what is going on here on Hilton Head.

A decade ago the new pioneers were not entirely dependent on the grapevine. But when my Lucy bought on Piping Plover Road back in 1961, communications were limited. I don't remember how it was at Port Royal Plantation and on Brams Point, but in Sea Pines the phone lines ran south only as far as the Beach Lagoon roads. Where Palmetto Dunes now spreads, communication was only by bird song, owl hoot, and alligator roar. Sometimes the limited phone service seemed little better than smoke signals in a high wind. Under Ellen and Larry Rogers and now Jim Littlejohn *The Islander* satisfied—and satisfies—a lot of curiosity once a month. Helen Brooks and a corps of other ladies have given us more frequent reports.

Still, the other day my neighbor Gus Watters had a lot of news to tell. I asked him where he heard it. In the dentist chair, he said. Undoubtedly Dr. Joe List may provide a good news service and fill the cavity of information while he packs in the amalgam. But it ought not to be necessary to have a mouthful of instruments to find out what is going on. Neither the medical center nor the beauty parlors nor the barbershop nor the grocery store quite suffice as media. So there should be a real welcome for *The Island Packet*.

There is more news to report as there are more of us. The day when you could put the whole resort population at one cocktail party has passed. The decibels grow higher but not clearer. Times have changed even around the earliest of those who were beckoned here by such solid sirens as Charles Fraser and Fred Hack. We grow more formal even in our relaxation. The tuxedo and the mink stole are no longer intruders. We've been here long enough to have our own items of nostalgia. I even have an authentic letter, *circa* 1962, signed "Charlie," not "Charles." Sometimes firstcomers here have regarded themselves as the elite. Often people who had been here six years thought of themselves as like Charlestonians, who have been there three hundred. That changes, too. Increasingly, as land prices rise, the First Families of Hilton Head are those who couldn't be here at all if they hadn't come early.

More change is coming. Possibly BASF,* viewed as a dark Leviathan soiling waters and breathing fumes, may be put to flight. Possibly such a proposed substitute as a "Six Flags Over South Carolina" tourist attraction, which would need five thousand attendants to care for the visitors, might be pollution-free, though it could be flung-beer-can-prone. A sports equipment industry center, making the gadgets of recreation, might prove play triumphant over poverty.

Here we all need to be pessimists enough to guard our optimism

* Badische Anilin Soda Fabrik, a German enterprise which in 1970 was contemplating the establishment of a large petrochemical complex at nearby Victoria Bluff.

about the future. But we don't need to become the claque of the prophets of doom. I believe this island's charm is ancient and eternal. Of the first I am sure. The most appealing brochures about this lovely country were written long before Charles Fraser, Fred Hack, and Bill Gregory began to produce theirs in technicolor.

Before I first visited the island I had read two such accounts, which have never been bested. Charlotte Forten, the lovely and perceptive mulatto from Philadelphia, who came here in 1862 to teach the little freed children, wrote one. She put a passage in her now-famous journal about a horseback ride through the sea-island country: "first through an avenue of beautiful trees—mostly live oaks draped with moss—and then for miles through the Pine Barrens. The air was soft, Italian, only a faint murmur could be heard among the pines,—hardly 'the sound of the sea.' The ground was thickly carpeted with ferns of a most delicious green, and to crown all we found Azaleas of a deep pink color and perfect fragrance. Found also sand violets, very large purple ones, and some kind of grass which bears an exquisite fine white flower, some of the petals tinged with a delicate lilac. . . . The brightest and most delightful experience must come to an end, and at last too soon we emerged from the Pine Barrens and came out into the shell road. It was like leaving Paradise."

Another such passage on perfection was sent home from this country by Abraham Lincoln's private secretary, John Hay. He wrote a White House colleague in April 1863: "I wish you could be down here. You would enjoy it beyond measure. The air is like June at noon and like May at morning and evening. The scenery is tropical. The sunsets unlike anything I ever saw before . . . singularly quiet and solemn. The sun goes down over the pines through a sky like ashes of roses, and hangs for an instant on the horizon like a bubble of blood. Then there is twilight such as you dream about."

Those sunsets will be here for a while. Certainly I count upon them beyond my terrace on Calibogue. And I count on *The Island Packet* to tell all that happens on this island under its sun.

July 9, 1970

So Fair a Shore

Whatever may be the fate of BASF in this age of ecology, the odds are against the enterprise in history. The Port Royal area was always about to be "developed" after the pattern of Charleston and Savannah—or Hoboken. Sadly or gladly, that didn't happen.

The first Europeans who saw this land wrote like port authority publicists. René Laudonnière, who came with Jean Ribaut in 1562, wrote that his "pinnesse," which had been driven up the coast before him, informed him of a "mightie River which in bignesse and beautie" exceeded one they had seen earlier: ". . . wherewithall the Captaine was exceeding joyfull, for his chiefs desire was to finde out an Haven to harbour his shippes, and there to refresh ourselves for a while. Thus making thitherward wee arrived athwart the sayde River, (which because of the fairnesse and largeness thereof wee named Port Royal) wee strooke our sailes and cast anker at ten fathom of water; for the depth is such, namely when the Sea beginneth to flowe, that the greatest shippes of France, yea, the Arguzes of Venice may enter there."

The expectation was aroused again by the occupying Yankees at the end of the Civil War. A soldiers' city had grown here "blooming

9

out in the most extravagant display of fancy lettered signs." An immense hotel was under construction to accommodate bustling Northern visitors coming on regularly plying vessels, which it was believed would be coming forever. A railroad was projected from Port Royal Sound to Branchville, South Carolina, connecting with "the whole railroad system of the South."

Whitelaw Reid, the young journalist who later became editor of the *New York Tribune,* wrote on a visit here then: "Everybody seemed possessed with a mania for speculation. That a great city must spring up hereabouts has been laid down as an axiom. This is the best harbor on the coast while that of Charleston is positively bad, and that of Savannah is contracted and not easy of access. Situated midway between the two, the speculators insist that it ought to fall legitimate heir to the trade of both. Besides, the Carolina sea-coast must have a seaport, and Charleston is so utterly ruined, they argue, and so odious to the nation that Northern trade and capital would discriminate against it, in favor of its younger rival."

Actually the Northerners who came turned out to be more interested in fish and game than industrial boom. Their "in-migration" lately has been one more intent upon beauty than urban sprawl. Those constituting it have brought more cash than chemicals. Most important they have brought a faith that a serene place is possible on a spoiled continent. I think history supports that faith. I hope the poet of the marshes, Sidney Lanier, was prophetic about this lovely Low Country when he wrote of sunrise in this region:

> Oh, never the mast-high run of the seas
>   Of traffic shall hide thee,
> Never the hell-colored smoke of the factories
>   Hide thee,
> Never the reek of the time's fen-politics
>   Hide thee,
> And ever my heart through the night shall with
>   knowledge abide thee,
> And ever by day shall my spirit, as one that
>   hath tried thee
> Labor, at leisure, in art,—till yonder beside thee
>   My soul shall float, friend Sun,
>   The day being done.

July 16, 1970

Fat Cat Island

"Fat cat" has been the noun and "plush" the adjective of those who undertook to suggest that newcomers of the last decade on Hilton Head have been only concerned for their own serenity and careless of the welfare of others. It is an easy legend to conjure up. Hilton Head is plush with guarded trees and the sleek spread of golf courses. And many of its houses are plush in terms of the beach cottages of the past. Air conditioning has been invented and is now peddled to the buyers of mobile homes.

We do live in an age in which onetime grudging bankers are now giving the impression that every man can have his own Aladdin's wonderful lamp in the form of a credit card. But the impression that Hilton Head is a compound of the overopulent needs some revision. Also it needs to be noted that some of those who have flung the word as an epithet at Hilton Headers are better heeled than most of the residents of the island.

The results of a questionnaire circulated on the island some time ago asking recipients to give their income brackets have never been reported. Perhaps they have never been found. But casual observation by the informed suggests that the number of the very rich even

11

in the most "plush" plantation houses is small. There are some palaces, but few. The great American fortunes are not represented in wide estates here. Most of the residents are people of moderate means, including many who have retired on strictly limited incomes. And the "plush" facilities are available to them only because they are open to everybody. The Plantation Club in Sea Pines undoubtedly looks like an establishment of the nabobs, but it is about as exclusive as Grand Central Station. The kind of condominiums built and building are based upon something like the slogan of the late Huey Long, "Every Man a King." What they promise is that, by clustering, any middle-class American can look like a millionaire.

Certainly the conventions which provide most of the push for the "plush" are not companies of the multi-rich. Rather, they are composed of congregations which could not gather except for expense accounts provided by their companies. Undoubtedly, many of the island's retired businessmen, service officers, and others are appalled by the mounting prices of the real estate around them. Many of those who came early could not have afforded to come late.

But what Hilton Head chiefly proves is that serenity can be assured in more places than Newport and Palm Beach. Families still find it necessary to work to supplement limited incomes. Some survive only in terms of Dean Swift's statement that they live by taking in each other's washing—as insurance men, building and loan promoters, assessors, real-estate salesmen. One man in a most "plush" area sells Christmas cards. An admiral is a haberdasher. The wife of a general clerks in an antique shop. So does the lady of a retired A. T. & T. executive. A onetime insurance big shot has worked as a golf-course ranger. Other "fat cats" are busy trying to make both ends meet.

But the greatest myth is that the "fat cats" of Hilton Head are not concerned about their less-fortunate neighbors. Undoubtedly the island has its share of the complacent, the selfish, and the unconcerned. But in terms of good works the "plantations" have a good record which at least matches those of other communities hereabouts.

Let those who are without sin cast the first nugget.

July 23, 1970

The Eternal Young

Summer increases the number of the young on Hilton Head. Some come bringing more helping hands, and others bring hands which more powerfully propel beer cans. Long locks have become more evident on the boys as well as the girls. Some grandparents are apologetic about the hair of their heirs. But, in a colony of the retired, the summer young add a decorative touch, like the flowers which arrived before them. They deserve more than fastidious commentary.

The young are not strangers to the island—nor are their ways. One of the best pictures of them in both fascination and revulsion was drawn as long ago as 1838. It does not seem out of date in 1970. Then Frances Anne Kemble, the popular actress, drew it in her journal. On her way to indignant observations of American Negro slavery on the vast sea-island plantations of her husband, Pierce Butler, she sailed along this shore. She made tart reports in her diary. Though only twenty-nine herself then, the famous Fanny seems to have been on the far side of the generation gap.

Coming down the coast in a not-very-seaworthy old boat, she stopped at Edisto Island, "famous for producing the finest cotton

13

in America." There she made a disdainful note: "While we were walking, a young man on horseback passed us, whose light hair, in a very picturesque contempt of modern fashion, absolutely flowed upon the collar of his coat, and was blown back as he rode, like the disheveled tresses of a woman. On Edisto Island such a noble exhibition of individuality would probably find few censors."

She herself was more censorious as she sailed on southward: "Our party, on leaving the island, had received an addition of some young ladies, who were to go ashore again in the middle of the night, at a stopping place called Hilton Head. As they did not intend to sleep, they seemed to have no idea of allowing anyone else to do so; and the giggling and chattering with which they enlivened the dreary watches of the night, certainly rendered anything like repose impossible; so I lay devoutly wishing for Hilton Head, where the boat stopped between one and two in the morning. I had just time to see our boarding-school angels leave us."

It is difficult to think that the young man who looked in 1838 like a hippie to Fannie would be too old in 1861 to ride in the cavalry of the Confederacy. Those boarding-school angels must have had chattering children or grandchildren of their own when the Yankees poured ashore from the sea and Port Royal Sound. The young grow old and old grow older, not altering the process by objections. On Hilton Head, as everywhere else, the generation gap seems changeless and everlasting.

Fortunately, however, there are some changeless things to be seen late and soon and by old and young. The South Carolina poet Paul Hamilton Hayne was just a boy in Charleston when Fanny Kemble passed there complaining about the accommodations. Complaint is eternal. But Hayne wrote of things which do not change:

> The great constellations rose and set;
> I knew them all, and worshipped all I knew;
> Yet from their empire in the pregnant blue
> Sweeping from planet-orbits to faint bars
> Of nebulous cloud beyond the range of stars,
> I turned to worship with a heart as true,
> Long mosses dropping from the cypress tree.

July 30, 1970

The Gentlemanly Serpent

In this time of much concern abut preserving the ecology and protecting the wildlife, few generous gestures are extended to the snake. Bird watching has become, particularly on islands like this one, a popular spectator sport. But only naturalists and small boys seem eager observers of the serpents. Hardly any kind words have been spoken about the crawling creatures since God gave them a bad name in Genesis. At least a part of the basis for the sanctification of Patrick was that he rid an island bigger than this one of all its snakes. A similar process may be going on here as bogs become building lots and sleek green golf courses run where the bushes provided cover. Maybe they are saints who direct the bulldozers and the dredges hereabouts. Still, at this time of hiatus from hibernation, even snakes, if carefully avoided, may deserve some consideration.

William Bartram, the eighteenth-century naturalist who studied the flora and fauna along this southeastern shore, wrote deferentially even of the rattlesnake as "a wonderful creature, when we consider his form, nature and disposition." He saluted it with respect and admiration.

15

"I have," he wrote in the 1770s, "in the course of my travels in
the Southern states (where they are the largest, most numerous and
supposed to be the most venomous and vindictive) stept unknow-
ingly so close as almost to touch one of them with my feet, and when
I perceived him he was already drawn up in circular coils ready for
a blow. But however incredible it may appear, the generous, I may
say magnanimous creature lay as still and motionless as if inanimate,
his head crouched in, his eyes almost shut, I precipitately withdrew,
unless when I have been so shocked with surprise and horror as to
be in a manner riveted to the spot, for a short time not having
strength to go away, when he often slowly extends himself and
quietly moves off in a direct line, unless pursued when he erects his
tail as far as the rattles extend, and gives the warning alarm by
intervals, but if you pursue and overtake him with a shew of enmity,
he instantly throws himself into the spiral coil, his tail by the rapidity
of its motion appears like a vapour, making a quick tremulous
sound, his whole body swells through rage, continually rising and
falling as a bellows; his beautiful particoloured skin becomes speck-
led and rough by dilatation, his head and neck are flattened, his
cheeks swollen and his lips constricted, discovering his mortal
fangs; his eyes red as burning coals, and his brandishing forked
tongue of the colour of the hottest flame, continually menaces death
and destruction, yet never strikes unless sure of his mark."

Bartram himself seemed almost caught in the paralysis of that
long sentence. But his admiration is evident. Not quite so much
approval can be expected from others. Still, the same hand which
made the lamb and the tiger perfected this gentlemanly killer which
the naturalist described. Other snakes hereabouts deserve less fascination and fear. If few of them can be so arrogantly urbane as the
rattler, they deserve more than hard heels on their heads. We may
miss them when all their hiding places are cleared and the rats
multiply in freedom from their menace. I haven't seen a good-sized
snake on Hilton Head in more than a year but I watched three rats
boldly assembled just outside the porch of a Garden Court Villa in
the Beach Lagoon area of Sea Pines during a cocktail party. They
were, of course, more impertinent than poisonous. They looked like
ragged roughnecks stubbornly determined to enjoy the feast to
which they were not invited. They will sneak in where serpents fear

to crawl. They'll steal from the larder and die stinking in the walls.

While careful where I step, I prefer the snakes. Some of them may be desperadoes, but the real, insolent ruffians are the rats which may be expected in mob proportions when the serpents disappear.

August 6, 1970

Happy Hurricane

So far in this year's early beginning hurricane season no such wind has ruffled a sea oat on this shore. Not since 1964 has there been such a storm over Hilton Head as then sent its settlers scurrying inland and upland. I remember what a convivial time one body of refugees had at Allendale—including Siemers, Whites, Vails, Royces, Youngs, and others. The motel operator gave us a private dining room. If treasures had been left behind, bottles were brought along. Lasting friendships were made. When the hurricane had passed and we drove back to the island, bright sunshine greeted us. But then Dora, celebrating a party of her own, turned around and hit Hilton Head harder the second time than on the first blow from which we fled. Nobody was hurt. But it was evident, to revert to a frayed adjective, that no "plush" shore provides certain protection from the big blows.

Nobody has it so "plush" as Aaron Burr did in the summer of 1804 when he sailed by Hilton Head. A little way down the coast he found the sanctuary which he needed in the hue and cry which followed his killing of Alexander Hamilton in their famous duel. He wrote in August to his daughter Theodosia Burr Alston, then living

in South Carolina. He told her: "I am now quite settled. My establishment consists of a housekeeper, cook, and chambermaid, seam-
stress, and two footmen. There are, besides, two fishermen and four
bargemen always at command. The department of laundress is done
abroad. The plantation affords plenty of milk, cream, and butter;
turkeys, fowls, kids, pigs, geese and mutton; fish, of course, in abundance. Oranges and pomegranates just begin to be eatable. The
house afford madeira wine, brandy and porter. Yesterday my neighbor, Mr. Couper, sent me an assortment of French wines, consisting
of Claret, Sauterne, and Champagne, all excellent; and at least a
twelve months' supply of orange shrub, which makes a most excellent punch. Madame Couper added sweetmeats and pickles. . . .
We have not a fly, moscheto, or bug. I can sit a whole evening, with
open windows and lighted candles, without the least annoyance
from insects; a circumstance which I have never beheld in any other
place. I have not even seen a cockroach."

Such felicity did not last. Less than two weeks later he wrote
Theodosia again: "On Friday last, hearing that Mr. Couper had
returned and was very seriously ill, I took a small canoe with two
boys, and went to see him. He lay in a high fever. When about to
return in the evening, the wind had risen so that, after an ineffectual
attempt, I was obliged to give it up, and remain at Mr. C's. In the
morning the wind was still higher. It continued to rise, and by noon
blew a gale from the north, which, together with the swelling of the
water, became alarming. From twelve to three, several of the out-
houses had been destroyed; most of the trees about the house were
blown down. The house in which we were shook and rocked so
much that Mr. C. began to express his apprehension for our safety.
Before three, part of the piazza was carried away; two or three of
the windows bursted in. The house was inundated with water, and
presently one of the chimneys fell. Mr. C. then commanded a retreat
to a storehouse about fifty yards off, and we decamped, men,
women, and children. You may imagine, in this scene of confusion
and dismay, a good many incidents to amuse one if one had dared
to be amused in a moment of much anxiety. The house, however,
did not blow down. The storm continued till four, and then very
suddenly abated, and in ten minutes it was almost calm. I seized this
moment to return home. Before I got quite over, the gale rose from
the southeast and threatened new destruction. It lasted great part

of the night, but did not attain the violence of that from the north; yet it contributed to raise still higher the water, which was the principal instrument of devastation. The flood was about seven feet above the height of an ordinary high tide. This has been sufficient to inundate great part of the coast; to destroy all the rice; to carry off most of the buildings which were on low lands, and to destroy the lives of many blacks. The roads are rendered impassable, and scarcely a boat has been preserved. Thus all intercourse is suspended. . . . I apprehend that the roads on the whole coast as far north, at least, as Cape Hatteras, are in the same condition."

However, all winds pass. In the same letter in which he reported the storm to Theodosia, he mentioned his adopted daughter, Nathalie DeLage Sumter, of Stateburg, South Carolina: *"Madame j'ais bien diner,* and *j'ai fait mettre mon* writing desk *sur le table a diner.* What a scandalous thing to sit here all alone drinking Champagne—and yet—(*madame je bois a votre santé et a celle de monsieur votre fils)*—and yet, I say, if Champagne be that exhilarating cordial which *(je bois a la santé de Madame Sumtare)* songs and rumour ascribe to it *(a la santé de Mademoiselle Sumtare)* can there be ever an occasion in which its application could be more appropriate, or its virtues more. . . ."

The winds blow and we can still hope there will be good wines after storms. Colonel Burr set a precedent that may still be applicable today. *Á votre santé* to all on this same shore.

August 13, 1970

Unwanted Generation

Maybe Hilton Head should follow the example of another island. In England the Establishment, whatever that may be, has banned an edition of the *Ladies' Home Journal* because it contains an unwelcome article about Princess Margaret. Well, now comes *Time* with a long piece about the American minority composed of persons over sixty-five. They (or many of us) are labeled by the news magazine as "The Unwanted Generation."

"Strangely enough," the once provocative but now ponderous magazine says, "the aged have a lot in common with youth; they are largely unemployed, introspective and often depressed; their bodies and psyches are in process of change, and they are heavy users of drugs."

Not all on this island, who have sometimes been aghast at the antics of the young, will care for the supposed similarity. But it is too late to keep *Time* out. Perhaps its entry should be welcomed as instructive.

Few of the "aged" on this island are unaware that some of their contemporaries are having a pretty hard time. Not all Americans can count their Social Security checks as just their liquor money.

21

They are everything to too many. And all of us must recognize that the clock and the calendar have not been abolished. But this particular "unwanted generation" is aware that it was once damned or blessed as the "Lost Generation," which had F. Scott Fitzgerald and Ernest Hemingway as its participants and prophets. We had our poet who sang:

> My candle burns at both ends;
> It will not last the night;
> But, ah, my foes, and, oh, my friends—
> It gives a lovely light.

It is true that the youngest of this trio, Hemingway, would today be seventy-one. But they were the patriarchs of a generally younger Lost Generation. The rest of us, as their readers, were the flappers, the drugstore cowboys, the first automotive generation, the boys and girls of the jazz age. Many of us were too young and then too old to be troubled by any wars. We burned no schoolhouses. We had no draft cards to burn. We didn't go on trips with LSD, but the Good Lord must have protected us survivors from some of the Prohibition potations we drank.

The same kind of fingers were shaken at us as are now still pointing out the hippie young and the Unwanted Generation. A good many of us survived, as our numbers, which sometimes seem ominous to the planners, psychologists, and politicians, indicate. And a lot of our friends and relatives and some of us had it pretty hard even in middle life in the Depression.

It is sad that some of our contemporaries are not having it "plush" now that the calendar is blowing hot on the backs of their necks. But anybody who thinks many old people were not having it rough when we were young must have been born not only young but blind as well. Maybe those in the Unwanted Generation are, as *Time* says, "heavy users of drugs" like those at the other end of the generation gap. The elder generation when it was "unwanted" by us hardly had aspirin for its aches and pains.

Possibly we are living too long to suit the actuaries, the Medicare appropriations, and the Malthusians. But no demand for the reversal of that process comes from the "aged." Some of us may look a little unduly preserved in this cosmetic age. But few of our lady companions want to look like Whistler's mother. "Unwanted?" Ask Charles Fraser, Fred Hack, or Bill Gregory. The Bank of Beaufort, along with similar institutions, says, "Senior Citizens are among our favorite people." Ask those who—too often, it is true, in a jerry-built fashion—have made a nursing-home industry, with more beds than there are in hospitals. Some undoubtedly only want the elderly in order to exploit them.

Of course, there are problems about those over sixty-five as there are about those under twenty-five. Most of the young, like the young in the past, will outgrow such idiocies as now involve them. The elderly do not expect eternity on this earth. But despite the growing number of the elderly, despite the tragedy which involves too many of them, the old folks never had it so good.

And sometimes they would have it better, if some of the erudite or just plain impolite whippersnappers didn't keep telling them (us) that they didn't.

August 20, 1970

G. Washington's Coach

Traffic has thickened across coastal Carolina. The big new connection being built below Yemassee on Route 17 suggests that more, faster, and maybe bigger vehicles will be moving along this coast. Still the little blue-coach route markers point to where other travelers came and moved. The silhouette of the coach on these little signs for tourists along the roads hereabouts recalls a vehicle gone, but one which ought not to be forgotten. Even in this day when people are collecting antique automobiles and airplanes, there may be some interest in George Washington's coach, which came this way in his "lumbering entourage," as one writer described his Southern presidential tour in 1791. His coach was certainly the Cadillac or the Imperial of his day—as an imported vehicle, maybe the Rolls-Royce or the Mercedes 600.

As a collector of antique vehicles in his time, William Meade (1789–1862), third bishop of the Protestant Episcopal Church in the Diocese of Virginia, got the coach, an English one, after Washington's death. In it, the Bishop reported, George and Martha rode not only in Fairfax County, Virginia, "but travelled through the length and breadth of our land," including two different routes across

24

South Carolina: one along the coast, along the King's Highway which is now Route 17, and one from Augusta, Georgia, northward by Columbia and Camden. On a part of his journey through the Low Country, Washington visited a rice plantation which looked to him, as one not given to poesy, "like fairyland." Still most of his coastal journey, he reported without enthusiasm, was "a dull way between the uninterrupted scenery of sand & pine barrens."

But to get back to the coach, its manufacture, its service, and its fate. Bishop Meade reported: "So faithfully was it executed that at the conclusion of this long journey, its builder, who came over with it and settled in Alexandria, was Proud to be told by the General that not a nail or screw had failed. It so happened, in a way I need not state, that this coach came into my hands about fifteen years after the death of General Washington. In the course of time, from disuse, it being too heavy for these latter days, it began to decay and give way. Becoming an object of desire to those who delight in relics, I caused it to be taken to pieces and distributed among the admiring friends of Washington who visited my house, and also among a number of female associations for benevolent and religious objects, which associations, at their fairs and on other occasions, made a large profit by converting the fragments into walking sticks, picture frames, and snuff boxes. About two-thirds of one of the wheels thus produced one hundred and forty dollars. There can be no doubt that at its dissolution it yielded more to the cause of charity than it did to its builder at its first erection. Besides other mementos of it, I have in my study, in the form of a sofa, the hind-seat on which the General and his lady were wont to sit."

Maybe the ladies of sweet charity on the island, such as the operators of the Bargain Box, can pick up some ideas from the Bishop's experience. Certainly the Bishop's revelation indicates that the love of the antique and ingenuity in benevolence are not entirely new. They are certainly not entirely gone. Perhaps some of our clergy and good women ought to put in early bids for Strom Thurmond's automobile or the airplane in which Governor McNair flew to Germany. There's no telling how many ashtrays could be made out of them.

August 27, 1970

Antiquity of Gossip

Every now and then even on so sedate a sea island as Hilton Head the antennae of the elderly in residence receive either amazing reports or false alarms about scandalous goings-on on this shore. At least one imaginative lady at a cocktail party seemed rather pleased as well as puritanical about the weird word she had received that even an insulated island might be a Peyton Place. She sounded like the man who had heard of the wild behavior in suburbia, bought a house, and after he moved in wanted his money back. His expectations had not been realized. But if grounds for gossip, like everything else, come over the James F. Byrnes Crossing, that will not be new or strange.

Wanton Eves were suspected in this Eden when the newcomers to it included, in addition to the soldiers, many missionaries. They formed a diverse company from the North, intent upon the salvation of the Union-occupied sea islands but ready to have some pleasure in the process. General Quincy Gillmore, noted artillerist who graduated first in his class at West Point, had as his assignment the breaking down of the defenses of Charleston up the shore. He found, however, that he had as frustrating a task in shepherding the missionaries, teachers, nurses, other lady abolitionists, and their male companions in his theater of operations. A man of scientific brilliance, he was described as "a fine, wholesome-looking, solid six-footer, with big head, broad good-humored face, and a high forehead, faintly elongated by a suspicion of baldness, curly brown hair and beard." Also, those who described him said, he blushed easily.

And perhaps with reason. Romance flourished on the captured shore. Gillmore's associate in charge of the diverse civilian population, General Rufus Saxton, took possession of "a fine, airy, large-windowed, many-porched Southern residence." To it, looking "quite radiant," the pretty, famous mulatto diarist Charlotte Forten wrote, he brought as his wife a schoolteacher who had come from Philadelphia. "A strange marriage, it seems to me," Charlotte Forten wrote cryptically.

There, innocently, they loved to play charades, in which they were joined by a lady whose very good looks prompted gossip. She was Jean Margaret Davenport Lander, then a popular Shakespearean actress. Mrs. Lander was dramatic on and off the stage. Earlier she had gone to the White House to tell of a plan to assassinate the President which she said had been confided to her by a handsome Virginian. Then, as a young war widow, she had offered her services as a nurse. She was rejected by the superintendent of women nurses, Dorothea Dix, who had stipulated that her aides be not only thirty but also "plain looking." La Lander was, however, welcomed to the islands by General Saxton.

No specific scandal was alleged in Mrs. Lander's case. But tongues were wagging in paradise. Miss Forten, who wanted to work with the soldiers as well as with the children, was piqued when she received word that "she not join the regiment just now." She wrote in her journal: "He fears scandal. There have been of late very scandalous reports of some of the ladies down here, so of course as usual, *all* must suffer to some extent." Charlotte did suffer when she returned from a visit to the North and received a "very inhospitable reception" at the landing. She and another returning woman "were told that an order had been issued by General Gillmore forbidding any lady to land unless provided with a pass from himself or the Secretary of War." Charlotte got ashore but only after spending the night on the boat "watched closely meanwhile by no less than three lynx-eyed guards."

General Gillmore evidently was determined to have no reason for blushing. When a body of Negro troops set out on an expedition to Florida he instructed their commanders: "You will see that no females accompany your command, and will give strict orders that none shall follow except regularly appointed laundresses who will be allowed to accompany the baggage of your respective commands." Apparently laundresses could be better trusted than missionaries.

General Gillmore did not take Charleston. Perhaps he was relieved when he was transferred to the active and wholly masculine front along the James River in Virginia. Saxton apparently lost the fine house he had occupied and in which he and the ladies had played charades. A brief season ended leaving twenty thousand Yankee boys behind in the Beaufort cemetery. There was more earnestness than scandal on the sea islands during the period of their living and dying here. But no situation, no place, is secure from gossip. And maybe the sad truth about us humans, even on Hilton Head, is that we find it more interesting than military dispatches or even real-estate brochures.

September 3, 1970

Change the Name?!

Memo to the Master of Erudition, one Jonathan Daniels:

"I have a very serious subject. I note that 'legally' (Post Office designation) we live on 'Hilton Head Island.' To me this is redundant, and the name "Hilton Head" is more euphonious, distinctive, attractive, and shorter. Do you think we should undertake a campaign to acquire this name, or am I as usual taking another unpopular minority stand, like being a Republican in South Carolina?

Tom Howard

"Or am I ——— in the wind again?"

Dear Tom:

I am not erudite enough to know which way the wind blows. I respect minority stands, however. I'd better. If you are a Republican in South Carolina, I'm a Democrat in Sea Pines. I salute you as an expert in nomenclature. But I remember from my bawdy boyhood a popular schoolground (not schoolroom) oration. Supposedly it was originally delivered by a passionate orator in the Congress about a name change proposed by early advocates of euphony. The

29

speech recited all the outrageous acts which might be done to sacred things but ran to the clarion peroration: "Change the name of Arkansas? Hell, No!"

Majority or minority, this is my view about the old name Hilton Head Island. I note from your stationery that you are still, despite your presence here, chairman of the board of the Fort Knox National Bank. Boy, that sounds like you are banking with the national gold hoard in the basement. To bobtail the name of Hilton Head Island as you propose would seem to me almost like changing the name of your institution to the Bank of Skid Row.

We live on an island and don't want anybody to miss the fact —least of all ourselves and our new friends here like you. Some of us are not sure, as the population grows, that we even like the bridge which turns our island into a more and more crowded peninsula. Your bobtailed name would no more indicate our happy presence by the sea than does Caesar's Head, South Carolina (altitude 3,115 feet).

I'll admit I'm a conservative in this matter. Democrat though I am, I would have kept that cape named Canaveral. I wouldn't have changed the name Sixth Avenue to the "euphonious, distinctive, attractive," and entirely unaccepted Avenue of the Americas. I hope places like Oshkosh and Dubuque will cling to the names of their heritage.

Hereabouts we can swiftly change the names of inns. Sometimes the names of streets change before the stationery of residents on them runs out. We've lost some old names like Old Woman's Folly, which once constituted a large part of Sea Pines (and in some cases may still). I like Robbers Row and wouldn't change it to something more euphonious like Predatory Passage. I don't agree that the traffic circle by the Sea Pines office should be made the Sea Pines Runaround.

Having said so much, may I reassure you. If you address a letter to Hilton Head, South Carolina, it will get here without the full name attached. And if you want to make a crusade for change, you may be encouraged to know that name changes have been made before. Earlier, the island was called Liburni after the Latin name for its shape like a small ship or galley. It was Ile de la Rivière Grande, then called Escamacu, after an Indian tribe. It became Isla de los Osos (the island of the bears). Captain Hilton described the landmark bluff, not the island which is Hilton Head: "The said head-land is bluft, and seems steep, as though trees hung over the water." After Hilton it was long called Trench's Island (even Ile de Tranchées), after a man who used the island as a cattle grazing ground. It was still Trench's Island on a war map published as late as 1861.

I still stand with the Arkansas orator: Change the name of Hilton Head? Hell, No! Still I don't count on all things, including names, being eternal. I would still love the island if its northern and southern points ran from Hack's Headland to Fraser's Folly.

I only hope that none will succeed in tagging it as Die Insel der Fatten Katzen.

September 10, 1970

Lost Fruit

Only a few hereabouts like John Postell still have lemon-bearing trees. Maybe most of them began to disappear in recurrent, rare incidents of real cold weather like one which prompted John to pick his lemon tree's plentiful crop quickly and pass the fruit around to his friends. But nothing seems so clear as that in the early days in this sea-island country such fruit trees were numerous and fruitful.

Sir Charles Lyell, famous British geologist and observer of all nature, came through this sea-island country in 1845. He commented on the beautiful verandahed houses in Beaufort and on the shade of the trees about them. He spoke especially of the "orange trees laden with fruit." On a Georgia sea island, not much south of here, Aaron Burr wrote his daughter in August 1804 that the oranges were just beginning to be eatable. Frederick Law Olmsted, who came South in the 1850s as an observant abolitionist before he began his great career as almost the first important American landscape architect, spoke of oranges in this corner of South Carolina. One February he wrote of ripening oranges hanging on the trees around a plantation house he visited.

Perhaps the reason for the absence of fruit trees in the new developments was demonstrated this summer. Ruthven Vaux, who maintains a mini-plantation on Calibogue Cay, has a very realistic scarecrow guarding her vegetables. But fruit trees call for more active defense measures. In her orchard, which contains fig, pear, and peach trees, with some grapes on the side, she had the prospect of some especially beautiful peaches.

As they ripened to perfection, she determined that no body or beast was going to get those peaches but herself. She certainly did not mean to have them consumed by any impertinent raccoons. So she sat herself on guard as the darkening hour of raccoon depredations approached. She fixed her chair at a perfect vantage point. Then with a gun across her lap she waited any invasion. She waited and waited. The night became more and more dulcet. A soft breeze murmured across Broad Creek. Ruth fell asleep. Suddenly she awakened with the gun still across her lap—and at the ready. There was not a raccoon in sight—or a peach. The big-eyed beasties had worked while Ruth slept.

There is, however, nothing new about troubles with the guardianship of fruit. Long ago Thomas Chaplin, a planter in this neighborhood who liked to entertain poets, made a diary entry on the subject. Chaplin, who probably gave his name to the community in the middle of the island, on May 10, 1854, wrote of a little slave boy he had put on guard.

"More robery [sic].—discovered that my little rascal William, who I had minding the crows off the watermellons [sic] had been the worse crow himself, and does the thing sistematically [sic]. He turns over a mellon, cuts a hole on the underside large enough to admit his hand, eats out the inside, when he finds a ripe one, then turns the mellon back again, not breaking it off the vine, there it lays looking as sound as ever. No one would suppose it hollow. In picking some—we found no less than 23 or 4 in this fix. Cunning, very."

There have been a lot of generations of little boys and raccoons since that time. The predatory are always with us. Maybe in this day when we are not content just with fruits "in season" we had better let Gene Martin guard them at the Red & White. There, hopefully, the fruits are safe from everything except the ladies who pinch 'em. No grocer has ever found a guard against that.

September 17, 1970

Storm Season

June, too soon.
July, stand by.
August, come it must.
September, remember.
October, all over.

Hurricane song.

This is the time of year when on this island anybody who writes about hurricanes should do it with fingers crossed. Still, there is some basis for reassurance. A good part of the "hurricane season" is behind us, and meteorologists estimate that in any year there is a 74 percent chance that no big blow will hit the South Carolina coastline.

Nobody in his right mind is going to speak lightly of these visitations, which take their name from the Caribbean Indian word *hurrican*, meaning "evil spirit." About 136 such storms have struck this area since records began to be made, sketchily at first, in 1686. That one brought blessing as well as bane since it not only smacked this coast but also disrupted a Spanish attack in the neighborhood of Beaufort.

The catastrophic storms here have been rare. There were whoppers in 1752, 1797, 1804, 1811, 1813, 1846, 1881, 1885, and the lulu of 1893. The worst hurricanes hereabouts in this century were those of 1911, 1916, 1928, 1929, 1940, and 1959. In twenty-one hurricane seasons big storms came twice. In ten years three hurricanes hit. As late as 1964 there were tropical storms on this coast in each of the three months of the hurricane season, only one of which, Dora, by an unexpected turnaround, hit Hilton Head Island.

This area looks back to its worst storm as the one of August 27–28, 1893. Then about two thousand people were killed in this part of South Carolina. One account of it said: "Hundreds of corpses were strewn among the farms, unknown except to the vultures which flocked about them. Whole families are wiped out in some places. The coroner has sworn in an army of deputies, and these are hunting for the dead." It was said to be four days before songbirds reappeared. A phenomenon was that trees, stripped of leaves, re-leafed in the fall. Even a less severe storm, which came from the westward into Beaufort in October 1929, caused such flooding that during its peak the waters of the Savannah River broke through the swamps emptying at Port Royal.

Fortunately, islands are not left unwarned as they were in 1893 and even later. The only safe hurricane rule, however, for islanders is "git" inland and upland. Hurricanes apparently have not changed in the centuries. William Bartram, the naturalist who came this way before the American Revolution, described one in which he was caught without warning while on a botanizing excursion: "Being heretofore so closely invested, by high forests and deep swamps . . . I was prevented from seeing the progress and increase of the approaching tempest, the terrible appearance of which now at once confounded me; how purple and fiery appeared the tumultuous clouds swiftly ascending or darting from the horizon upwards; they seemed to oppose and dash against each other, the skies appeared streaked with blood or purple flame overhead, the flaming lightning streaming and darting about in every direction around, seems to fill the world with fire; whilst the heavy thunder keeps the earth in a constant tremor. . . . The forests behind me bend to the blast, and the sturdy limbs of the trees crack; I had by this time got up a-breast of the grove or hommock, the hurricane close by, pursuing me, I found it dangerous and imprudent in the highest degree to put in there, as the groves were already torn up, and the spreading limbs of the ancient Live Oaks were flying over my head, and carried about in the air as leaves and stubble. . . .''

Bartram finally made it to the plantation of a friend: "all their buildings on the plantation except his own dwelling-house, were laid almost flat to the ground. . . . He had nearly one hundred acres of the Indigo plant almost ripe for the first cutting, which was nearly ruined. . . . The great Live Oaks which had been left standing about the fields, were torn to pieces, their limbs lying scattered over the ground: and one very large one which stood near his house torn down, which could not have been done by the united strength of a thousand men. But what is incredible, in the midst of this devastation and ruin, providentially no lives were lost. . . .''

Bartram even saved his flower specimens from the storm. Others have not been and may not be so lucky.

Rule 1: "Git."

September 24, 1970

Romulus and Remus

As entrepreneurs of the second rank on Hilton Head Island (neither yet presides over debts of $15 million), Wilbert Roller and Louis McKibben may be setting the design for Hilton Head Island. Their proposal, as tentative as a toe in the crack of the door, does not relate to fairways and lagoons, to wildlife protection and architectural regulation. They confront much more mundane— maybe more fundamental—matters, such as costs and taxes, services and controls. And specifically what they want is a town established smack dang between the compound of Sea Pines and the stretches beyond the interlocking, almost-Venetian lagoons of Palmetto Dunes. Beyond would be the terra unincorporated of the villages of black folk and the developments of Port Royal and Spanish Wells.

Some questions may be raised as to the boundaries of their dream town, which leave out practically all of the rich and the entirety of the poor. But problems do arise on an island governed largely by the modern magic wands of Prosperos. Maybe it is time for some Calibans to shake off their bonds. Undoubtedly the costs of security rise. There may be restiveness beyond guarded gates. Erosion bites at the platted and unplatted places. Unity confronts pollution from across the bridge, but an ever-increasing number of johns are flushed independently on the island.

As reformer, Wilbert Roller eloquently expresses a growing conviction that more services should be provided "for the money we are now spending." There are those who think Mr. Roller might be a good guardian of any purse, public or private. Mr. McKibben might be helpful in that process. And if they need any help, such a citizen within their proposed boundaries as Norris Richardson might provide aid in this regard.

The town, however, seems a little exclusive in its proposed frontiers. Many of the lieges on the feudal plantations would be denied the right to contribute to the funds Mr. Roller would like to see guarded. Many of the scattered poor and blacks would be denied the services he would like to see provided. And the problems with which he would have a municipality deal are those of everybody between the point of Coggins and Braddock and that one where Brams Point sticks an elegant toe into the juncture of Broad Creek and the Intracoastal Waterway.

The possibility is that as pioneers the Roller-McKibben vision is incomplete. There may even be people restless for services within the "plush" paternalism of the plantations. There are certainly some people lacking services outside them. The island as a whole should be concerned with the support of the bulging medical center, the library, the day care center. The volunteer fire department should hardly stop short at any city limits provided.

One Roller-McKibben municipality would in the long (not very long) run hardly suffice. The place called Hilton Head Island could be fragmented by many towns with different names, perhaps different post offices. And there could be a multiplicity of city officials ready, willing, and possibly able to make sure in diversity that services are provided for the "money we are now spending." Some "Articles of Confederation" might have to be drawn to prevent confusion between the various colonies established. If Hilton Head Island has reached the town stage, a lot of trouble might be avoided by making one town of one island now.

Not all will agree the need is now. As is the case with many pioneers, Roller and McKibben may have trouble in enlisting enthusiastic proselytes. That should not deter them. And they should not be dismissed as dreamers or visionaries in their proposal for the public good. As Founding Fathers, they should not limit their aspirations. Rome was not built in a day.

Think broadly, Mr. Roller.

Dream expansively, Mr. McKibben.

But please keep Hilton Head Island intact.

October 1, 1970

Acorns on the Roof

The acorns drop from the live oaks *pong pong* on my roof. They clutter the terrace, And it is good to note at sunset on Calibogue that an acorn half an inch high on a paved surface can cast a shadow nearly three inches long. Maybe these finger-like shadows are portentous. The old folks used to say that many nuts in the fall forecast a hard winter.

We do not really need to fear that on Hilton Head Island. I like to hear the acorns hit the roof when I'm in bed. They do not make quite the music I remember when, as a child tucked in, I listened to the rain falling above me on a tin roof. No better music than that has ever been made.

Of course, the old prediction of cold weather ahead when nuts are plentiful was based on the idea that beneficent nature provided a special supply for the squirrels and other creatures when a long winter was before them. Apparently nature is suffering from the generation gap. Today these young squirrels on Hilton Head Island aren't bothering to cache the nuts. They prefer to poach on the bird feeders. I'm sure some may see an analogy in this to a human generation which just doesn't give a damn in a time when they can count on welfare and Social Security if and when winter comes—which they sometimes seem to doubt.

Nowadays the acorns just get swept away by Johnny White and his crew. It is a long time since those days when, as Father Juan Bautista de Segura reported from this still-wilderness shore, the Indians at this time of the year scattered through the forest to collect the acorns and other wild fruits. They were both thrifty and generous, the good padre said. "Their provisions were held in common and it was their custom to give away their food without demanding anything in return." There might be a disturbing contrast in that, too, in these times.

However, maybe the acorn indication of a hard winter is irrelevant here to both squirrels and men. One of the blessed things about Hilton Head Island is that it does have the seasons. Houses here do not have chimneys merely for decoration. The open fire here can be as pleasant as the sun. The smell of burning oak and pine adds a bouquet to the glasses filled before it. Still, the acorns may be right. I don't remember how plentiful they were a year ago, before the freezing time we had last winter. There could even be snow, as there was a few winters ago.

Then its fall was spoken of as almost an unheard-of event. That, of course, was incorrect. Weather records on the island do not go far back into the past. But Yankees have been cold here long before the recent migration. Way back in January 1863, a lady missionary to the freed folk in this area wrote that on January 25, 1863, the weather was so warm that one hundred and fifty people, brightly arrayed, were baptized in the creek. But on January 28, she recorded in her diary: "A memorable day because we had a snow storm—in miniature. When I got up this morning some of the roofs had a white layer upon them, but it did not stay on the ground. The 'storm' lasted but a little while. Towards eve, there was another slight attempt at snow, which was unsuccessful. A cold, dreary day."

Whatever the acorns may say, we will have such days again. People will worry about their camellias. Other trees and plants may suffer. But after days fit for open fires, days suitable for baptizing or good golf will come again. And the little winter dreariness only makes more precious the quickly intervening sun. The cold that the acorns may foretell is one of the blessings of this island, saving it from the monotonous, unseasoned weather of southern Florida.

As the acorns *pong pong* on the roof I hope they are predicting some cold weather. It's a part of the diversity which adds to the charm of this island. We can count on days which will point one of its greatest assets: that is knowing that, however chill it may become down here, it is luxurious beside the weather up north. Pleasure lies not only in weather where we are but in the sense of superiority in the comparison between occasionally tingling weather here and the steady frigidity endured by our less-fortunate or more-foolish friends.

Let the acorns fall.

October 8, 1970

Plat-eye

Something—maybe poetry—has been lost in the supposed disappearance of superstition from this shore and its islands. And Sheriff J. Ed McTeer, in his fine book *High Sheriff of the Low Country,* suggests that the loss has come lately. He writes: "In nights only recently past, the throb of drums wafted out of the swamps on the breeze, to float across the farm lands and the islands and tell the whole night of this thing that must never be forgotten. Thousands and more sat and listened, remembering tales by fathers and grandfathers of the spirits and hags, the things that go bump in the night. This was the darkness of voodoo, satanism, the black magic known as 'Root.'"

Not all the magic promised evil. There was a blue root "for protection against evil of all kinds and help, in love affairs." And the whole weird business was presided over by Root Doctors. According to the Sheriff, tinted sunglasses were "the traditional badge of the Root Doctor." Superstition may be disappearing in the sea islands or, as the Sheriff says, it may be the " 'in' thing today all over the nation." Root Doctors and other practitioners need no longer grub in graveyards at night for the materials for their potions. They can buy them wholesale from factories in Baltimore.

Unfortunately, in his report, the Sheriff, who says he has forty-five years of association with witchcraft hereabouts, does not write of "Plat-eye," which has the greatest power. The famous South Carolina writer DuBose Heyward defined this dreadful thing: "Plat-eye is a spirit which takes some form which will be particularly apt to lure its victims away. It is said to lead them into danger or lose them in the woods and, stealing their wits away, leave them to die alone."

That was nonsense, said Heyward's friend, a bottle collector, before Plat-eye called him for taking a half-pint flask from a grave in a Negro cemetery. Maybe all magic is nonsense. That is the view taken by dull, unimaginative people. Some of them don't even believe in fairies, let alone Plat-eye. Fortunately, not all folk are like that. And there seems to be some evidence that if magic, conjured up from the Congo, is disappearing in the vicinity of Hilton Head Island, newcomers here are intent upon fostering a magic of their own.

There are certainly here enough dark glasses, which made "the traditional badge of the Root Doctor." And now spreading like magic are the copper bracelets warranted to keep off arthritis and rheumatism. Their prevalence is perhaps to be expected on a golf island of older folk, where athletes and arthritis often come in combination. There is a tradition behind them. Long ago crones and gaffers (who seem to have disappeared in this century) carried big horse chestnuts, called "buckeyes," which guaranteed the same protection.

Now the custom becomes venerable. When Mary Ellen Mulford got her first ruddy bracelet long ago, Emerson had to send to England for it. And it cost five dollars. England was a natural source of origin. There civil servants coming back from years in the tropics to the dank and rheumatic little island remembered that in Africa canny natives wore copper bracelets and other ornaments to keep off the evil spirits. Others brought tales from another hemisphere that Aztec or Inca slaves in the copper mines left skeletons behind them unscarred by arthritis. Maybe such slaves didn't live long enough to get arthritis, but that is, of course, irrelevant.

Now you can pick up testimonials by the double handful on Hilton Head. Tales are told of a lame-armed golfer who wore a copper bracelet and won a tournament. You don't have to send to England for them now. You can buy them on the way here at Stuckey's. Or on the island you can for $2.50 buy them from Wallace Palmer at the Pro Shop in the Plantation Club (made and guaranteed in Atlanta). One gentleman on the island made his own out of pennies. Some are dubious about this last, there being zinc as well as copper in the coin. One lady wears one on her wrist and another on the opposite ankle. Perhaps unfortunately, they are not yet prescribed at the medical center. But you can get them at Capin's Pharmacy—without a prescription.

Of course, there are some skeptics abut this as about everything else. Sheriff McTeer quoted one contemporary Root Doctor as doubting that man had really landed on the moon. That was too much magic for him. But many here bless the bracelets even if they leave a green stain on fair arms. The certain thing is that there is faith in this world. Faith will move mountains. It may ease a joint.

When magic is missing this island will not be the same. Fortunately, there does not seem to be much danger of that now.

October 15, 1970

Condominium, the Gem of the Ocean! *

It doesn't require many years
On Hilton Head to be pioneers!
We found the land unspoiled and spacious,
Here was room for all the gracious,
Coming from the crowded towns
Where no such pleasantness abounds.
Here planners platted to make sure
Serenity would be secure.
No room here for realty faker,
Limit people to the acre.
This is one shore none shall wreck,
Keep on guard the architect!
Lock one gate, police the other,
Bar the roughneck and his brother.
Elsewhere explodes the population,
No beer cans here, or copulation,
Save behind their shuttered blinds

* Revived by request.

46

By gentle folk with gentle minds.
So certain here was the felicity
That golly but it got publicity!
There was the picture not much later
Of *Grande* Charles with his alligator,
Strolling on the greens so fair,
Both evidently debonaire.
Wide went the tidings, muted, bland,
That here was last left promised land.
In bank and bar the word was spread
Of hydrocephalic Hilton Head.
The lots were taken grab by grab,
When architects lagged you could get prefab.
For some who filled the beaten track
Were lot, plan, and house in one pack.
By sound and sea such houses rose
With blinds you can see but cannot close.
The land of course remained restricted,
Only the wildlife was evicted
To make more room for planes and men
Where once were wood and swamp and glen.
The lots grew fewer, higher the price:
How to pack more people in paradise?
Then suddenly the answer came
Wearing a not-to-be-mispronounced name.
By golf course and beach front, by the lagoon,
These warrens for wanderers rose toward the moon.
So an endless island may be attained,
Who counts the loss by so much gained?
They miss the dream who only see
The cut down trees and the masonry.
Scorn those who say condomini*um*
Is only a word for a probable slum.
Hail these dreamers, great reformers,
Such men are our best performers.
Upon high purpose their plans are bent.
They build Appalachia for the afflu *ent!*

October 22, 1970

Cry for Rape

HILTON HEAD
ISLAND

The boats get bigger. The captains and crews (generally wives) take the Coast Guard courses and learn the ways to follow directions carefully marked in the sounds and the waterways. Often they are like golfers following the well-defined ways from hole to hole. Also, if you are new on the island and curious, real-estate salesmen will take you on guided tours by the best existing houses and the most inviting still-for-sale lots. In all such cases it is like pursuing the paths indicated in the sea and shore brochures. Fortunately—and increasingly fortunately—few find their ways to the secret and most lovely places on Hilton Head Island. The ecology of the eye could be destroyed if the secret places got on a beaten path.

It is probably disloyal to reveal the discoveries of such an explorer as Bill McKecknie of Calibogue Cay, who found a terra incognita in his own backyard. Most of his neighbors head out regularly to sound and sea, some sitting on lofty bridges above high-powered engines. Bill has a boat for the sea. But more significantly he also has a bateau, solidly built out of cypress by Sollie Campbell, who constructs craft for oyster gatherers. With the outboard motor

48

pulled up, it only requires four inches of water. At high tide it can go to places where at other times the marsh mud is exposed.

His most beautiful voyage is through the almost-lost area between his canal side of Calibogue Cay and the water-lapped margins of Six Oaks Memorial Park on Plantation Drive. He knows the creeks which even at low tide meander through the marshes. And beyond the marshes they run by wooded promontories where the lack of underbrush marks the habitations of the deer. The sides of the creeks rise straight up from the water, obviously, McKecknie thinks, cut out long ago by slaves to permit the movement at high tide of barges filled with rice and cotton. The slave boatmen often filled the woods with song. High trees with half-exposed roots line the banks. They give a cathedral cover to the creeks, and the moss hangs down, like curtains across a nave, almost to the dark water.

The poles of some old fences stagger on the shore. Sometimes even now cattle, loosed in the woods, come down to the edges of the creeks. Bulls look menacingly at the few boatmen who have found the way to the wet edges of the brambled pastures. In the spring the love calls of alligators rise like the croaking of monster bullfrogs. On cold days the herons perch on the sunny side of trees snugly out of the wind. Occasionally a marsh rabbit stares at the intruding boatman. Birds sing, emphasizing the amber quietness, their feathers no brighter than the streaks of penetrating sunlight.

Somehow this is Hilton Head Island before the strangers came. This is the island of the long, silent interval between slave song and real-estate ballyhoo. The place seems as eternal as the new graves on the shore, which rest above the seeping tides. And McKecknie as discoverer, knowing the creeks hidden in tide better than the marks in his hands, seems eternal, too. On this brief "waste" between developed streets only his outboard motor seems to differentiate him from Charon navigating his ferry on the river Styx between this world and the next.

There are stories of buried treasures on this island. Some were so secretly hidden that those who dug the holes for the hoards were dispatched in accordance with the theory that dead men tell no tales. Some creeks are lost in the memory of dead men, too: those who dug and those who sang, those who picked the cotton and harvested the rice, and those who on their piazzas only watched the loaded barges in the sluggish streams. Such forgotten creeks are buried treasures, too, safe so far from the planners who give a gardened order to once-wild loveliness. Ecology here is not a solemn science but an almost wanton rioting in shade and sun, tide flow and marsh growth.

McKecknie's big backyard seems both safe and secret. But it stretches only a mile or less between air-conditioned houses (designed to protect the ecology of the comfortably retired), a paved highway thick with trucks, and garish directional signs. Maybe Bill McKecknie should have kept it secret, and no passenger of his should be a blabbermouth about beauty. Other such hidden places should be kept hidden. Their appeal is too great. Sadly, the virgin wilderness almost cries aloud for rape.

October 29, 1970

Secession Syndrome

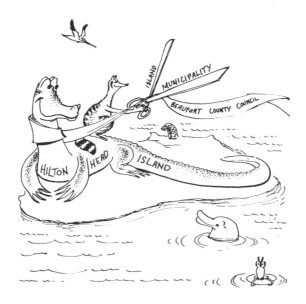

There seems to be a restlessness hereabouts and not only in proposals to pull one small chunk of Hilton Head Island into a separate and independent town. Maybe we confront the secession syndrome. Possibly it is endemic here.

There was the hothead of Edisto Island who cried long ago that if South Carolina did not secede, by God, Edisto would! And there was the opposite view about secession expressed by James Louis Petigru that South Carolina was not big enough to be a republic and was too big to be a lunatic asylum. Maybe there is a middle ground between these two extremes in recently murmured resentment that Hilton Head has been relegated to hind tit in the government of Beaufort County. Secession seems out of date. One opinion recently given was that if South Carolina fired on Fort Sumter again, all the United States would have to do would be to close the Charleston Navy Yard. Then Mendel Rivers himself would lead the repentant procession back to the Union and the Union treasury.

Still if there is not secession action, there is secession muttering. Some South Carolina politicians have been talking in high indigna-

tion about Washington meddling. Even Columbia is a far place up
the road and has sometimes seemed closer to the Rhine River than
to Port Royal Sound. There is a really Broad River between the
Hilton Head–Bluffton community and the seat of power in Beaufort
County. So in a state where secession was first and foremost honored, naturally, some muttering goes on in the lost area south of
the Broad River and Port Royal Sound. Maybe, it has been said, this
area would be more at home in Jasper County, which is not cut off
by formidable waterways and by the apparent feeling of Beaufort
County.

A few years ago Hardeeville felt that way. That town chose Jasper
as its happy home. And as a matter of fact, Jasper County itself
earlier seceded—or was separated—from the Beaufort District.

Muttering here was magnified when the county-seat powers withdrew tax funds from the Hilton Head Island promotion of what it
considered its best interest. The Beaufort powers disagreed. Hilton
Head might pay much in taxes but it was told to shut its mouth or
lose its share of promotion funds. Undoubtedly the county satraps
could do this with a sense of self-righteousness because island newcomers could be considered as carpetbaggers doing nothing for the
county but carting in the cash.

Probably few in this southern part of the island are quite ready
to secede. They cherish the old name Beaufort. It is hard to tell why.
Though Henry Somerset, Duke of Beaufort, was a lord proprietor
and gave his name to the town, he is regarded as deserving little
recognition in history. Even of the modern town of Beaufort the
current edition of the *Encyclopedia Britannica* only says bluntly: "*See
Port Royal.*" Still, Hilton Head Islanders would much like a shorter
road to the lovely old county-seat town. At present, though it costs
fifty cents to enter Savannah, that city seems to be holding out more
welcoming arms.

As carpetbaggers maybe, as strangers until recently, newcomers
on Hilton Head Island are eager for welcome, anxious to be loved.
They have, however, a prejudice against being politically spat upon.
Shall it be "Hail to Jasper" or a growing sense that Beaufort is
home, market town, fair harbor, and the seat of hospitality. The
Yankees have not this time landed on the shore with hostile intent.
They are not yet so acclimated that secession is in their tradition.

Probably they will back no secession movement en masse. But they could slip away one by one, day by day, on visits to other places for warmer welcome. That could be a real Beaufort County pity.

November 5, 1970

Dancers of the Deep

Probably the only time to talk about sharks is when people have hung up their bathing suits. Fortunately, even in the swimming days, the big, frightening fish are always "somewhere else," according to Jacques-Yves Cousteau, who has picture-hunted sharks in all the seas.

In his beautifully illustrated new book, *The Shark: Splendid Savage of the Sea* (Doubleday), he reports: "In Europe, the waters of Senegal, West Africa, are thought to be dangerous. But, in Dakar, you will be told to avoid the Red Sea and Djibouti. Djibouti prides itself on never having had a single accident, but people there will tell you that Madagascar is infested with sharks, thirsting for blood. And, on the island of Madagascar, if you are on the west coast, the sharks are dangerous on the east coast, and vice versa."

Something of the same sort undoubtedly applies to stories of their prevalence between Florida, Hilton Head Island, and Cape May. Sharks reported off Sea Pines may really exist only in the waters around Port Royal, also vice versa. Unfortunately, however, Cousteau reports, sharks "are everywhere in tropical or temperate waters, and some species, such as the Greenland shark, even live

54

in glacial oceans. They are found at great depths, as well as on the surface and even in the estuaries of rivers and in some fresh-water lakes in Latin America. It is, therefore, possible to encounter a shark wherever man ventures on or under the sea, and the attack may be fatal."

Strangely, however, Cousteau, while pointing man's ancient and present fear, comes forward with a book full of admiration for this creature—for "the metallic beauty and invincible strength of that incomprehensible monster—the shark." As diver, he writes, "The blue tranquility of his form surrounds me with the sensation of a web of murderous yet beautiful force. . . . His silent circling is a ballet governed by untraceable mechanisms. . . . His configuration is perfect. Suddenly, the idea that he deserves killing comes to me like a shock and instantly shatters the spell. Murder is the real function of this ideal form, of this icy-blue camouflage, and of that enormous, powerful tail. . . . He is really a superb animal, almost seven feet in length, and I know, since I have often seen them before, that his jaw is lined with seven rows of teeth, as finely honed as the sharpest razor."

Superb and beautiful as he may be, this hardly sounds like the description of a welcome neighbor in any waters off Hilton Head Island or anywhere else. Stories, true or false, about these "hounds of the sea," as the Greeks called them, have "contributed toward creating a psychosis of the shark in all the sailors of the world and even in men who are simply interested in the sea, without the slightest intention of ever going near it." One seagoing superstition was that even sighting a shark presaged the death of a member of the crew. The danger and the terror can both be exaggerated, however. Underwater explorer Cousteau, who has not only encountered sharks but gone out to seek them, reports finally that, "All things considered, diving in tropical waters (where sharks may lurk) is actually much less dangerous than riding a motorcycle." Lately on this island certainly, sharks have seemed less menacing than some mini-men on mini-bikes.

Finally this veteran diver reports: "Sharks belong to the undersea environment. They rank among the most perfect, the most beautiful creatures ever developed in nature. We expect to meet them around coral reefs or in the open ocean, even if it is with a twist of fear. Their absence means disappointment for the divers, while their appearance is disquieting. When their formidable silhouette glides along the populated coral cliffs, fish do not panic; they quietly clear the lord's path, and keep an eye on him. So do we."

And a non-diver can take comfort in the fact that in cold climates and warm ones more people are hit by lightning than are bitten by sharks. The snake is a more-present danger. And the automobile is a deadlier monster than the most rapacious creatures of the deep.

Don't throw away your bathing suit.

November 12, 1970

Arrival of the Armada

Coming late, this has been in general a beautiful autumn on Hilton Head Island. And there is no reason to feel that this is a bad sign, as it turned out to be in the island's momentous year of 1861. That year, as reported in diaries of the time, a gentle October made way for a golden November. Slaves slowly picked a cotton crop which promised to be the biggest the oldest men could remember. Weather conditions had been perfect. And by the end of October even the threat of all hurricanes seemed safely past. But a bigger blow was coming.

On October 19th, a great Union fleet, built in haste, sailed from New York. Despite its magnitude, it was a fair-weather fleet. Admiral Samuel F. DuPont, who was to command it, described vessels being altered from trade to war: "It is like altering a vest into shirt to convert a trading steamer into a man-of-war. Except that there is a vessel and a steam engine, all else is inadaptible; but there is no help for it—the exigency of the blockade demands it." Some other vessels had been built in fifty-eight days. Some were ships chartered for the expedition. Among them were ferryboats and a steamer which the Admiral said was "never in her best days adapted to sea voyages."

Weather wary, the armada ran into trouble off Hatteras. So rough was the sea that the signal was sent from the flagship to commanders of other vessels to disregard the order of sailing and take care of their individual commands. Several ships sank. Many were damaged. Off Charleston, however, the fleet sailed on with a moderate breeze and a smooth sea. At last it came to its appointed destination off Port Royal Sound. There for a moment the weather seemed to show Confederate sympathies. Afterwards General Thomas F. Drayton, the Confederate commander, reported that Union attack on November 6th was delayed because the weather was "very boisterous." There was a heavy westerly wind.

But November 7th was the kind of day those delight in who love Hilton Head Island. One Union officer wrote of "a glassy sea." General Drayton reported: "At last the memorable 7th dawned upon us, bright and serene; not a ripple upon the broad expanse of water to disturb the accuracy of fire from the broad decks of that magnificent armada advancing, in battle array, to vomit forth its iron hail, with all the spiteful energy of long-suppressed rage and conscious strength."

The beautiful day became the most spectacular one in the history of the islands. A Union historian, who apparently was also an observer, wrote that "so great was the cannons' roar that it was distinctly heard at Fernandina, seventy miles away. There was deafening music in the air, which came from far and near and all around; heavy clouds of dust and smoke, due to our bursting shells and the enemy's fire, partly obscured the earth-works, while our vessels were but dimly seen through the smoke from their own guns which hung over the water."

One of the first of the many visiting correspondents who have come to report the Hilton Head Island scene wrote then for the *London News* that "the rising of the dust on shore in perpendicular columns looked as if we had suddenly raised from the dust a grove of poplars." His image would have been more native if he had written of a grove of pines.

Certainly it was a beautiful day, even if those on shore, already scurrying to get away, would have preferred a hurricane. For them, good Hilton Head weather was then bad Hilton Head news.

November 19, 1970

Tournament

There is every reason in the wonderful world of golf why the Heritage Golf Classic on Hilton Head Island should be regarded as something special. The game can be and is, of course, played at inland clubs. Pinehurst and Augusta get along very well at some distance from the sea. But the very word *links,* even in some modern dictionaries, has as its first meaning "sandhills especially along the seashore"—a word derived from Scotland, as so much of the game of golf is. Furthermore, an English golfer named Harold Hilton, whose relationship to Captain William Hilton is at least obscure, nearly fifty years ago made a reluctant admission: "To put the matter in the very plainest language, American players of the present day are better golfers than their British cousins."

Charles Fraser, as archivist as well as architect of this arcadian playground, has dug up the facts about the ancient play of golf in this neighborhood. He found evidences of the game here long before millionaire playboys in the late years of the last century began to lay out crude courses in New York and Newport. Tradition at least carries the play in South Carolina and Savannah as far back as 1786—a year in which there was more excitement about a new-born republic than par on any course. More romantically, the documentation includes the invitation to a Miss Eliza Johnston to a ball given by a Savannah golf club in 1811.

This entry of a lady into the story is an important item in the consideration of the Heritage or any other tournament. Most tournaments, or tourneys, in the Old South derived from Scotland, as golf did, via the Waverley Novels of Sir Walter Scott. Sir Walter's novels were so popular that a distinguished South Carolinian of the time said that the young gentry divided their time between "outdoor amusements and the Waverly Novels." Sometimes they put the two together. Tourneys then followed a fashion borrowed from *Ivanhoe.* Palmetto knights of the *chiv-al'-ry* (never pronounced *chiv'-al-ry*) rode to the lists on thoroughbred horses, carrying lances which they aimed at wooden rings instead of each other. South Carolina newspapers enthusiastically covered such tourneys in which "all the beauty and bravery of the parish" gathered on the "lush and spacious greensward" before Low Country "castles." The elders and the girls cheered as the knights vied for the honor of crowning "the Queen of Love and Beauty."

Maybe something of the romantic is lost in the modern golf tournaments in which cash, rather than the lady, is the prize. Perhaps today ladies casually clad in very expensive clothes only add their presence to the galleries or serve as chauffeurs for the pros. Going back to the ancient times which the Old South emulated, it is probably too much to expect a re-creation here of such a gathering as that on the Field of the Cloth of Gold (the French name, *Camp du drap d'or,* seems less poetic) at which Henry VIII of England and Francis I of France took knightly parts. Probably we have moved a long way from such a time when "ladies gorgeously clad, and knights showing by their dress and bearing their anxiety to revive the glories and the follies of the age of chivalry, jostled mountebanks, mendicants, and vendors of all kinds."

Still, evidently the tournament is everlasting whether played with mace and broadsword or driver and niblick. And certainly no better place could be found for the gathering of the skillful and the admiring than Hilton Head Island. The Cloth of Gold may be missing, but quite as lovely are the fairways, which a recent writer, not otherwise entirely complimentary, described as being as sleek as a fawn's flank. In the big crowd expected possibly some mountebanks and mendicants will slip into the galleries. But the ladies will be at least as lovely as those who watched more bloody jousting long ago. The elders will be as enthusiastic. The players won't creak in armor. The same kind of cheers will rise for the victor. And—God willing—the same good sun will shine on the colorful company gathered for the show of skill.

It is too bad that neither Richard Coeur de Lion nor Barnwell Rhett nor Bobby Jones can be here. Each of them would enjoy the spectacle with the thousands assembled. In varying ways we keep old patterns intact in a changing world. The tournament is eternal.

November 26, 1970

O Say Can You See?

Three young boys of the Sea Pines Academy at the end of their day lowered, briskly, ceremoniously, carefully, the American flag. Their impeccable attendance to the flag would have pleased Warren Vail who, while no super-patriot, has a profile somewhat like that of the American eagle. And sometimes, when he is displeased by anything on this island that he loves, he seems to carry, like the eagle, arrows in his hand.

Recently he has been much disturbed by what has seemed to him the careless treatment of the flag here by some of those who, in evidence of their patriotism in a troubled time, display the national banner before their houses. He reports neglected flags flying in the night. Frayed flags drooping in the rain. Flags faded and forgotten. So Warren secured a copy of rules on flag etiquette. They are not complicated. As everyone should know, the universal custom is that the Stars and Stripes should be briskly raised at sunrise and ceremoniously lowered at sunset. There are some official exceptions to this—such as the night flying of the flag at Fort McHenry where the Star-Spangled Banner was seen only by the rocket's red glare. The flag should never touch anything beneath it, such as the ground, the floor, or the water. The best rule is that those who display flags in respect should take care of them in responsibility.

Flags can be endangered even by those who seem to love them best. Recently, an automobile painted with the stripes and stars of the flag was seen here on the island. Possibly, its owner considered himself a special patriot. His car made the flag look like an automotive joke.

The best warning about flag abuse lies in what has been done to the Confederate flag by some of those who whoop loudest at the playing of "Dixie" and cry stridently that the South will rise again. They have turned the Stars and Bars into bumper stickers. They fly Confederate flags as decorations on hot-rod autos. They have made it a symbol not of a dignified Lost Cause but of a raucous, often rowdy, chauvinism. *Chauvinism,* as not every child need know, came from the name of Nicolas Chauvin, whose demonstrative patriotism and attachment to Napoleon came to be ridiculed by his quite-as-patriotic comrades in arms.

Nicolas Chauvin casts a long shadow not only in France but also in America, particularly the South. Sometimes those of his kind treat the flag as a private possession peculiarly their own and hardly shared by all their fellows under it. The real meaning of the American flag—or the Confederate flag—can be more distorted by some who ceremoniously display it at Ku Klux Klan and like assemblies than by any who in human forgetfulness leave it hanging dank in the night and the rain.

It is a good thing for Warren Vail to urge the respectful care for the flag on this island in particular and in this country in general. Some rules as to its flying and its care should be known and obeyed. But in hardly any other thing is it more true than that in the flying of the flag the spirit is more important than the law. Most of all, it needs to be flown always in remembrance that our flag is the banner of a land founded in the faith that "all Men are created equal, that they are endowed by their Creator with certain unalienable Rights, that among these are Life, Liberty, and the Pursuit of Happiness—That to secure these Rights, Governments are instituted among Men, deriving their just Powers from the Consent of the Governed. . . ."

The first rule is that that faith be raised with the flag. If it is not, only a piece of cloth is flapping in the wind.

December 3, 1970

Jewel on a Thistle

Fortunately, it is not necessary to be an ornithologist to watch birds, nor an entomologist to watch butterflies. In each case it would probably help. Certainly a man who associates butterflies with the blooming of flowers has a right to be a little puzzled by the great number of butterflies which have been hovering about Hilton Head Island this fall. Few of them are spectacular creatures, but their presence has added much to the autumn scene.

They have been flying about here for a long time. The Spaniards who followed Columbus must have seem them. So also Jean Ribaut, though he left no reports of their dancing presence. It was on this coast, though farther northward, that Sir Walter Raleigh's captain, John White, grandfather of Virginia Dare, painted his famous picture of the beautiful swallowtail butterfly, which he carried back to England in 1587 as a first evidence of the beauties of this strange new world.

In the British Museum today this painting still keeps the brilliant colors in which it was painted by this artist-sea captain. Nearly a century after it was painted the author of a quaint scientific book, *Theatre of Insects*, wrote of White's painted butterfly that "the roundles of the inner wings are sky-colour, insomuch that you would think they were set with Saphire stones; the eyes are like Chrysolite." A century later the early American naturalist William Bartram, in his travels through the primitive South, wrote much not only about fighting alligators, leaping fish, queer beasts, but also of the butterflies flickering in the air above them in numbers and kinds equal to the birds. He added details about butterfly hunting by the Indians. But probably the most enthusiastic reporter of the colorful insects was Fanny Kemble, the young, lovely actress-abolitionist, during her unhappy stay at her rich planter husband's cotton plantation on a nearby sea island.

She wrote in 1839 of a spring ride in that sea-island cotton country: "Lovely blossoms are springing up everywhere—weeds, of course, wild things, impertinently so called. Nothing is cultivated here but cotton; but in some of the cotton fields beautiful creatures are peeping into blossom, which I suppose will all be duly hoed off the surface of the soil in proper season; meantime I rejoice in them, and in the splendid, magnificent thistles, which would be in flower gardens in other parts of the world, and in the wonderful, strange, beautiful butterflies that seem to me almost as big as birds, that go zigzagging in the sun. I saw yesterday a lovely monster, who thought proper, for my greater delectation, to alight on a thistle I was admiring, and as the flower was purple, and he was all black velvet fringed with gold, I was exceedingly pleased with his good inspiration."

Fanny only mentioned the dazzling creatures casually in another passage, but she put it in proper sea-island scene: "The Acacias are swinging their silver censers under the green roof of these wood temples; every stump is like a classical altar to the sylvan gods, garlanded with flowers; every post, or stick, or slight stem, like a Bacchante's thyrsus, twined with wreaths of ivy and wild vine, waving in the tepid wind. Beautiful butterflies flicker like flying flowers among the bushes, and gorgeous birds, like winged jewels, dart from the boughs. and—and—a huge green snake slid like a dark ribbon across the path while I was stopping to enjoy all this deliciousness, and so I became less enthusiastic, and cantered on past the little deserted churchyard, with the new-made grave beneath its grove of noble oaks, and a little further on reached Mrs. A's cottage, half-hidden, in the midst of ruins and roses."

Perhaps such a passage is too brilliant to be conjured up by a few fall butterflies. It is good to know that such a scene is possible still. And it may be instructive to learn via Fanny that that "thyrsus" of Bacchante was a flowering staff attributed to Bacchus, god of wine, and to the crew of women—Bacchae—who accompanied him and took part in his rituals. Certainly that indicates where a few frail butterflies in the late autumn sun can lead the imagination of a lady—or a man.

December 10, 1970

The Pine Cones Fell

Suddenly, on a single night not particularly marked by winds, the big pine cones fell in profusion on Hilton Head Island. Undoubtedly this sudden cone-fall was an annual occurrence which foresters could explain. Being city folk, however, most new residents on the island merely noted the unusual incidence of cones in their driveways and on their pine-straw lots and lawns. Some thought about collecting them for the children in cities far away. Others wanted them removed as litter. But those who retained some of the backcountry thrift of their rural ancestors recognized them as the best kindling to be collected for the good open fires which bless households on this shore on the brisk winter days.

Except in the case of some magnificent specimens, like one which was struck by lightning here last summer, the pine doesn't get as much credit hereabouts as it deserves. For those who come from the North, the palmetto, as a palm, is symbol for desired climate. The live oaks carry the moss which festoons the island. Still, begging Mr. Kipling's pardon, each of us holds here a little "dominion over pine and palm." And in recent years, with the growth of the paper mills and the spread of their tended forests, the pine has become a Southern symbol even more important than the magnolia.

Maybe the pine is momentarily in ill repute. The huge barges of pine pulpwood, strangely moving in both directions up and down the Intracoastal Waterway, may seem to be the materials for the making not only of paper but also of stink. The view of the belching stacks of Union Bag across the Savannah Wildlife Refuge on the way to the airport is no longer regarded as deserving of aesthetic approval. Times have changed since citizens of Savannah and Georgetown happily declared that the odor broadcast from the tall stacks "smelled like prosperity." Prosperity had become commonplace, and pollution is cast in the role of the major villain of the times.

The pine is certainly not to blame for its uses and misuses. Pines cover thousands of Southern acres which were eroding into the rivers. They are important on shores like this one. For years in Europe, particularly along the Bay of Biscay, pines have been planted to protect the eroding shores. Even here some are planted on bare beach-front lots to help justify the high prices they are bringing. Also the pines, which have been a source of pollution by smell, have long been regarded as a source of special perfume. Even the ordinary "old field pines" in the woods running back from the shore have a fragrance in their abundant resin which has sometimes given them the additional name of "frankincense pines." The one certain thing is that there is no more delightful odor than the smell of pine burning in the wide fireplaces on Hilton Head Island when the occasional cold days come.

So welcome the pine cones that have been falling here. They look big to Eastern city eyes. In the West, enormous cones—sometimes a foot long and six inches in diameter, weighing more than four pounds—are almost commonplace. Ours suffice. They are big enough for decorative purposes. And they make almost the best kindling in the world. Perhaps they are not quite so good as the sticks of fat "lightwood" which the late Win Dow gave to friends last Christmas and which are now produced on a commercial scale. Those on sale in the stores are packaged more slickly, but they lack the charm of Win's hand-bound bundles tied with red ribbon bows.

Certainly next best are the cones. And now is the time to fill empty liquor cartons with them, pile the cartons in the carport, and almost eagerly await the weather that calls for the fires. Certainly such fires, set off with the cones under good stout logs of pine and oak, are as decorative as holly and mistletoe. Also, they provide a warmth which neither oil nor electricity can produce. The yule log is over-sized and out of fashion. But as an accompaniment of wassail, which certainly is not out of style on this island, hardly anything compares with the sight, the smell, the feel of blazes set off with pine cones.

And the time to collect them is now. They are the pine tree's gift to us all.

December 17, 1970

The Beloved Imposter

Is Santa Claus coming to Hilton Head? Is he coming anywhere?

There has seemed to be some doubt about it. Indeed, in recent years there has seemed to be almost a concerted movement to take Santa Claus out of Christmas as an old imposter about whom children should be warned and all Christians admonished. He had no place, some preacher said in a Carolina town, in a parade heralding the approach of Christmas. And in Baltimore, a priest used the occasion of a Christmas party for little children to denounce Santa Claus and at the same time make a pretentious Christmas gift. He announced, as if he had wrapped it up with a red ribbon, that he "gave Christmas back to Christ."

The form of his gift was a Christmas sermon in which he undertook to disillusion the children about Santa Claus. Undoubtedly, from a theological and scholarly standpoint, the well-meaning priest thought he did a good and necessary job. The old elf was unmasked, and the priest reported he has received many letters of commendation. One which he made public was from a father who wrote that "you go out and work like a dog to buy your kids presents and Santa

Claus gets all the credit." It seemed time to the priest to unmask Santa Claus as a pagan, an elf, a hobgoblin, and also apparently as a grabber of Christmas credit.

Maybe a pious deed was done. Maybe a pagan has been killed, even if a demon has not been exorcised. Now perhaps the father who resented Santa Claus getting the credit for the gifts he bought can spend Christmas as the undisputed center of his Christmas scene, expanding in the doctrine that it is better to get thanks yourself than to see delight and wonder on the faces of others. It may be time to unmask the whole company of the pretenders, the fairies, the elves, all the good little people who have up to now had hiding places in the hearts and minds and imaginations of children and of those adults, too, who decline to grow grim and stern about the property rights of the theologians on Christmas Day.

Undoubtedly, such theologians know "the law." They keep "the truth." Well, they've been keeping it now for two thousand years. They were keeping it when Jesus was born. And no people more clearly received—and soundly deserved—the scorn of Jesus than those who stressed the laws and lost the spirit. It was Jesus himself who said that the children, not the priests, know best the way to the kingdom of heaven. Also, it was Jesus who said that one who gave to the least gave unto Him. The clear teaching of that is that any who give joy in His spirit (even such a disreputable old pagan as Santa Claus) give for Him and give in His service. Of course, it is literally true (and was no surprise to the children when they were told) that Santa Claus had no place in the Christmas story. That story was filled by angels and shepherds and by wise men who gave a baby in a stable such strange gifts as gold and the ingredients of incense and perfume. Santa Claus was not there. And neither, so far as the record goes, were any solemn priests. The Pharisees and the Sadducees, who were most sure they knew the law and the truth, were not even mentioned. What the angels sang was not the solemn law but tidings of great joy.

Of course, Christmas is Jesus' day—not Santa Claus's. The little children bowing their heads every time the priest mentioned Jesus' name knew that. They have not been deprived of the Christmas story. Neither have little Methodist and Baptist children. Santa Claus is not pushed into the Saviour's place. Indeed, Santa Claus is most welcomed in homes where Christ is most worshipped. It is not unchristian to let Santa Claus help the children celebrate the birthday of their Lord. Christ has not lost His day—or His world. He does not need any man—even one in vestments—to give it back to Him. An ordinary man does not presume to say, but it could be that Jesus does not think Santa Claus is the chief despoiler of the Christmas spirit at Christmas time. There are possibly some greater offenders against His day and His spirit than children who hang up their stockings and parents who watch the children empty them on a morning in which young delight and young wonder do not seem impiety, heresy, paganism.

There are other Christmas interlopers. Pride and selfishness, hardness of heart and meanness of spirit remain even on Christ's birthday as in all the year around it. His day is stained by the sins of gluttony and drunkenness, envy, even hatred.

His world is divided, and people in division sometimes make hatred of each other seem a virtue. The peace which His day proclaimed is still denied. In such a world it seems at least a sad service to Christ or Christmas to direct particular indignation at Santa Claus.

The one heartening thing in Christendom is that Santa Claus does come. He will come next year, too, and the next; and on Christmas days in all God's years so long as there remain the eager hearts of children, homes of love around them, faith in glad tidings, exceeding great joy, all these things which still make the world worthy of God's love. Perhaps among these good things the faith in Santa Claus, which is the faith in good and loving giving, is only a small item. Maybe historically and theologically, Santa is a disreputable, phony old pagan, perhaps a hobgoblin, an elf who consorts with such a covert company as the fairies. He does seem sometimes to have imposed some tall tales upon the minds of children. Certainly some preposterous stories have been circulated about the travels of his reindeer in an age of supersonic planes. He could stand a visit to the barber. He might begin to realize that his continuing addiction to red clothes seems a little suspicious, if not sinister. His residence close to the North Pole puts him in a position which might concern those who are most concerned about security.

Hobgoblin, pagan, elf—he may be all those things. The important thing is that he comes on Christmas morning. He will pass this way.

And it will be time to stop him as an itinerant intruder on the birthday of Jesus when those who would stop him can show that they add more joy, more kindness, more love to the celebration of the birthday of Our Lord than Santa Claus himself.

December 24, 1970

Year's Happy Ending

As chronicler of the adventures of two bewildered noblemen cast upon an island by a mysterious tempest, the poet recorded this exchange:

> GONZALO: Had I a plantation of this isle, my lord—
> ANTONIO: He'd sow it with nettle-seed.

Obviously then, Hilton Head Island cannot push Bermuda out of mind as the scene of *The Tempest*. No such prickly shrubs have been planted on this gardened shore. Even the thistle on this island is a beautiful plant in the springtime when black-winged butterflies occasionally alight. Yet, as the years too swiftly pass here, possibly, in New Year's retrospect 1970 may be recalled as the *anno Domini* of fresh, good unity. It was welcome. Sometimes this precious body of land has seemed to run not only between the sounds of Port Royal and Calibogue but also from one paranoid point to the other. In the face of the threat of BASF, Capulet appeared ready to embrace Montague and vice versa. Like pioneers mounting the palisades to repel incursive savages, island colonists confronted BASF. To guard their estuaries, ladies rushed to man mimeographing machines, to stamp communications, to collect petitions. Gentlemen composed propaganda and collected the munitions of battle.

Of course, not all was unity on this island of diversity. It would be dreadful if this were a stereotyped shore. Many disagreed with Romulus Roller and Remus McKibben when they appeared, perhaps mistakenly, to wish to set themselves up as the founders of a city. They withdrew with grace in the face of opposition of persons reluctant to serve as the wolf's paps. Now Fred Hack's Shipyard Plantation will have simpler sailing on the seas crowded by so many people with a compulsion for condominiums.

Surely, the happiest agreement was in the male and female rush to help Charles put on the Heritage Tournament. Charles seemed that week like Ariel in command of the elements. The week which began with cold and rain turned into weather like a golden syrup when the play began. The pros presented a great show, but the spectacle was made possible by real amateurs. They were the assembled citizens in special costumes, glad to pay to use their willing hands. There are other tournaments here and there and every year. But no such body of eager volunteers has been assembled since Tom Sawyer let the boys of his Missouri neighborhood help him whitewash the fence.

Maybe this was a Mulford year. Emerson led the embattled retirees recently escaped from regions they had helped pollute. They met the threatened blitzkrieg of Governor McNair and the chemical storm troopers. And Mary Ellen led the ladies in their multiple tasks in support of the tournament. Other thanks seem in order. Orion Hack taught a people—whose language is limited to golf, boats, the stock market, and the price of building lots—the new vocabulary of ecology. Some thanks are due to friends who made sacrifices far away. A monument to Walter Joseph Hickel should be erected, possibly in one of the island's circles, by popular subscription, bearing some appropriate inscription, such as: "Here lies Hickel but where in the hell is BASF?"

Now we move along into a new year. The island has become big enough to tolerate in the Bank of Beaufort such a man as Jim Gray, who is permitted to say that this island is not the only place worth visiting. And speaking of travel, Lawyer Joab Dowling now seems to be commuting from Hilton Head to Beaufort instead of from Beaufort to Hilton Head. We grow. The medical center is expanding. One thing certain in this community of lights and shadows, recently diagnosed by Dr. Donald Gatch, is that the presiding physicians here are in no danger of malnutrition. The Bargain Box is going to get a new building to house its old clothes and shelter Almeda's chortle. The Post Office will get more space as the island gets so big that Mary Scheider can no longer read all the postcards anymore.

Gene Martin is running a supergrocery which seems almost like a free dispensary to those who once paid the prices charged by Norris Richardson. Tom Howard needs some sort of prize for nomenclature. Pete Hall has added something to the art of salesmanship since he had his picture printed in *The Islander* wearing the expression of a man who dared anybody to buy a lot in Palmetto Dunes. And *The Islander* itself deserves some recognition for its new series of love stories about Liz and Charles Rousek and Walter and Margaret Greer. *The Island Packet* certainly should be rewarded for development of a new system of simplification of the division of words at any point and between any letters. And I throw a kiss to Rosalie Stone—but from a safe distance and in readiness to duck behind a condominium.

All I would like from the new year would be the right to the epitaph:

> When I am dead, I hope it may be said:
> "His sins were scarlet, but his books were read."

Happy New Year!

December 31, 1970

Pattern in the Stone

Those who now enjoy the gardened Low Country of South Carolina may well remember over their clubs and their cups that once there was not merely a South of sun and slavery. Also, even if rare, there was a most aristocratic ideal. Fortunately, it is wisely monumented in Saint Michael's Churchyard in Charleston. More lusty, even rambunctious, heroes are remembered. Often there seems more color in the hotheads who danced into war as into a waltz. But South Carolina reverently remembers, too, a man with whom most of its citizens violently disagreed without denying him due respect when he died.

James Louis Petigru lies close to John C. Calhoun, who led the state into war. Petigru, was walking the city's streets alone as it began. He mistook the bells which rang so loud on December 20, 1860, for a fire alarm, and when he was told that instead they had announced secession, he cried, "I tell you there is a fire; they have this day set a blazing torch to the temple of constitutional liberty, and please God, we shall have no peace forever."

His view was rejected. Yet, in three years the city, in the midst of war, honored its man of dissent at his burial. His epitaph remains a perfect statement of the aristocratic ideal, which remains as important as it has always been in the South as on earth. Never was so much engraved on so little stone. It is:

JAMES LOUIS PETIGRU
　　Born at
Abbeville May 10, 1789
Died at Charleston March 9th, 1863

JURIST, ORATOR, STATESMAN, PATRIOT

Future times will hardly know how great a life
　　This simple stone commemorates.
　The tradition of his Eloquence, his
　　Wisdom and his Wit may fade;
But he lived for ends more durable than fame,
His Eloquence was the protection of the poor and wronged,
His learning illuminated the principles of Law—
　　In the admiration of his Peers,
　　In the respect of his People,
　　In the affection of his Family,
　　His was the highest place;
　　　The just meed
　Of his kindness and forbearance,
　His dignity and simplicity,
His brilliant genius and his unwearied industry,
　Unawed by Opinion,
　Unseduced by Flattery,
　Undismayed by Disaster,
He confronted Life with antique Courage
　　And Death with Christian Hope.

　　　In the great Civil War
He withstood his People for his Country,
　But his People did homage to the Man
Who held his conscience higher than their praise;
　　And his Country
Heaped her honours on the grave of the Patriot,
　　To whom, living,
　His own righteous self-respect sufficed
　　Alike for Motive and Reward.

In a time of stridency, when sometimes, in the collapse of consensus, repression seems the proper medicine for dissent, that stone is as pertinent as it is permanent. The pattern in the stone cannot safely be neglected in an opulent world in which ideals sometimes seem only old-fashioned. It is worth a trip to Charleston just to stand by this stone.

January 7, 1971

Lilliput or Monopoly

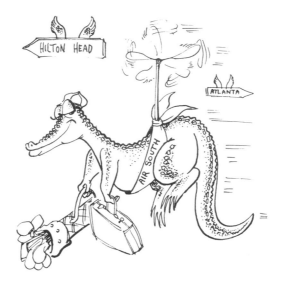

Of course, there is nothing more commonplace than flying. Some neighbor or another is nearly always high above the Atlantic, the Pacific, or Jersey City. Ginny Linton went to darkest Africa to get the German measles and was practically turned out on the veldt because other air tourists were pushing for the hotel rooms. It is only a one-martini trip between Atlanta and Savannah. Sometimes there seem more hijackers now than there were passengers when many of us were young. Hardly anybody remembers the proudly possessed "short snorters" of World War II. Those one-, five-, and ten-dollar bills were signed for transatlantic flyers by others who had made such trips. They were the certificates of the daring. Now in a world filled with senior citizens and schoolboys going to world's ends for weekends, they seem as out of date as speak-easy cards.

Still, it is an adventure to fly over and around Hilton Head Island, particularly with such a pilot as island visitor Charles Czermak, Atlanta radiologist, who seems to resent the fact that he wasn't born a bird. Many people come into the slick new airport on the north end of the island. But too few case the whole joint from the air—or so it seems. Certainly the air above us is not crowded, though jet trails streak the sky. Coast Guard helicopters chug over the beaches, and recurrently bug planes do unequal battle with pests below. There is a sort of double-vision experience in an island air-reconnaissance for an island man. The eye-level vision is given a sort of fourth dimension of appreciation.

It is hard to realize that Hilton Head is almost two islands, with Broad Creek (and it is broad!) stopping just short of the old cemetery, where it might easily cut through Folly Field to the sea. From the air, the island, including creeks and landscaped lagoons, looks as if there were more water than land within its limits. But what an amazing undeveloped area of forest land lies across much of the north end of the island. Plenty of wilderness, with a capacity to contain a metropolis, still waits to be turned into building lots. Also, in this place of palms and pines, winter reveals a large forest-land area of deciduous trees, gray in the midst of surrounding green. Considering the tomato tales, amazingly little land seems set aside for cultivation except in the long neat rows on Jenkins Island.

There lie the real-estate developments, one after another—Port Royal, Palmetto Dunes, and Sea Pines—all looking like parts of a gardened game of Monopoly. Will the lighthouse at Harbour Town mean an advance or a penalty in play? What about the water towers looking like white toadstools? How many houses equal an inn? What is the play-money price of condominiums? Certainly those of us who are tiny pieces in the game are put in perspective. Even former generals and robber barons are pygmies. The trucks and cars are the toys children collect by the dozens. Boats are things suited for the bathtub. The lagoons are like those in Japanese gardens kept on window sills.

From the playpen to the philosopher's barrel: High above it we see our land like Lilliput. It might be even more interesting if we could become Lilliputians and see our scene like Brobdingnag. We could all be giants then. Yuccas in such a case would reach to the sky, and sparrows would be interplanetary planes. From both trips we might gape not at how big the universe can be but at how small a space could contain a universe. Depending upon the point of view, we are monsters or mites. Packing all the necessary nerves into a gnat's eye may be a problem at least equal to that of casting the constellations into infinity. NASA can put men on the moon, but nobody dreams of men walking into the last chamber of the nautilus, where presumably the music is.

Apparently the oxygen is getting a little thin up here with the altitude. Better come down toward earth. Anyhow, flying low over Hilton Head Island you can, if the trees aren't too thick, pick out your own house and wonder how all those problems and delights can be packed into so small a box. The smoke that comes far off from the Union Bag factory might be the steam from a tea kettle. And, also across water, Foot Point is still only a green site for serenity. It would be good if on a clear day you could see forever but that is not always certain—up or down.

January 14, 1971

Durable Illusion

The pollution explosion seems to have quieted down. And maybe the polluters after first protests of innocence and announcement of purposes for good are just "laying low" like Br'er Rabbit. That would make pretty good sense for them. It has worked before and may very well work again.

Writing in 1956 of the Santee (the only South Carolina river included in the Rivers of America series, published by Rinehart & Company), Henry Savage, Jr., was optimistic. In a two-page passage he listed the plants and places which were pouring sewage and every sort of effluent into this tidal river system. The Santee system of streams, he thought, could assimilate a far greater pollution load than other rivers of comparable volume.

"But even so, its ever growing pollution load was fast approaching its assimilative capacity. The awful threat posed by that approach brought legislative action in both the Carolinas—laws which will protect their rivers from new, untreated sources of influction and gradually reduce the load they are already being called upon to bear. Thus an enlightened, conservation-minded public came to the rescue of the Santee waters. . . ."

This suggestion that South Carolina was made safe fifteen years ago does not quite jibe with situations disclosed in recent months. And those polluting plants Mr. Savage listed have been joined by more and more along the Santee and other rivers. That "enlightened, conservation-minded public" has certainly not been as energetic or as vigilant as the promoters.

Other rivers were going to be saved thirty years ago. Writing about the Hudson in 1939, in the same series of books, Carl Carmer sounded both practical and poetic about the situation: "The people of the big valley know that cleaning Hudson water will take time— but they know, too, that it will be done. The recalcitrant towns love the river and are aware of what its waters, if purified, could do for them and their children. There will be beaches on the Hudson and people will sit on them in the sun and they will swim in the water.

"There will be boating for everybody, the people say. Up and down the navigable length of the river there will be basins— 'Marinas' the Survey Commission calls them in its report. In a marina a man can moor his boat, whether it be a canoe with an outboard motor or a yacht, and he can buy supplies, and from it as a home port he can take his family on proud journeys along Henry Hudson's River of Mountains.

"The time will come—the people have dreamed it—when the river running down from its high source among the ancient rocks will ripple beside green parks and winding level roads all of its way to the tall gray city at its mouth."

The man who wrote about the Delaware River presented himself as neither a prophet nor the son of a prophet. Of the fate of fishermen he simply reported: "Growth of industry along the river wrecked a flourishing New Jersey occupation. . . . Upstream factories poured their waste into the Delaware: acid from the tanneries, sewage from the cities, and oil from mills poisoned the stream. Fish ceased to spawn in such vast numbers in the Delaware. Fishermen who once had dipped out, by hand seines, three thousand catfish in a single night found that the species had almost vanished. . . ."

Of course, near the Delaware you can still get the best fish in the world at Bookbinder's Restaurant in Philadelphia. Planes bring them now from further and further away. But the streams most of us watched and were supposed to tend have become the nation's septic tanks. They were already becoming that when these men wrote in warning and hope—even confidence. They have thickened in filth and may grow more and more foul tomorrow and dirtier nearer and nearer to the last estuaries.

We have been warned. We have been alerted. We have been aroused. Well, Theodore Roosevelt, the great conservationist, did that more than sixty years ago and look where we are now. And imagine where we could be sixty years from now with the same poor old rivers and millions more people to foul them. Nothing is more polluting than the false promise and the false hope, unless it be the strictly limited interest span of the so-called enlightened, conservation-minded public.

January 21, 1971

Love and the Yucca

Not all of us can be poet-scientists like Nancy Butler. As a matter of fact, not all the scientists can be such a poet as she is, and certainly not all poets can put her learning into their lines. Most of us come from paved canyons to this reservation for the retired. We confront nature with serenity and maybe, if we look hard, with some astonishment.

Take the two ubiquitous symbols of our shore: the yucca and the Spanish moss. They look like fairly simple things to start with in our exploration of the nature at our doors and in our trees. Both are actually astounding.

Up near Charleston recently the report was that the Spanish moss was sick. It was not suggested that the oaks might soon lose their drapery, but on some trees the moss seemed somehow puny.

There have been no adverse reports about the yucca. Their growth requires no such green thumb as Alva Hines possesses. Over in the sandy land on Piping Plover Road they multiply like weeds, which they may seem to some to be. They flourish on Calibogue. Johnny White moves them as if they were sticks requiring no care.

They thrive wherever they are stuck in the ground. And considering the complexity of their propagation, that seems mysterious.

Some people (notably, for instance, the late Mrs. Franklin Roosevelt) do not like Spanish moss. It seems to them dreary, ghostly, portentous. Gray-bearded ghosts are in the trees. Others wonder about its addiction to the oak and its discrimination against the pine. Certainly, hung between eyes and a sunset, it adds strangeness to beauty. It seems almost alive in the wind. Sometimes fallen pieces of it do look like small dead creatures on the roads.

Still, these simplest things are strange: Spanish moss is not a moss. And—now hold your hats—it belongs to the same botanical family as the pineapple. And, so the book says, the pineapple plant resembles some yuccas in general appearance. So far as is known, however, neither man nor beast ever found sustenance in the yucca or the moss.

Without such a relative as the pineapple, the yucca is the more amazing plant, particularly in connection with its sex life. There is a real story of fidelity here utterly different from that of other flowering plants and of the promiscuous butterflies, bees, hummingbirds, and other flying creatures which attend them. The yuccas's white, bell-shaped, pendulous flowers are fertilized entirely by one faithful aide. Each species of the yucca has a yucca moth adapted to it and to it alone.

Here is the scientific story of this pretty natural process: The yucca moth emerges at the time of the opening of the yucca flowers. The timing of the tryst is important because the flowers frequently remain open only for a single night. The lady moth gathers pollen from one yucca flower, rolls it into a ball, flies to another flower, lays four or five eggs in the pistil (the ovule-bearing organ of a seed plant consisting of the ovary with its appendages), and inserts the pollen mass in the opening thus formed. The larvae eat about half of the two hundred seeds produced by the plant. The yucca can be fertilized by no other insect, and the moth can utilize no other plant.

The yucca has not generally been cast in a romantic role among the plants. The magnolia and the myrtle have been greater favorites with the poets. Ladies prefer the camellia and the japonica, the azalea and the rhododendron. The bristling yucca seems inhospitable, even austere. Evidently, however, appearances are deceiving.

The homely yucca depends upon the tender attention of so fragile a creature as its one and only, very special moth for the survival of its species. And there could be some sort of parable in the strictly limited embrace of the plant and the moth. Anyhow, here they grow and bloom for recurring welcoming evenings with their attentive flying assistants in procreation. If there ever was a case in which it could be truly said that "they are made for each other," this is it.

Besides this romantic attachment, the Spanish moss is just an intruder on a tree.

January 28, 1971

Beauregard's Ballistics

This is the month South Carolinians were once sure would be "a date that will live in infamy," as a later statesman said of another occasion. On February 1, 1865, William Tecumseh Sherman began his march from Savannah across the Carolinas. In bitter remembrance, that march has seemed to have been illuminated all the way by a succession of burning mansions leading to the big bonfire in Columbia where eighty-six blocks (366 acres) and 1,386 buildings were destroyed in flames. Not until recently was it safe for a wag to say that South Carolinians ought to build a monument to Sherman, who made it possible for almost everybody in this area to say that their ancestors lived in great plantation mansions but that Sherman burned them down.

It was not until 1923—fifty-eight years later—that a real South Carolina aristocrat, who had been a boy in 1865, dared to write of this pyrotechnic time in terms of its comedy as well as its tragedy. I. Jenkins Mikell performed this improbable task in his rare little book *Rumbling of the Chariot Wheels*. He wrote not only of Sherman's march but also of the beginning of the war when the word came to guard all the rivers at Charleston's back door in this sea-island

country. What he wrote of the Edisto River and Edisto Island applied equally to the Broad River and Hilton Head.

"The Artillery Company of Edisto Island—strictly of an amateur
nature—composed of wealthy planters and their sons, each of
whom was a law unto himself, organized as a pastime, was ordered
to the duty of 'repelling the invaders.' With its thirty odd men and
two shining, brass-muzzled loading cannon—or was it only one?
—six pounders, they left their gun shed and marched the five miles
to their post. I do not know but what most, if not all, of them rode
in their buggies! At any rate, they finally arrived, prepared to shed
their blood for their country.

"They made camp, or at least their body servants did, each soldier
being provided with one, and then sat down to a two-hour dinner.
It was really too bad, but, as it was so late in the afternoon, it was
scarcely worth while to begin soldiering until next day. The day
began with a dispute with the officer of the day as to who should
or should not 'walk sentry' during meal hours. This was compro-
mised finally by no one doing sentry duty during meals. All con-
gratulated each other on the happy settlement of that dilemma.
Orders from Head Quarters were then read. In brief, 'Sink every
ship attempting to cross the bar. Spare none. Show no mercy.' The
men then gave three cheers—and took a drink.

"Time passed and no ship appeared, so none were sunk. The
monotony of camp life was soon broken by the announcement that
General Beauregard would visit the camp on the following day, on
a visit of inspection. Then there was bustle and confusion. The
cannon was polished until it was dazzling, shoes were cleaned, hair
cut, faces shaved, everything was put in order. The General arrived
and was accorded military honors. His first act was the inspection
of the artillery commanding the river. Going up to the shot piled
in pyramidal form, he gazed in silent awe at the sanguinary prepara-
tions for the defense of Charleston's back door. Saying nothing, he
took a six-pound shot in each hand and tossed them to and fro, from
one hand to the other, back and forth, gently laid them down in
place, gave the salute that signified inspection was over, then retired—to dinner. There has ever been some discussion as to the
significance of the General's tossing the cannon balls to and fro.
Some ill-natured and critical persons construed it as poorly veiled
contempt of the whole 'lay out.' The matter will go down into

history among the unsettled things of war. Soon after, the camp was broken up, and the men ordered to a less exposed position."

Of course, by 1865 the war turned out to be no gentleman's picnic. Sherman came. He held to the principle that the war could be terminated sooner by bringing it home to a civilian population. A recent military historian wrote: "Aside from condemnation and acclaim, it is on his deliberate exploitation of this principle that he has been called the first modern general." Now certainly he seems old-fashioned. The boys on Parris Island are carefully taught how to extinguish a city and with no more compunction than Sherman's bummers felt when they put a torch to a barn. And no general in his right mind is going to toss their bombs back and forth from one hand to the other. It would certainly seem puzzling if anybody did.

February 4, 1971

When Audubon Came

Beanie Newhall and Nancy Butler are only two of those on this island who have helped make John James Audubon seem a very close neighbor in history. Sometimes, while as close as his framed prints on Hilton Head walls, he has seemed little more than a transient in this area in comparison with such locales as the Feliciana parishes in Louisiana. An Audubon biography at hand has neither South Carolina nor any South Carolina place in its index, while New Orleans is pointed to on a dozen pages.

It is well to show that Audubon was more than a brief visitor here. It may be better if the remembrance of him here helps make clearer the scene of his time in this Low Country. Too often in a conventional history this warm land has seemed to have been occupied almost exclusively by hotheads ardent about the business of creating war. Beauty and learning concerned its people too.

It would be interesting to know more about the six gentlemen of Savannah who subscribed for Audubon's great book before he took the coach for Charleston in the fall of 1831. There is more known about the Charleston he visited than is generally printed. That was, of course, when the state was angrily talking of nullification, which would be a sort of prelude to later civil war. But there were people in Charleston besides the politicians. The Reverend John Bachman, Lutheran minister, was then waiting to meet Audubon, whose collaborator, friend, and in-law he would become. Others in the city toward which Audubon moved included Edmund Ravenel, John Edwards Holbrook, and Joel Poinsett. Poinsett, like the earlier Charlestonian Dr. Alexander Garden, is remembered by a flower. The others are scarcely remembered at all. It was a time of intellectual flowering.

Bachman was one of those welcome Yankees who came South to contribute much to knowledge and learning. Holbrook, born in Beaufort of visiting Yankee parents, returned to Charleston to become professor of anatomy in the Medical College of Charleston and to become the great authority on reptiles and fish. Edmund Ravenel was the native who pioneered in the study of shells. Across those years at his plantation, "The Grove," on the Cooper River, he entertained a succession of the great students of nature. Audubon, Holbrook, and Bachman shared his interests and his company. Later he was to entertain the great Jean Louis Rodolphe Agassiz, who for two years was professor of comparative anatomy at the Medical College of Charleston and maintained a seaside laboratory on Sullivan's Island. What conversation there must have been in the company of such men!

None of them were to escape the tumult of their times. The outbreak of the war put an end to Holbrook's scientific activities. In the midst of war his wife, Harriott Pinckney Rutledge (how South Carolinian can you get?), died while he was serving as a medical officer in the Confederate army. Ravenel was chairman of the political meeting in Saint Thomas' Parish, November 10, 1860, which endorsed secession, but he showed far greater interest in resolutions concerning oyster boats in the Wando River. Bachman tried to maintain a middle ground in the furious argument but, when at last South Carolina met to enact an ordinance of secession, it was he who opened the meeting with prayer. Throughout the war "he was a soldier of mercy, giving his entire time to the sick and dying." Much against his will he was persuaded to escape from Charleston by the last train before the evacuation, but he ran into Sherman's incendiary army up the road.

Audubon, who had known South Carolina in its days of intellectual ferment, did not live to see the disaster which overtook his friends. And the creative period in which these men looked at the world about them with such eager, inquiring eyes has been almost as little marked as the plantation grave of Edmund Ravenel above which, until recently at least, there was no stone. Probably nothing is left of the thousands of fruit trees he planted in the years when he searched for shells and fossils. Only few recall that in Ravenel's happy years such was his eagerness about science that he even drained his rice reserves that his friends might study animal remains at the bottom. Remembering such a halcyon time as that when Audubon first came to Charleston is like searching for such fossils now.

February 11, 1971

Smoke and Longevity

Smog didn't have a bad name when people feared the miasmas. Stuart Thompson brought proof of this in a rare little book he owns: an abridgement of *The American Gazetteer* by Jedidiah Morse, D.D., who is properly accorded the title of "father of American geography." Stuart's copy, published in 1798, is frayed and faded but packed with useful information about American places, all presented in alphabetical order.

In it, Charleston seems almost the healthy, happy, charming 1798 duplicate—or model—of Hilton Head Island in 1971—with one major difference. Dr. Morse (whose son invented the telegraph) wrote, "The continual agitation which the tides occasion in the waters which almost surround Charleston—the refreshing sea breezes which are regularly felt, and the smoke arising from so many chimneys, render this city more healthy than any part of the low country in the Southern states."

There are fewer chimneys in Charleston today but there are bigger ones. And few, even of the most persistent polluters of the air, are now advocating the stuff which comes out of them as an aid to health or longevity. However, Dr. Morse attributed much to the combination of tide and breeze and smoke. He informed his fellow Americans in the 1790s:

"On this account it is the resort of great numbers of gentlemen, invalids from the W. India Islands, and of the rich planters from the country, who come here to spend the sickly months, as they are called, in quest of health and of the social enjoyments which the city affords. And in no part of America are the social blessings enjoyed more rationally and liberally than here. Unaffected hospitality—affability—ease of manners and address, and a disposition to make their guests welcome, easy and pleased with themselves, are characteristics of the respectable people of Charleston."

Then Dr. Morse gave the clincher on Charleston's remarkable virtues: ". . . and what evinces the healthiness of the place, upwards of 200 of the white inhabitants were above 60 years of age." That was 200 out of 10,000—one not-quite senior citizen to every 166 other persons. A little checking on this remarkable longevity in old Charleston seemed indicated. Of the four South Carolina signers of the Declaration of Independence, only one, Thomas Heyward, Jr., attained the age of sixty. One of the four died when he was thirty.

The chances of longevity in those old days in South Carolina seem better when the larger group of thirty gentlemen who represented South Carolina in the Continental Congress is considered. The age of one of them is not known, his birth date being uncertain. But of the other twenty-nine, the age of sixty was attained by fourteen. Three got to be seventy or more. A relatively obscure one of them, Thomas Bee, lived to be eighty-seven. Pierce Butler lived to be seventy-eight, and Christopher Gadsden, often Butler's violent political enemy, reached the age of eighty-two.

The bell at last tolled for them all—as it does "for thee." Now, day by day, year after year, we can rejoice at the lengthening of the average life expectancy. But that does not mean a longer life span for the creature man. A leading authority states that at the end of the eighteenth century the expectation of life at birth in North America and northwestern Europe was about thirty-five or forty years. By 1960, in this most-polluted area of the world, it had exceeded seventy years. But listen: "There is no evidence that the span of human life has increased since the beginning of recorded history. Expectation within the span goes up but the span remains the same."

Begun in Charleston or Hilton Head, now or nearly two hundred years ago, a little study of this life span is a fascinating business. No specific figures have been worked out for residents of Charleston, Sea Pines, Port Royal, Palmetto Dunes, Bluffton, or Baygall. But man is still expected to outlast all the creatures except the box turtle and the giant tortoise. The lion lives nine times as long as the mouse. Dogs survive longer than cats. Ants and gray squirrels have about the same maximum life span. The sturgeon is expected to long outlive the goldfish. The blue jay's chances are sixteen times longer than the canary's. Some botanists figure that blue green algae outlast man and almost everything else.

But the bell tolls, and nobody has yet found a way to eliminate the clapper. Invest your money in nursing homes but don't forget to buy a cemetery lot.

February 18, 1971

Promoter's Progress

Stuart Thompson opened some old vistas into the past when he produced that copy of the *American Gazetteer* of Jedidiah Morse, published in the 1790s. One was a sort of tale of two cities—or at least two hopeful towns.

The Beaufort District, the Reverend Mr. Morse noted, between the Combahee and the Savannah rivers, was divided into four parishes—Saint Helena, Saint Luke, Prince William, and Saint Peter. It contained 18,753 inhabitants, "of whom only 4,346 are whites." Its chief place, Beaufort, was "A pleasant town, of almost 60 houses, and 200 inhabitants; who are distinguished for their hospitality and politeness. It has a fine harbor, and bids fair to become a considerable town." Its fortunes did not look too good at that moment, however, for "the courts which were formerly held here, are now removed to Coosawhatchie." Also, Beaufort's location was indicated by Dr. Morse as "situated 26 miles from Purisburg." Now that is from nowhere.

That town, also spelled Purrysburgh, was, Morse wrote, " a handsome town of S. Carolina, Beaufort district, on the eastern side of Savannah river, 37 miles from the ocean, and 20 from the town of

Savannah. It contains between 40 and 50 dwelling-houses, and an Episcopal Church. It took its name from John Peter Pury, a Swiss who settled a colony of his countrymen here in about the year 1733, with a view to the culture of silk. The mulberry trees are yet standing and some attention is still paid to the making of silk."

The *Dictionary of American Biography*, which gives the town founder's name as Jean Pierre Purry (1675–1736), describes him as a "colony promoter." He was the first to enunciate the theory, one sketch of him says, that "the ideal climate exists at or near the latitude of 33 degrees." David Ramsay, in his *History of South Carolina* (edition of 1858), said that Purry preached and promoted the idea that "countries laying in the 32nd degree of North Latitude, (the site of Palestine and of South Carolina) are remarkable for their fertility; the production of the most valuable commodities, and other good qualities." (The 32nd and 33rd degrees of northern latitude span the area between Charleston and Hilton Head.)

Some historians have made Purry out as something of a charlatan or a fumbler in the colony-building business. One sketch by an authoritative source reports that Purry, with a party of pioneers, came to South Carolina "to select the town site, Yamasee Bluff on the north bank of the Savannah river, some twenty miles above the place where Savannah was later to be founded." He had produced, its author said, a "Carolina fever."

That proved to be a mortal disease for him, for he died in Carolina in July 1736. Later South Carolina historians, in describing the remains of the "Purrysburgh Cemetery," wrote of the developer as "a Swiss who was inspired by rumor to print broadsides advertising the glories of Carolina, and who, under the English king's bounty, persuaded several hundred German-Swiss colonists to settle here. In a few years malaria had killed them or driven them to other sections. Purry's methods are described in Rousseau's *Confessions*."

Ramsay wrote: "The Swiss emigrants began their labors with uncommon zeal and energy; highly elevated with the idea of possessing landed estates. But in a short time they became discontented. Smarting under the pressure of indigence and disappointment, they not only blamed Purry for deceiving them, but repented leaving their native country."

It has taken some time to vindicate Purry in his notion that the ideal climate in the world is that between the 32nd and 33rd degrees of northern latitude. Purry was ahead of his time and certainly subject to the attentions of mosquitoes. He could hardly have dreamed when he died at sixty-one, a disappointed man among his complaining colonists, that his advertisements, which stirred a "Carolina fever" in the first half of the eighteenth century, would be repeated in technicolored confidence by other colony developers two and a half centuries later. Or that the new colonists, who got only such land grants as they were willing to pay for, would outtalk the developers in praise of the ideal shore between the perfect degrees of latitude.

Along with Jean Ribaut and Captain William Hilton, poor, damned, doomed Jean Pierre Purry needs remembrance. The first two just came here and went away. Purry stayed and died for his illusion, his deception, or his ideal.

February 25, 1971

Point of Departure

"I have to see the Orient," she said. It was a sort of assertion of a duty. Evidently, on Hilton Head she felt remiss about having neglected such a portion of the planet on which she had been a resident for a long time. Possibly such a feeling by many people explains the fact that so many of those who have found final satisfaction on this island make it one from which such a high ratio of residents travel season by season to the ends of the earth.

The fact is, however, that Hilton Head Island, which for so many—too many, some begin to feel—has become the most desirable final destination, is also one of the most active points of departure. The Bank of Beaufort did not set up a travel department for a community halted in happiness. The road from Hilton Head Island leads not only to Bluffton but also to Mexico, the Isles of Greece, Carcassonne, and Stockholm. It also runs to bird watching in New Guinea and to safaris in darkest Africa, which is fortunately now illuminated by the lights of good inns. It goes to greater warmth in winter, and to cooler summer days. Some in love with this island may still sing in lines remembered from Edna St. Vincent Millay that:

101

It may be that the flower for me
Is this beneath my nose.
How can I tell
Until I smell
The Carthaginian rose?

So there were a couple this winter who went south to look at other islands. They drove through the treeless tundra of Florida. Beyond was the even-more-depressing tangle of resort towns receiving the effluvium of America over vast highways smogged with both carbon monoxide and the smoke of brush fires. Off the throughways, the still-clogged roads and streets ran beside the endless honky-tonk of filling stations, bigger burger places, bars, Laundromats, discount stores, and neon-marked funeral homes. Beside them was the mass of mobile-home parks, the rows of identical, minuscule villas, the tiers of multiporched condominiums. Cheap housing is not to be scorned. Undoubtedly it provides heart's desire to many occupants who have as much right as the rich to the sun. A single geranium at a door as well as a walled garden may please the eye and warm the heart. But even the gardened places seemed besieged. In the most exclusive area of Boca Raton (Rat's Mouth), "For Sale" signs hung on many mansions. Some of the high rises seem more vulgar than the trailer camps. The biggest cafés are filled with people guzzling like maggots on a dead whale.

The islands below would be better. Along the Florida shore the tall towers for the rich made an interminable Manhattan. Some of the islands were better. But the oil refineries got to many of them before the developers. From the sea, Puerto Rico is made more beautiful by the torches of flame above the stacks of the long-established duplicates of BASF. And though every traveler, including yourself, adds to it, the pollution of people makes the future of the world look like Miami Beach—even Coney Island. Somehow the islands under other flags than our own seem safer in loveliness. For all their poverty, there is a special beauty and dignity and gaiety about the people of black Haiti. The carriage of young women is improved where they carry burdens on their heads. The multicolored store clerks in Curaçao add much to the charm of the jewelry they peddle. Even the taxicab drivers at island wharves are no more strident than American billboards. The San Blas Indians build their privies over the surf, but the swimmers in the waters about them are Americans in expensive bathing suits. In all this island circle, the most beautiful places seem to be those to which the Americans have not yet swarmed. But the jets are disgorging everywhere.

It is a good sign that Hilton Head Island is a place of people much given to travel. Not many of its retired people are stuck-in-the-mud folk. At a recent cocktail party here three couples discovered that they would be in Athens at the same time. More will meet in Paris, Hong Kong, and Tahiti. They have fun moving. But they come back with reassurance to their own blessed island. They should come back with warning, too. The bridge is open to Bluffton and beyond, and, despite the sworn dedication of Hilton Head's developers, only God knows what may come across it—or how soon.

March 4, 1971

Who Was Audubon?

Even in this era of the environment, there are probably few places where the name Audubon is spoken with more admiration than on Hilton Head Island. It would be nice if here we could find out who Audubon was, Of course, all know about the man and painter, and also the legendary figure who now seems almost the personal guardian of the birds. But who was he? Could he really have been Louis XVII—the lost dauphin of France?

Stuff and nonsense.

His father, the *Dictionary of American Biography* positively asserts, was Jean Audubon, a French sea captain in the Santo Domingo trade. In 1783 he was engaged by a firm of colonial merchants at Nantes to take charge of their West Indian trade, which centered at Les Cayes, Santo Domingo. He resided there almost continuously for a period of six years and, as merchant, planter, and dealer in slaves, amassed a considerable fortune. During these years his wife, Anne Moynet Audubon, whom he had married in 1772, remained in France. The mother of the great Audubon was called "Mlle Rabin" and was "A Creole of Santo Domingo." It is thought that she died within a year of her son's birth. In 1789 Captain Audubon, with the boy, who was called Fougere (or sometimes Jean Rabin), and a younger half sister, called Muguet, returned to France. His wife received the children tenderly, and in 1794 they were legalized by a regular act of adoption by Jean and Anne Audubon. Captain Audubon was said to have been "a prominent local figure in the Revolution."

Audubon's birth date is given as April 26, 1785. Possibly it is only an irrelevant coincidence that a son was born to Louis XVI and Marie Antoinette on March 27, 1785, who in June 1789 became dauphin of France on the death of an older brother. With the execution of his father Louis XVI, on January 21, 1793, this boy became for royalists the king of France. But by that time he had been imprisoned for five months by the revolutionists. What happened to this child between that time and his reported death on June 8, 1795, is surrounded by much mystery. Many believed that he escaped or was rescued and that the ten-year-old boy buried in an unmarked grave in the cemetery at Sainte Marguerite was not the dauphin. In the years following, countless pretenders presented themselves as the lost dauphin. One story is that the boy Captain Audubon pretended to bring back from Santo Domingo was actually the boy-king, whom the Captain, under the cloak of his revolutionary political position, was able to save.

Audubon, the painter and naturalist, made no pretensions in his lifetime that he was the lost dauphin. But legend makers have clung to some cryptic remarks he made. Once he said, "My own name I have never been permitted to speak." Once, referring to an old boat on the Ohio which nearly went down in a storm, he declared, "Her name, like mine, is only a shadow." Certainly, despite his poverty in later years, when he first came to America in 1803–4 he "lived the life of a country gentleman, essentially free from money cares."

Audubon needs no legend to support his fame. The Bourbons would be more enriched if he were in fact one of them. Certainly the happy ending would be served if the little prince, supposedly mistreated in a most horrid aspect of the Terror, did not die of "a scrofulous affection" in prison, but instead escaped to beautiful freedom and creation in American fields and woods, in its wilderness and on its rivers.

Stuff and nonsense this story may be. But it is the sort of romance that many of us would much like to believe.

March 11, 1971

Sunrise on Calibogue

The happy people on the Broad Creek side of Calibogue Cay have an air of proprietorship about their sunsets. They hang them up to decorate cocktail parties. Chuck Carpenter regards them as a more valuable addition to his property than the massive sea wall he has had to build. Down the shore they continue an essential part of the commercial decor of the Quarter Deck bar at Harbour Town. They are properly added to the price of town houses on the quay nearby.

In all but the most sullen weather, the sun and the sky marshal their forces to go on dress parade for their admirers on the creek bank. They point the western horizon with the same splendor which the earliest Indians knew, which the discoverers saw from their tiny ships, which slaves faced as they came wearily home from the fields, and which John Hay wrote home about to Lincoln's White House in the midst of the war. They are worth remembrance and promise the delight of constant renewal. Superspectacles, however, which a lie-abed along this west shore of Hilton Head Island may miss, are the almost secret sunrises which there decline to be blatantly pyrotechnic.

Indeed, almost deviously, with stealth, the sunrises come to Calibogue. They leapfrog the woodland, appearing first perversely on the most western tongues of the marshlands. The most distant marsh from the rising sun comes first alive in copper and gold, in wheat, in flame. At low tide the earth beneath marsh grasses becomes ebon in contrast with the gold growth above them. At high tide the painted plants seem to rise straight out of the radiant water. On the creek shore the sun slips through almost secret vistas among the trees, like bright fingers moving through the dark, tangled coiffeur of the woods. The vistas and the fingers change as moss swings on the trees. Like a tide coming in, the waters change their colors in the same reverse pattern, running back in slowly illuminated little waves toward Point Comfort and the still-hidden sun. To the last it keeps in hiding, only to appear when it fully dresses the day.

The Broad Creek sunset is arrogant in consciousness of its flamboyance. The sunrise there is shy, undressing slowly to show its beauty. It is not easily or quickly possessed. Undoubtedly on the eastern sea side of Hilton Head Island, the sunrise is brazen enough to those whose houses first face it. There it comes like its sister sunset arrayed in all its harlequin colors, prying immediately into every cranny and corner, roughly rousing the sleeping like a brass band outside the window playing "When the Saints Go Marching In." There it makes dark shadows of every tree, bush, and bird feeder. It throws the black images of huge toadstools beyond tall water towers. But transformation overtakes it as it enters the forest. Its light is subdued by moss and leaf. Then, heralded only by the muted music of bird song, it moves surreptitiously across little creeks, by tree-margined lagoons, through clearings where only small beasts await it. Egrets and lizards welcome its warmth. It makes bright splotches like the white tails of disappearing deer. Some stumps are made to look like thrones. Only where the golf courses stretch is a way prepared for this sunrise to skim and skip.

Certainly when the sunrise first reaches Calibogue Cay, Point Comfort, Harbour Town, and the Baynard shores there is no loud cry of Chanticleer about it. There no one could suspect that a rooster on a dunghill crowed to cause its coming. Where the gold marsh sits on a black stage or a blue estuary, the rising sun whispers to the morning, it kisses the marsh, very gently it dresses the waters. It wipes away the mist as a lover might wipe away a tear. It awakens the world with a caress. It plays tricks with tides, high and low, and with the moss and the wind. It moves quietly, with grace, to shining water, to the gorgeously naked marshes. But it advances certainly and arranges surely the debut of its daughter the day.

March 18, 1971

Towers and Toilets

Long ago there was the old rhyme pertinent to nothing:

> Dr. Broadus built a house
> Fifty stories high
> And every story of that house
> Was filled with chicken pie.

The verse is pertinent on Hilton Head today in connection with possibilities which Beanie Newhall and a lot of other lovers of this island fear. Undoubtedly, high rises here might be filled with goodies for their promoters, but they could make a mess like fifty stories of spoiled chicken pies for everybody else.

Implicit in the promises to early settlers in the developments, who by their coming brought others, was one that people would be strictly limited to the acre. As something containing horrible possibilities, lot buyers then were forbidden even to build duplexes. With condominiums, developers themselves long ago moved into multiplexes. Now comes the threat at least of skyscraper settlements. Indeed, one already in prospect is a multistoried structure

which looks like a pigeon roost for people. Now there is talk that
the Holiday Inn people may build one of their tall-and-taller hostel-
ries here, adorned undoubtedly by the tall, garish sign designed
originally to stop tourists in their tracks. Whatever such a sign did
to the sweet shoreline of pine and oaks, it would make nonsense
out of efforts to keep even the roadside signs on this island designed
for quiet handsomeness.

Maybe such a Manhattan skyline as now marks much of the shore
of Florida would rise in proof of the popularity and prosperity of
Hilton Head Island. It is appalling to contemplate what they might
do to the lands about them. A mathematician could figure the multiplication of sewage which would flow from each cute little apartment in the sky. Maybe more and more wells could run the water
up to them. Certainly not even the least-fastidious promoter would
want to provide wall-to-wall deserts for sale.

Already there is talk of more golf courses. Certainly, as people
are packed skyward, they will be needed. Perhaps it is time to build
more and more beaches. The time could come when golfers would
not only have to queue up at the beginning of play but also move
in a sort of bumper-to-bumper procession across the fairways to the
greens. The whole shore from Port Royal to South Beach could
become as crowded as the present beach before Coligny Circle on
the Fourth of July. Coney Island here we come!

This island and its developers got pretty upset when BASF threatened to establish its chemical and oil complex on Victoria Bluff.
That could have been a disastrous thing. An oil tanker might have
spilled oil on the beaches. Chemical effluent might have polluted
all the fishing, swimming, and boat waters hereabouts. But even an
oil tanker might be outclassed in filthiness by the multi-flushing of
multi-toilets down from the towers for tourists.

Of course, a high rise might be designed in beauty. The new
lighthouse in Harbour Town rises a little way but in the greatest
charm. Height itself is not necessarily a menace. But it might as well
be admitted that people and people packed on top of people,
charming as they may individually be, could certainly alter the ecology of this island, of which we are all supposed to be the guardians.

This is not written by a man who really seriously wants to blow
up the bridge which long ago transformed this island into a popular
peninsula. Those who live here welcome progress. ("Progress, yes;

pollution, no.") Those who remember the days when there was no doctor hereabouts welcome the recent doubling of the size of the medical center. It is good to have more and better stores. Let the golf courses spread, the houses rise, the boats multiply. But high rises are invitations to invasion, plans for people-pollution.

Beanie Newhall has blown a whistle which should be harkened as something louder and more meaningful than a bird cry in a swamp. So far the developers of this island have done a beautiful job. They have shown themselves eager, and at great expense to themselves, to protect this shore in grace, cleanliness, and beauty. They are threatened now with forces that could push them as well as crowd the rest of us.

Blow, Beanie, blow! But we need a bugle as well as a lady's muted whistle.

March 25, 1971

House Tour

Not sweet charity but self-preservation started the house tours in Natchez. Perhaps the tour-of-home procession which now runs across this Southern seaboard did not begin in that old town on the Mississippi shore. But Natchez brought national attention to the enterprise when it opened its old houses to paying visitors in 1932. No oil had been discovered on the old, worn plantations then. Cotton prices had hit bottom. Doors of great houses opened with more hope than expectation.

They have been open every year since to a lengthening line of ladies wearing gloves and some tourists in T-shirts. Big cars and long buses clot driveways built only to accommodate buggies. But the Natchez Pilgrimage has survived division, and troubles, too. That story may not be needed as instruction on Hilton Head Island, where no tensions of hunger attend the display of delectable houses. It may be interesting only as something distant and strange but relevant to the tour-of-homes tale all the same.

In the stagnant old Mississippi town, which in 1932 had five thousand less population than when its sons left the big houses in 1860 to go to war, Mrs. Balfour Miller took the lead in the Pilgrimage like a lady at the head of a parade. Handsome, childless, full of energy, and mistress of old and quietly lovely Hope Farm, she organized the first Natchez Pilgrimage as an activity of the Natchez Garden Club. She went, slim in her crinolines, inviting Mississippi, the South, and America to "Natchez, Where the Old South Lives." That year, in Natchez and elsewhere, the Old South was practically starving; and Yankees, as well as Southerners, with the price were more than welcome.

And they came. They filled the Eola Hotel. They followed the costumed ladies of Natchez through the double doors at Gloucester; under the six high-fluted columns at D'Evereux; through the garden of gazebo, box, azaleas, and japonicas at Arlington; even under the cast-iron balcony over the door at Homewood where then (except at Pilgrimage time) Mrs. Kingsley Swann, a rich Yankee settler, turned back the tourists with a vigor amazing (and amusing) to the natives.

The whole affair was a great success. Newspapers far away rejoiced to print pretty pictures of costumed Natchez ladies standing decorously in doorways and, less decorously, flying in swings just high enough to show that there were limbs of flesh beneath the billowing skirts of dimity. The City Bank and Trust Company of Natchez, which knows good business when it sees it, presented to Mrs. Miller a silver tray engraved in token of the highest civic service. The years marched by—1932–1933–1934–1935–1936—and all went as lovely as a bride descending a wide mahogany staircase in a Natchez mansion. Then schism ran like a crack in old masonry through the Natchez Garden Club. Suddenly, there were two garden clubs, two Pilgrimages, no more mansions, and only one Natchez.

A sad policeman in the town diagnosed the trouble: "The Garden Club took in folks that didn't even have a flowerpot. They ran it. And some of the folks that own the biggest places need the fees the tourists pay to see them to eat on."

There was something to this in those old lean days. The original Natchez Garden Club divided the money from the Pilgrimages, one-third to the club for "the preservation, beautification and restoration of historic Natchez," and two-thirds to the owners of the homes shown on the tours. In the Pilgrimage Garden Club, organized by the seceding homeowners, after the payment of all expenses, three-fourths of the money went to the homeowners and one fourth to the club for some civic purpose. The money made a difference —so did control. There were over a hundred members in the Natchez Garden Club, but the houses worth visiting are limited to perhaps less than twenty-five. The flowerpotters might certainly have been in control. From such a possibility of a tyrannical majority, ladies in Natchez seceded in 1936, as did gentlemen in Natchez in 1861.

Apparently now the wounds are healed. Some of the plantation owners who then much needed the fees take sustenance now from royalties in oil discovered in their eroded fields. A little prosperity has a placating effect even in graceful halls. No such dangers threaten the tour of homes on Hilton Head Island. Self-interest presumably is a stranger here. This whole island is just one big, happy flowerpot and hopes to remain so.

April 1, 1971

Curious Silence

As spring comes on Hilton Head Island it is easy to understand the amazement of Harriott Horry Rutledge Ravenel about "the curious silence respecting flowers" in early South Carolina. The thousands of visitors coming to the Carolina gardens at this season are properly impressed by the antiquity of their beauty. But as South Carolina counts its centuries, they came late. The first landscaped garden in America was designed in 1740, certainly a while ago, but there had been seventy years of settlement and living here before that.

Mrs. Ravenel quoted and commented on the description of an ancient road by John Archdale, who was sent as governor in 1694: ". . . the land is mixed with brackish mould, it is beautified with odoriferous and fragrant woods, pleasantly green all the year as the Pine, Cedar and Cypress, insomuch that out of Charles Town for three or four miles called the Broadway, is so delightful a Road and walk of great breadth, so pleasantly green that I believe no Prince in Europe with all their Art, can make so pleasant a sight for the whole year."

Mrs. Ravenel footnoted this old report in 1906: "But not a word of the yellow jessamine, the magnolia, the sweet bay, of the gay catalpa trees which must have filled the woods with odor and color then, as they do to-day."

But the gardens were coming on mightily in the years after Archdale wrote. A hundred slaves worked ten years to complete the forty-five-acre garden and sixteen-acre lawn at Middleton Place. Such botanists as Dr. Alexander Garden and André Michaux came to live in Charleston around the time of the Revolution and shared their love of flowers with rich planters. South Carolinians remember that Eliza Pinckney successfully introduced the growing of indigo at about the same time the Middleton Gardens were developed. She ran great plantations but she tended, too, the beauty of her gardens on the Wappoo Creek. Certainly she broke the "curious silence respecting flowers" in a letter inviting a friend to visit her in the spring: "The majestic pine, which imperceptibly puts on a fresher green, the young myrtle joining its fragrance to that of the Jessamine of golden hue, perfumes all the woods and regales the rural wanderer with its sweets, the daisies, the honeysuckles, and a thousand nameless beauties of the woods, invite you to partake the pleasures the country affords.

"You may wonder how I can at this gay season think of planting a cedar grove, which rather reflects an autumnal gloom and solemnity, than the freshness and gayety of spring. I intend to connect in my Grove the solemnity of summer and autumn with the cheerfulness and pleasures of spring for it shall be filled with all kinds of flowers, as well wild as garden flowers, with seats of camomile, with here and there a peach tree, orange, plumb, etc."

Certainly there is no "curious silence" about flowers in South Carolina now. Its gardens have had a world's applause. Annually, with the spring, huge buses pour delighted visitors to the gates before the jeweled paths. And they go away still filled with wonder at the flowering beside the mirroring streams. Spring is the beautiful explosion. But Eliza Pinckney was right in seeing the beauty of the whole surrounding year. The winter isn't only marked with solemnity of green pine and cedar and cypresses. Camellias flower from November through April. Then the azaleas come rioting into bloom. Afterwards gardens are filled with the delicate pinks of mountain laurel. Then the rose and the magnolia. The orchestration—certainly not the silence—of flowers fills all the Carolina seasons.

Perhaps the pioneers were too preoccupied with practicalities to speak or write much about the flowers. Few of us today have the labor of a hundred slaves or the leisure of a decade or the wealth of cotton and rice to carve out great aesthetic acres. But there can never have been any real silence about flowers here. Even an unattended yellow jessamine bush by a rural roadside speaks—or sings—for itself.

April 8, 1971

The Brothers Drayton

Of course, everybody who has done enough homework to qualify him for residence on Hilton Head Island knows about the Drayton brothers who here provided the classic example of brother against brother in the Civil War. Such scholars of their locale know that General Thomas Drayton commanded the Confederate forces on the island in November 1861 and that his brother, Percival, was in command of the U.S.S. *Pocahontas,* which moved with the fleet to capture the island for the Union. But there seems an appalling lack of knowledge around here about the two brothers before and after the battle.

Indeed, the ignorance is so great that some cynics have been able to make a malign mythology to the effect that the brothers took opposite sides to make sure that, whatever side won the war, the properties of the Draytons would be secure. That really does smear a good story of brothers in arms against each other.

The two Draytons were born in South Carolina of an aristocratic and distinguished family. Their father was William Drayton (1776–1846), soldier, lawyer, congressman. Their mother was Ann, of the distinguished Gadsden family. Their grandfather, William Drayton

(1732–90), was first judge of the United States District Court of South Carolina. This grandfather William was born at Magnolia, a plantation on the Ashley River, today famous as Magnolia Gardens. It would be difficult to find two boys more ancestrally tied to South Carolina.

Thomas, the older brother, graduated from West Point as a classmate of Jefferson Davis. He resigned from the army and became a planter and a railroad builder as president of the Charleston and Savannah Railroad, which he regarded as the most effective means of unifying the South. His younger brother Percival went into the American navy as a midshipman and stayed in it. At the outbreak of the Civil War, Thomas, as brigadier general, was made commander of the military district about Port Royal. Percival was then on ordnance duty in the navy yard at Philadelphia. So devoted was he to the Union that on February 25, 1861, he requested that his name be entered in the naval register as a citizen of Philadelphia. The brothers met in combat before the year was out.

Percival wrote that rather than interfere with the success of the Union, he was ready to sacrifice every relative (presumably including his brother Thomas), painful as that would be. The South Carolina legislature proscribed Percival and declared him infamous. But in the Union navy Percival advanced in the blockading squadron off the Carolina shore and in attacks on Fort Sumter. Farragut warmly commended him in a letter to the secretary of the navy for his part in the operations in Mobile Bay. Regarded as one of the ablest officers in the Union service, he was made chief of the Bureau of Navigation, a position approximating that of the navy's chief of staff.

Thomas did not do so well. Transferred—after his defeat here—to the front in Virginia, he won no praise from his superiors. General Robert E. Lee wrote Thomas' old classmate President Davis, "He is a gentleman and a soldier in his own person but seems to lack the capacity to command." He was transferred to relatively inconsequential duties. When he returned home, he found his plantation damaged by Union soldiers and in part confiscated by the federal government. He moved to Dooly County, Georgia, where he tried to develop a farm. He was unsuccessful and became an insurance agent in Charlotte, North Carolina.

Percival died in Washington a few months after the Union victory he had helped to achieve. He was unmarried. Maybe Percival had been ready to sacrifice Thomas and all his other kin for the Union cause. He had borne the South Carolina decree which labeled him as infamous. But though his convictions seemed to him more important than kinship, he was one with whom, at the last, blood was thicker than water. By his will he left Thomas $28,000—a lot of money then in Dooly County, Georgia, and the Carolinas. It helped to sustain his brother in the crumpled South which he had not been able to help win.

Hilton Head Island and South Carolina historians remember the collision in arms of these brothers. The happy—or at least loving —end of their story should not be forgotten beside the wartime tale.

April 15, 1971

Pioneer Party

The sense of antiquity grows on Hilton Head Island. Sometimes now the arrival of the first retirees seems almost like the landing of the Pilgrim Fathers or whatever it was that South Carolina celebrated in its tricentennial last year. Nancy and Wally Butler properly celebrated old times gone but not forgotten recently in a Pioneer Party for those who arrived before 1962 A.D. The passage of time seemed properly marked by the contrast between the dilapidated cabin pictured in the lower right-hand corner of their invitation and current housing. News quickly spread. Less than a week after this celebration telephones crackled with the word that Ruth Vaux had sold the beach-front and lagoon house of Jay McDonald and Don Jones to Henry Haskell for $250,000.

Some were aghast and some appalled by this information, which still may be classified only as rampant rumor. The current idea has been that such a choice beach-front lot as Jay's and Don's was price-tagged at about $60,000. That would mean that the house, even with its panoplied pool and painted porcelain toilets, was a $190,000 item. Still, Henry Haskell, as a sailor who only occasionally runs aground on Buck Island, is regarded as a canny

121

businessman who generally knows which way the wind blows.

Maybe the span from antiquity to now was more certainly marked by the picture Wilton Graves presented in an advertisement in *The Packet* of the two-room Sea Crest Motel in 1954 beside a photo of the plush sixty-seven-room one of 1971. A newcomer to the island, Beverley Krampf, who is setting up an elegant emporium in Harbour Town, remembers coming to the early hostel, finding both of the rooms occupied, and feeling like a lost lady in a jungle.

But possibly antiquity is best marked by the information revealed in a recent issue of *The New Yorker* that Charles Fraser, the young developer, was twenty-one when he determined that Hilton Head Island need not be developed "in dissonance with nature." Now he has passed the great divide and is forty-one. Also, according to *The New Yorker,* he "has made twenty million dollars in the past ten years." Under his guidance and authority, the magazine says, 550 private houses have been built. *The New Yorker* did not mention condominiums. Charleston did not grow so fast or attain antiquity so quickly.

It is doubtful that the Butlers were setting the scene at their party for the organization of something like the "Sons and Daughters of the Island Settlers." But maybe some such organization would be in order. It could be an exclusive company, almost a sort of sea-island Cincinnati. A good many of those now living here arrived in this "high quality destination resort," or what *The New Yorker* calls "one of the creamiest resorts in America," after the 1962 date set up by Wally and Nancy. Now, according to the long article in the prestigious journal, Charles "figures he can blend fifteen hundred more houses into the trees." No mention is made of the blending which may be done by other developers. And so far as *The New Yorker* is concerned, the condominium is an unknown item.

Nostalgia certainly has its place on this sea island as everywhere else. Wilton Graves properly cherishes that picture of his two-room motel in the wilderness of 1954. Wally and Nancy happily welcome the old-timers, though Wally at least is not engaged in fighting off any newcomers who may wish to buy lots. Henry Haskell, by his investment, demonstrates a faith in the perpetuity of perfection. Pride in primacy is not generally regarded as improper. Also there is the line somewhere to the effect that the first shall be last and the last shall be first. It may be unfortunate that not all of us could in prospect have come over on the *Mayflower*. Some of the nicest girls are not Daughters of the American Revolution. Some of the ancestors of Sea Pines and Port Royal residents arrived in America after the slave ships stopped coming. Their oldest residents are Johnnies-come-lately compared with the citizens of Mitchelville and Baygall.

Still the Butler Pioneer Party was fun. But the chances are that the plumbing and the service are better in the Sea Crest Motel than they were when Wilton Graves first opened the two rooms on the shore. Hilton Head's future was probably indicated in those days when on an empty island Beverley Krampf needed a third room which was not there at the Sea Crest. That, sadly or happily, is the situation today, maybe tomorrow, and perhaps until the time when the whole island is room-to-room.

April 22, 1971

Fate of Kings

"What have we got to hate now that BASF has been driven away?"
And the bright-eyed one with the red lips and the sharp tongue said,
"We can always go back to Charles."

It is the fate of kings to receive both obeisance and abuse. And
long before Charles Fraser was cursed by some Carnegies and
courted by others on Cumberland Island, he could count on both
applause and impertinence on Hilton Head. This was undoubtedly
inevitable, and the cause was apparent even to such a recent, briefly
visiting writer as John McPhee, who gave much space to the Fraser
story in *The New Yorker.* He wrote: "He is Yahweh. He is not merely
the mayor and the zoning board, he is the living ark of the deed
covenant. He is the artist who has painted them [us] into the corners
he has sold them."

As Fraser himself would describe the combination of admiration
and antagonism, he is city hall. "I operate as non-elected mayor,
so I have to act as if I were elected." McPhee quoted him as saying.

"There is democracy of communications here but autocracy of
decision making. Our corporate contracts and deed covenants are
the constitution and by-laws of the community. The only way you

124

can have aesthetic control is through the power of ownership. We have more power than a zoning board has. I have centralized the decision-making process, but I'll listen to anybody." And McPhee added, in consideration of the composition of the community, "The marvel is not whom he listens to but who listens to him."

The marvel was in process of explanation while McPhee was here though the writer did not mention it. While McPhee was undertaking to describe the anatomy of the Fraser autocracy, Fraser was at work doing the sort of thing which explains its acceptance.

It makes Charles mad, he told McPhee, to be dismissed by some conservationists ("druids," as Charles calls them) "as a quote developer unquote." The truth is that behind the autocrat lies the artist. And that was and is now being shown by his creation of the Heritage Farm. This planted place cannot be expected to attract so many such potential lot buyers as gather at the Heritage Tournament. But it indicates that, despite the money maze which surrounds the operation of Sea Pines Plantation, Fraser is still a man primarily concerned with the combination of history, aesthetics and order, and charm on his plantation. It is no reflection on Fraser that this combination has become highly salable. But it may become more and more difficult to maintain as Sea Pines becomes big business in association with financiers and insurance companies whose devotion is exclusively to the dollar. Heritage Farm now indicates that Charles still has the dream of becoming and remaining the Prospero of a perfect island.

Harbour Town showed imagination closely tied to land sales. But the idea of creating here a garden which would be a living museum of the agriculture of the South Carolina past was—and is—a sort of art for art's sake demonstration of an imaginative man concerned with vastly more things than cash. Long, long ago, the growing of indigo, of rice, of sea-island cotton ceased to be profitable in this Low Country. There is no profit in growing them now. But their growth for the eyes of people now in Heritage Farm indicates an imagination related to a sense of history and an understanding of the need of man to take sustenance now from the past.

Whether he likes the word *developer* or not, Charles must operate under the money compulsions which have driven too many real-estate operators to the butchery of the earth. He himself has not always been as gentle with ancient marshes as some "druids" wish he had been. He has on occasion put unexpected clusters of condominiums (or "condominia") into what some earlier house buyers thought would be never-interrupted views. Sometimes his interests have seemed to go more to new people and new places than to older residents and scenes. Still, the amazing thing is how well the aesthetic and ecological faith has been kept in the face of more and more purchasers pouring over the bridge with more and more money in their checking accounts. And, fortunately, the "ark of the deed covenants" limits autocracy as well as gives it power.

Not all those who crack at "Prospero" Fraser are Calibans, who reluctantly do his will. Some merely need an occasional release from planned perfection. The best hunch about Charles is that he is basically more creative than acquisitive. And Heritage Farm is good and present proof of that. The only danger is—the only reason for restiveness is—that indigo, rice, and cotton were vulnerable to change. So might be a man with a dream.

April 29, 1971

Gentlemen's Agreement

In the face of the all-too-evident threat to the peace and beauty of all the shores of America, it has been proposed that protections for Hilton Head Island be provided by a "gentlemen's agreement" between the great landowners. Certainly all who know them know, too, that Hack of Honey Horn and Fraser of Magnolia Crescent are gentlemen and scholars even though they do not always grant as much to each other. As the developers of Hilton Head Island (for lack of a more euphemistic term), they have not only preserved the shores and the trees. Both have also given an historical accent to their enterprises.

Fred Hack keeps intact a whole fort which played an important part in the history of the island. Charles Fraser has assiduously collected records and memorabilia of the past, from ancient golf players to the ruins of a great old mansion. But somehow, in this talk of a gentleman's agreement, the quest for tradition does not go deep enough in history. The rule by the gentlemen on Hilton Head Island may be most closely traced to the Fundamental Constitution drawn up by the philosopher John Locke in the late 1600s. He drafted a plan for the government of what amounted to the real-estate development of Carolina by such elegant gentlemen as Lord Ashley Cooper and Peter Colleton.

It set up lordly estates, called baronies, and created titles, the highest of which were landgraves. Harriott Horry Ravenel, in her history of Charleston, wrote that the constitution "arranged for the proposed 'nobility' . . . in order to avoid a too numerous democracy." But she added, "This nobility was little more than a plutocracy, depending upon the amount of land owned by a man, which might be bought by him, without regard to birth or breeding, or service to the State. The titles passed by purchase as well as by descent."

William Francis Guess, in his more recent book about the state, says that Locke's plan "envisioned a timocracy, a state where rule and rank derive from property; not a feudality, where property and rank derive from a heaven-sent ruler." In recent times, only Bernard Baruch has been honest, presumptuous, or arrogant enough to call his estate "Hobcaw Barony." But the Hilton Head Island plantations qualify better as baronies. Such-named estates passed away, perhaps as Guess thought, because "the landgraves and the moss-draped baronies were foppish vanities." More probably it was because tougher planters disregarded them. But they remain a pattern not forgotten. The Hilton Head Island system may duplicate them under Landgraves Hack and Fraser and some other, lesser landowners entitled to less-noble titles.

Actually, of course, the rule of the landgraves was a sort of government by gentleman's agreement. But gentlemen died and landgraves passed away. Properties fell into the hands of other men who did what they damn pleased with them. And, of course, that could happen on this island now. Gentlemen with the best intentions about high rises and other threatening phenomena cannot control other owners and are not immortal themselves.

Nothing, certainly, can long protect land use except such unromantic, dull-sounding things as zoning and land-use regulations with the force of law. And at this point it would be possible to lay down regulations which would not unduly restrict property owners but would protect all from misuse by some other property owners. Maybe we can't, in all things, avoid here a "timocracy," which the dictionary defines as "government based on wealth or on love of honor." But we live in a situation where even wealth may be threatened unless law is provided to prevent its degradation by adjacent property owners. Certainly the love of the island, like the love of honor, calls for some protections.

We are not threatened now by the Spaniards coming up from Florida, as the landgraves and their underlings were long ago. But, certainly, we are threatened by the example of what has happened to once-lovely sections of Florida, which today look more and more like scenes of towers with slums at their feet. The probability is that nobody wanted to ruin Florida, but in wide areas somebodies did. Now many gentlemen, whose agreements would not have saved them, are overwhelmed. And some others are ready to use land in any way, however atrocious, to turn a pretty penny on an ugly scene. Gentlemen are both mortal and subject to erosion. Nothing will protect Hilton Head Island in the long run but the agreement, not merely of some gentlemen, but of all people, in rules fixed by law to guard beauty, charm, and serenity. There are gentlemen in our baronies, but the barbarians are already all too close to the gates —or the bridge.

May 6, 1971

Tree Houses

Certainly, the bulbous, column-supported "Sealoft," which has been on display by a swift-moving, tidal stream behind the library and the information center at Harbour Town has been entitled to all the *oohs* and the *ahs* it has received from appreciative visitors. With its steep circular stair (a ramp was put beside this one for less ascensional visitors) and its barrel-shaped bathtub, it was not merely unusual—it was unique. Indeed it somehow seemed the space age's shining evocation of the tree houses every boy once built or envied in American backyards. In its perfection, however, at something like $44,500, it emphasizes the line which Tootie Watters displays: "The only difference between men and little boys is the price of the toys."

But that apparently is no barrier to desire. Now it has been announced that on Deer Island, which was once left to the deer, seventy-five such elevated dwellings will be built with confidence of sale. Certainly no one can object to them as "high rises" as they are only treetop tall. Some residents of South Calibogue Cay may feel a little startled at the prospect of seventy-five identical mushroom (or toadstool) towers in their view where once there was only marsh and woodland. But to say the least, something new has been added and added in traditions of design which go back to such luminaries as Mark Twain, James M. Barrie, and Walt Disney—and, now, Edgar Rice Burroughs.

Part of the charm of Harbour Town as a replica of a Mediterranean seaport is that it looks as authentic as any of Disney's reproductions of fairy-tale houses and fairy-tale towns. Indeed, sometimes it seems as charmingly authentic as the Land of Oz on Beech Mountain, which is an exact replica of that imaginative kingdom down to the last detail of Dorothy's gingham dress. In many respects Harbour Town will be an inhabited Disneyland. Its occupants will serve the salesman as did the boys who helped Tom Sawyer whitewash the fence.

But the Sealoft community on Deer Island will be pure Peter Pan. There are few of us who have not wished at some time in our lives that Peter would come, attended by Tinker Bell, and take us from our drab, middle-class lives into the world where people never grow old (and, in this case, will be able to climb steep stairs eternally). Those who come to the Sealofts, of course, on this lowland island will not live as Peter and Company did, underground. Part of the promise to them is that they may watch from above the gamboling of the wildlife, the deer which will not be frightened away and the raccoon which may multiply by multiplied garbage cans. The alligators, if any, will sadly not be equipped with the eternally ticking, swallowed clock which in the case of Peter's crocodile provided adequate warning of approach. There will be no pirates—at least not in conventional costume. But few of the real and purchasable delights of an imaginative world will be lacking. It is not expected that the inhabitants of this Sealoft community will at first swing tree-to-tree from globular residence to globular residence à la Tarzan. But those who can make the steps—maybe with baby and groceries—will certainly be a people above and apart from their earthbound neighbors. So far these elevated people have no special name. Aldine Schroeder suggests that their description should be a word beginning with *syl*, like "sylvan." Brick Blackburn suggests that the name should derive from and follow the prefix *arbo*—as in "arboreal," meaning "inhabiting or frequenting trees." The name, of course, will not matter. It will be the lofty spirit that counts.

Certainly, as the occupants watch the wildlife below, they can count on people watching them in envy or amazement. There will be watchers as well as buyers. Every corporation executive who ever showed his teeth to competition—every general who once played Patton—was once a boy who sought the lofty solitude of the oak or the apple tree in his own makeshift mansion high above the ground. And, fortunately, there are now and always will be those with less-stiff knees and less shortness of breath who may prefer high branches to ordinary gardens.

One final thing: Buyers and sellers in this case above all others had better remember that this development warrants the caution not to throw out the baby instead of the bath water. That could happen even on Hilton Head Island.

May 13, 1971

Road Race

A-TOURING WE WILL GO...

The contests hereabouts multiply. The Heritage Tournament is only the greatest of a multitude of such golfing events each year. More and more sailboats are arrayed for racing in the creeks, rivers, and sounds. Now with $10,000 in prizes, a marlin fishing contest will soon start at Harbour Town. Acres of automobile parking are essential to participants and spectators at such events. But hardly anybody apparently remembers one item which gets a footnote in automobile history: "The American Grand Prize International Road Race" was inaugurated at Savannah, Georgia, in 1908, and continued as an annual event through 1916. It was won only once by an American car—a Mercer in 1914.

Those who impatiently await the completion of I-95 through this region might well consider the roads on which this event must have taken place. The first concrete highway in Georgia was an experimental five-mile strip out of Griffin, in Spaulding County, constructed in 1919. As late as 1940 the official state guide of Georgia carefully noted which roads were paved and which were not. Almost proudly, it declared that the road from Savannah to Thunderbolt was paved. The best of many other roads were like some of the still-unpaved streets which today surprise some visitors from wholly paved metropolises. The worst were described in bad weather as "loblolly bogs."

Savannah must have had some really early motorcar enthusiasts in 1908. Henry Ford had organized his company with a capital of $100,000 only five years before. His famous Model T was first produced in the year the Savannah race began. How many privately owned cars there were in Savannah that year is not known. But in 1908 a total of 49,952 cars had been produced in America. In 1909 more than twice as many cars were produced, though this year was a year of financial crisis. Though foreign cars won nearly all of the Savannah races, only 1,387 such cars were imported in 1908. Incidentally, maybe an item worth noting on this Mercedes island is that Carl Benz got the first prototype of that car rolling twenty years before Ford really got started.

The origin of this grand international race in Savannah is difficult to understand. Savannah was no center of automobile manufacture as Indianapolis was before it put on its first five-hundred-mile race in 1911. Though cotton had not yet been hit by the boll weevil, Savannah was a pretty sleepy Southern port in 1908. Nice ladies, like Mrs. Juliette Gordon Low, were still thinking in terms of the United Daughters of the Confederacy, not the Girl Scouts, which Mrs. Low founded in 1912. But there must have been some sporting characters among the gentlemen, thinking in terms of the internal-combustion engine as well as the sailboat and the duck blind.

On thing certain is that that race did not run from Savannah to Hilton Head, where a similar race today might end triumphantly at Port Royal or Harbour Town. No vehicles came to Hilton Head Island then. The only communication with Hilton Head in those days was by the biweekly Beaufort–Savannah steamer, which gave it equal stopping attention with Daufuskie.

In this day of more and more varied sporting events, maybe Hilton Head could lead to the revival or resuscitation of this exciting old race. Charles Fraser found and revitalized the area's oldest golf club. The same might be done for an old race. Some cars similar to those which participated in this early event must still be around in this day when antique automobiles are collected like antique sideboards. Perhaps I-95 could be used for such an event after it is finished but before it is formally opened to the roar on it of faster present cars, foreign and domestic.

Possibly, except at such places as Indianapolis and Darlington, such races have been outmoded. Unfortunately, a faster race than old Savannah ever saw can be seen almost every day now on Hilton Head Island on all of the main and most of the secondary roads. It deserves no prizes.

May 20, 1971

Island Primitive

Rumors roll on Hilton Head Island as regularly as the waves on its beaches. Sometimes they mount like the highest spring tides. So it was good to learn the true fact this week that Fred Hack had no intention of retiring from his post of command in the ordered development of this flourishing shore. Instead, with a new group and more money, he will move forward in carefully tended programs of development, keeping the same good guarantees which he initiated two decades ago.

Such a matter-of-fact, down-to-earth figure as Fred Hack does not fit into any technicolored image. He needs none. Unfortunately, however, some who have come to the charm he found have not carefully read Virginia Holmgren's authoritative book and her statement of his meaning here. It relates that way back in December 1949 Fred was the real first discoverer of the resort possibilities of the sleeping beauty which was this slumbering island. Then with his father-in-law, C. C. Stebbins, and his associate, General J. B. Fraser, he began land acquisitions here in March 1950. That seems both a long and a short time ago. Charles Fraser was just a college student then. Bill Gregory of Palmetto Dunes, young too, had no notions of turning a gun club into a sort of South Carolina Venice.

There was nothing exotic about Hack as a thirtyish young man when he brought his family to live on the island in 1950. There was only an informal ferrying service then. The regular state ferry service was not established until 1953, but perhaps appropriately then, presaging the future, the first ferryboat was named *Gay Time*. Fred pushed for the bridge which was dedicated in 1956. The kind of man Fred was is as important as the place and the access. Nobody was more native than he to the Southern coastal country. He was a man who knew the woodlands both by vocation and by avocation. He was in the ancient Southern tradition of the land surveyor made most famous by young George Washington, who surveyed the vast tracts in which he speculated. Also, Fred thought of that land as "my country," as Thomas Jefferson did of Virginia even after he was President of the United States.

But Hack was of the first generation of an amazing change in timberers. Over on the waterfront in Savannah in an unprepossessing-looking laboratory, Dr. Charles B. Herty was creating a woodland revolution. He demonstrated that the old methods of timbering which left a desert behind the axes and the saws was not only bad behavior but bad business. Not the torn forest but the tended forest paid off. Trees not only could but should be grown as a crop. Hack also saw that beauty was good business. With him to the island came his wife Billie, daughter of one of his partners, who loved the woodlands, too, and now knows the island paths and lanes and roads like the marks in the palm of her hand. And Fred's brother, Orion, began in the love of plants the tending of the earth which made him the "Conservationist of the Year" when that new precious thing called "ecology" seemed threatened in the clean air and water about him.

"He's a provincial," said one of Fred's best friends. The word in its proper meaning exactly suits him. He was born in a wide place in the road called Walthourville, Georgia, the son of a country doctor who knew what was in the hearts as well as what was within the hides of his patients. Walthourville (present population three hundred) was not far from more metropolitan Hinesville (population twelve hundred), where he went to school and into the surrounding forests. The word *provincial* has taken some beating from supercilious definers. It is set up in sharp distinction to *cosmopolitan*.

But, in the best and truest meaning of the word *cosmopolitan,* Hack is that, too. Some of those who think of themselves as cosmopolitans have a superficial knowledge of a planet but very little warm and close relationship to any place. Fred knows his cosmos, which is his world around him—the Southern woodland and the Southern island, the shore, the marsh, the swamp, and the rookerie.

Of course, he is in business to sell beauty and serenity. While he dependably promises that Port Royal Plantation will remain a place restricted to separate private residences, he is no King Canute trying to hold back the tide of condominiums. There will be place for them in his Shipyard Plantation. Clearly, however, he has sold the new group of developers on the safeguards he has promised to his purchasers. And in bringing these Southern investors into the still-beautiful picture, he may have added new defenders to this shore. Nothing is more necessary than that the business South learn that the good old beautiful South is the best new Southern business.

That may be a provincial attitude. But only as long as this province is protected will others wish to share it. What this island needs is more sound provincialism. Fred Hack can be just the man to provide it.

May 27, 1971

A Thrashing for Timrod

Those who have been troubled about problems of discipline in the Bluffton schools can be sure they have a sympathizer in heaven in the person of South Carolina's poet Henry Timrod. This sensitive, frail, convivial, and tubercular gentleman was not yet "the poet laureate of the Confederacy" when he arrived as schoolteacher in the Beaufort District in 1860, on the eve of war. Writers today describe Bluffton then as "a summer resort for rice planters." Still, in the area of thousands of black slaves, some white families remained the year round. The Church of the Cross had been built. And nearby Dr. John Kirk was building his elaborate plantation house with an entrance leading into a circular hall with a winding staircase. Glass for a huge cupola was stored in an already-completed upper room.

It is not clear in the record just where in Bluffton was located the school of Professor Hugh L. Train, a professor not dreaming of any problems of desegregation but plagued with some difficulties all the same. Timrod came to it as a young man who already had some reputation as a poet but who had not discovered how to make a livelihood from his muse (as, indeed, he never did). Before he arrived, he had written merry verses about schools and teachers. With tongue in cheek he wrote of the death of a tutor:

> Not a grin was seen, not a giggle heard
>   As the tutor breathed his last;
> Not a freshman uttered a jesting word
>   At the thought of labours past.

A little later he sang romantically of a remarkable student:

> Behold the youth whose mighty mind
> Leaves all competitors behind!
> He translates Latin, thinks in Greek
> Well-nigh as fast as one can speak.

Possibly it was as a homesick Charlestonian that at first Timrod found nothing comic or romantic in his Bluffton job. In starchy dignity he wrote: "I began school yesterday; and the boys set straight-away to see of what stuff I was made. Some of them being young men, were inclined to put on airs, but I met every demonstration with a promptness and decision, which astonished them very soon into proper behavior."

According to other historical versions, the situation was not quite so simple as that. A scholarly South Carolinian wrote that on the first day of Timrod's teaching the school bully refused to obey his smaller teacher. The poet-teacher, according to school rules, reported the incident to the principal, who insisted upon personally meting out punishment. Then: "After school was out, the bully armed himself with a stick, and hid in some bushes along the road. As Timrod passed the bully came out and threatened him with 'the damndest thrashing now that you have ever heard of.' Fortunately for Timrod the suspicious principal had followed him, and he thundered at the boy, 'You are right, sir, there is going to be the damndest thrashing you ever heard of, but you are the scoundrel that's going to get it!' "

Undoubtedly, there are cases in which many feel that such disciplinary methods are required today. The old scriptural line about rod and child seems to them more than applicable where the child becomes an overgrown child and children become a mob. But if old methods are not available, there is at least some comfort in the knowledge that the problems are not new, or not pertinent only to situations today.

Timrod survived them. Indeed, when he left to take on a tutoring job in Hardeeville, he missed Bluffton. There, he said, he found himself "among very good people, but far plainer and less pretending than the Blufftonians. I must say, too, that I prefer a little more polish than I have seen. . . ." He was sad because, "would you believe it, that though only sixteen miles from Bluffton, I have never been able to get a conveyance to take me thither."

Maybe by that time the bully of Bluffton was learning his discipline from both the Confederates and the Yankees. But the roadside thrashing he got from the principal was an engagement worth remembering.

June 3, 1971

Fifty-Year Reunion

Despite mounting evidence, nobody ever quite believes in his own antiquity. That may be especially true on this island. Ladies, well over the age of Mrs. Whistler when she had her portrait painted, go decked in the brightest colors, like the freshest flowers of the fields. Gentlemen emulate the painted bunting in the more brilliant plumage of the male. But time and change must occasionally be contemplated. Perhaps the best date to face them is the season when the college young come to Hilton Head Island to help with the summer activities and when an oldster returns to this island of the blest from exposure to a fifty-year reunion of his college class. On the way to such a regathering of the once-were-young, one elder expressed his amazement that he had attained so memorable a state.

"Fifty-year reunion!" he said with incredulity in his voice, and with no incredulity at all the young man at the other side of the supposed generation gap replied, "It will help you face reality."

"Or mortality," the old one added. Maybe the apprehensive senior-student faced both. The reunion of the class of '21 provided a good time for counting. Nineteen twenty-one was the year in which the century became of age. The class's members today are about

142

the age Civil War veterans were in 1917, the year the 1921 class entered college. World War II veterans won't get that old until 1998. Many of the 1921 boys in one way or another got involved in a war to make the world safe for democracy—indeed, safe for everything in the permanent peace promised beyond it. But some of the graduates then, despite their participation in a major episode of civilization, turned out to be no wiser than their world was. They took their places behind F. Scott Fitzgerald, Ernest Hemingway, and others in what was called a Lost Generation, composed possibly of pre-hippies.

Elders shook their heads then as now but they were not deterred from their purposes to hasten the perfectability of man. Women were given the ballot and were allowed to retain their pedestals, too. The virtues women were expected to bring to politics were fortified by Prohibition, which was to bring everybody to sobriety. America was a land in which it was proclaimed that everybody could get rich until it was suddenly discovered that everybody could get poor. The Depression was chiefly important as the basis for the determination that everybody must be protected. Now, on the other side of another war—or wars—for freedom, here on Hilton Head Island and elsewhere the beautiful people are confronted by the startling fact that there is little more than the width of a creek—if that much—between gardened serenity and the threat of pollution, between provident retirement and restless insurgency.

It may be a time for a reunion of the present with the past. They seem very different. There is a mask of similarity in the same ceremonies and collegiate folk customs, in the caps and gowns of durable survival from monasticism. Graduates today emerge from high-rise dormitories surrounded by vast acreages of parking lots. They move, attended by women and babies, in crowded cars, many of foreign origin. They—or the males among them—are bearded like brigands or cavaliers. Yet they seem to be turned out, like their grades, by computers. The proms and academic parades are much as of old, but now we usually graduate multitudes from stadiums where once fewer accoladed in halls.

The alumni are still given the perennial warning that dear old alma mater is in financial crisis and that the forces of darkness are at its doors. They still listen to fatuous speeches on irrelevent subjects. They are given a sort of rogues' gallery privilege of looking upon the portraits of old professors who, according to indestructible academic legend, students revered in their own college days. The legend is maintained, though their students actually hated some of them as sadistic so-and-sos who took their intellectual sustenance from intellectual triumphs over sophomores.

It is good that the old boys wear badges. Time does wither and fade. Also time touches some with fame and fortune and others with neither. The dead and the missing are recalled. The last are most mysterious. Some graduated and never have waved back or reported their addresses. They are listed almost like unknown soldiers in a military cemetery. But the living are ostentatiously happy and vociferously hearty. And they have much to recall about the wonderful generation of which they have been a part.

There is not a gap in it. If it went from war to war to wars, it can count its blessings: chain stores, installment buying, filter cigarettes, credit cards, golf carts, home freezers, air conditioning, radio, TV, automatic transmission and power brakes, dial telephones, detergents, traffic lights, motels, shopping centers, neon signs, seat belts, transatlantic flights, ballpoint pens, disposable diapers, Kleenex, presidential libraries, condominiums, film ratings, microfilm, mobile homes, screw-top bottles, cellophane, plastics, frozen foods, Polaroid cameras, penicillin, missiles, rockets, nuclear power, moon flights, computers, electric toothbrushes, and washer-dryers. Also, of course, we have added Social Security, Medicare, pension plans, stock options, consultants' fees, health insurance, the United Nations, and the Pentagon; yet the sense of security escapes us. Our frontier is our front yard even on Brams Point and Beach Lagoon Road. Our lighthouses, as at Harbour Town, are built for decoration, not guidance. *Love* is a word scrawled on the same wall with the word *pigs*. There are no unmentionable words and no inconceivable acts. It has been quite a trip without benefit of LSD, though that is said to be readily available.

Maybe we need a generation gap. The beard that hides a young face may be covering a blush for the elders. The past may be only a prologue, but it has been a procession from the Presbyterian idealism of Woodrow Wilson to the Quaker-in-arms of Richard Nixon. Democrats and Republicans have collaborated in frustration. We can write our history like a message on a postcard: "Having a wonderful time. Wish you were here."

A famous surgeon, graduate of the class of '21, was asked at a reunion what he was doing in his golden years. "Oh," he said, "I'm just doing little jobs on big people." Maybe the reverse of that is the history of the half-century to which, as loyal alumni, we cry, "Hurrah!"

June 10, 1971

Dionysus Last Seen

Dionysus has been much slandered. Of course, he was the god of wine, and puritans as long ago as the Greek mythmakers shook solemn heads at the possibilities implicit in the product of the vine. But he was originally, and is always, the god of the fruitfulness of the good earth. And in a world whose ecology is perhaps most threatened by the separation of men from the reality of the land upon which they depend, Dionysus is a figure who deserves remembrance and respect. A dreadful possibility is that we saw him for the last time here in the person of gentle Greyton Taylor.

Certainly he looked like a figure out of a good, ancient past one day last April when he came to plant two grapevines on Calibogue Cay. The vines were the sort of gift which the first Dionysus, like a primeval Johnny Appleseed, carried to all parts of the earth. His chariot on this occasion was a station wagon. In its back were buckets filled with rich soil and the tools of a man or myth devoted to fruitfulness. Though already fragile-looking, he climbed out like an eager workman, smiling shyly and warmly. He spotted the place in the sun where he wanted to plant his vines. With a steady foot he pushed his spade into the earth. He shaped the holes exactly to his expert liking. He clipped unnecessary tendrils from the small cuttings. Gently he put the vines into their holes and carefully pressed the earth about them. When he drove away, with no air of Dionysian mysteries, he left behind instructions, *Recommended Spray Program for Grapes on Hilton Head Island.*

There was certainly nothing mythological about this neighborly gift and visit. Indeed, the uniqueness of both emphasized the sweeping way in which all the poetry of creativity and fruitfulness have been so much lost, even here. But for his clipped New York accent, Greyton Taylor might have been a peasant or a god in the ancient tradition of the fruitful vineyards of man. Far from that, of course, he was a wealthy, successful American businessman—but with one tremendous difference from that familiar figure here. While no peasant and no god, he still kept the direct, loving contact with the earth, which the happiest peasants possess and the greatest kings may well envy. It is not entirely established by a round on a golf course, or by many rounds—not even by a hole in one.

Socially, intellectually, financially, Greyton Taylor fit snugly into the pattern of the retired or about-to-be-retired business executives or military chieftains who inhabit this place.

But, uniquely, no paper wall of stocks and bonds, memos and order blanks, pension fund or consultant fees separated him from constant creative contact with the good earth. In an age in which vintners are generally corporations with offices in skyscrapers, he remained the man close to the ancient symbols of earth and vine, grape and wine, planting and reaping with his own strong, slender hands.

Here on Hilton Head Island he did not leave his vineyards behind as many others leave gladly and casually behind them oil companies, utilities, textile plants, steel mills, paper factories, or the Pentagon. While living on Beach Lagoon Road, much of Greyton Taylor's real life was spent on lands he had acquired here for experimenting with the possibilities of grape culture in South Carolina. Perhaps that was a remote possibility. This island land, which can quickly produce condominiums, may not have such qualities as are to be found about the Finger Lakes in New York State. Perhaps such planting here was as financially futile as were the efforts of those who once wished silkworms and mulberry trees to work together in this country. But the desire and the dream were the precious possessions of a man who never meant to retire from his association with the earth and its fruition.

Old mythological figures disappear. Maybe there is no room in our time for those who know and hold tightly to their best meaning. As Greyton Taylor planted the two vines on Calibogue, he talked about the increasingly remote possibility of the survival of family-owned companies like his own and the family-handed-down heritage of devotion to personal participation in the fruitfulness of the earth. And he talked with less enthusiasm about the slick magazine advertisements of his wines than about the devoted cultivation by his companies of cuttings of the vines for others to spread vineyards across good, wide, fruitful areas.

Possibly the image of the good Dionysus disappeared here when Greyton Taylor died beside his vineyards in New York. Maybe the beginnings of vineyards he planned here will go back into weed and yucca, saw grass and thistles. But an enduring image will be left of man with his earth. And that begins, and can stay, nowhere except in each man's own spirit and in his determination to be a figure in creative relationship with the land on which he lives. Less than ever can we spare the best image of Dionysus in our times.

June 17, 1971

High and Low

The unanimous vote against the big foot-in-the-door of a first high rise in Hilton Head Island development clearly represented resident sentiment on the island. But the decision reached after a sort of Helen Hokinson session of the Hilton Head Island Community Association seemed wan in contrast to the glaring challenge presented by a young black man and a young white man in separate speeches on other subjects at the same meeting.

Charles Grant, young architect, and Joseph Brown, concerned island native, spoke out of an involvement for people which added weight to their words. Grant stressed a faith in public education as he enumerated the great needs of the island elementary school. Brown emphasized the basic health requirements of human beings here, particularly among his own black people, as he described the work to eliminate parasites which afflict so large a proportion of them. He told, too, of mobilizing young people in the summer to bring their hands, which might be idle, to work in the health program. Both spoke in moderate, unexcited, instructive fashion. Neither turned on any rhetoric. Yet only the dullest spirits present could have missed the human drama implicit in their messages.

They were applauded. No questions were required of either. But one tall man rose to express a general reaction when he asked to whom contributions to both causes could be made.

The high-rise discusssion followed. Almost everybody present was obviously against the skyscraper trend, which has made such a mess of the shores of Florida. There was a readiness for a general, if vague, mobilization against what Charles Fraser has aptly described as "visual pollution." But the discussion of the matter wandered off into sometimes expert, but generally emotionally sterile, discussions as to how high is high. Some present (maybe including this writer) were more irritable than effective.

Perhaps the trouble was that the problem of possible visual pollution came after, and in contrast with, the clearly demonstrated need for action against human pollution. That was described by the two young men with matter-of-factness requiring no eloquence for emphasis. They spoke to a company which had shown that it could effectively array popular opinion against a threat to clean air and water. Evidently it could, if it as passionately wished to do so, organize effectively against any visual pollution of its shore and sky. But the question really flung at those present at the meeting was whether the community of the serene and the secure here could mobilize its hearts as it has mobilized its fears.

Of course, people on Hilton Head Island want to protect the old patterns of its charm. Yet some changes will be inevitable as this island becomes more and more crowded. Some would hurry change and minimize damage. There were "experts" ready to dismiss as trivial the dangers from the wastes of a great chemical plant. There will be architects and designers who will aesthetically defend higher and higher buildings for more and more occupants per acre of land. After all, the Taj Mahal is 243 feet high. But nobody can defend an island where, as development mounts, so many people remain without plumbing, without safe wells, even without privies. Nobody—certainly not those elders who deplore the faults and failures of the young—can defend, in a rich community, an inadequate elementary school for children and the lack of the necessary tools and facilities for learning. Under able supervision, the children in this school have behaved well. They deserve a better chance.

It would be a sad day when—or if—Hilton Head Island lost the charm of people living close to the good earth, in the shade of trees, within the immediate sound of bird song. It would be tragic if gentle folk who are now ready to fight to save themselves from the pollution of air, water, view, were not also ready creatively to save their neighbors and themselves from the greater pollutions of ignorance and disease. High rises may be a threat. Low standards for many are a real danger to all. The worst high rise here would be a mounting contrast between towering facilities for some and continuing deprivations for so many others on the same beautiful shore.

June 24, 1971

Traffic Tunnel

Possibly there should be rejoicing in this neighborhood over signs that I-95 is coming toward completion. It will make shorter and swifter the ways from all parts of America to Hilton Head Island. Maybe the road time saved will make amends for the old feeling that from anywhere on earth the longest part of a trip to our island is the lap from Stuckey's to the bridge. The monument is already up at Point South, where decorated facilities will be provided for those who emerge from the green tunnel of the interstate to pause, eat, drink, or sleep before they set out again on the huge highway—which seems designed for a combination of speed and somnolence, or dispatch and boredom.

The one thing now most certain about the great highway which will "serve" this lovely area is that none who ride can see the land through which they pass. Here will be, as everywhere else, the road-building design of hiding America from those who ride to see it. Heart's desire in highways is apparently one wide, never-changing tunnel of interminable pavement and grass and nothing else. They are like one endless memorial park in this day when the style is cemeteries without monuments. The purpose is not to mark the

152

resting place of the deceased but to ease and cheapen the way of living lawn-mower operators. Such efficient, perpetual care seems best to serve instant forgetfulness.

Undoubtedly some of the old monuments in American graveyards were grotesque. Some of the epitaphs on them have served comedy. And, of course, billboards along highways are now classified as offensive. But the idea that removing the billboards will alone beautify the highways of the United States is an absurdity when the only substitute for them will be interminable dullness hiding all roadside charm as well as roadside horrors. Even an automobile graveyard of rusty wrecks and crumpled steel would provide some relief from sameness on our bigger and indistinguishable grass tunnels called interstates. Maybe some of the fastidious were offended when roads ran by slums and through gasoline alleys. They also ran by farmhouses, churches, orchards, mills, all the aspects of American living, good and bad, and as varied as the now-hidden American landscape.

Once, old-fashioned road builders in South Carolina and other places, too, would twist a highway to save a lovely tree. Now the bulldozers make ready for the pavement in disregard of hill and dale. Only destination seems to get any attention. And destination may be now all that American travelers at high speeds are concerned about. Still, somehow our great anesthetic highways ought to get some attention. Undoubtedly there are some supposed landscape men employed by the billions-spending highway departments. Apparently, however, their chief achievement has been to learn how to plant the seed of trillions of blades of identical grass by shooting it out of monstrous air guns.

The highway people piously hide all signs but their own, which can sometimes compound the mazes of their interchanges. They admit to human needs other than speed by abrupt announcements that food, lodging, and gas can be acquired at certain exits. Certainly this hardly meets the specification of Dr. Samuel Johnson that any landscape is improved by a good inn in the foreground.

"Ban the Billboards!" has been a demand popular with the self-appointed keepers of America the Beautiful. Some billboards have properly deserved their place as items of visual pollution. But the notion that the absence of billboards, or of any other signs of human activity or eagerness, will be beautification enough is pious nonsense and negative idiocy. Beauty of highways or anything else requires a creative relationship to life and nature. Our embalmed boulevards certainly do not meet that requirement. Indeed, the clamor of billboards has some merit beside the interminable triteness of the bigger and bigger American roads.

I-95 will help men move through this lovely Low Country like missiles in space. And perhaps all that men want is to be rocketed across unchanging pavements to identical motels. But there does seem a possibility that those who move in America may want to see it. And if that desire anywhere exists it will take more than bulldozer minds to meet it.

July 1, 1971

The End of Innocence

Manhattan must have been a lovely woodland island when the Indians sold it for pocket money and maybe a jug or two of liquor long ago. Hawaii was once a flower on the surface of the Pacific. Maybe there are no islands anymore. Even quiet Martha's Vineyard has begun to protest some of the company which threatens to engulf it. Hilton Head has not yet reached the point at which, in the midst of a crowd of thousands, a black man with no clear motive undertook to assassinate an alleged racketeer playing the role of devoted protector of his people. Looters have not yet run wildly through our streets or woodland lanes.

But to state it matter-of-factly, this island in recent months has seen arson and robbery. Within recent days a "practical joker," who was in fact a criminal idiot, has drugged the drink of children. Earlier this island was shown to be a scene of marijuana smuggling. A dwelling house was fired into with bullets striking near a sleeping child. And now double rape. All this—and, of course, undiscovered more—has happened with scarcely an arrest in any serious case.

Naturally, the sense of serenity which lured so many here has almost been succeeded by forebodings of defenselessness. Possibly, much of the growth in crime here was inevitable with the growth in population. Other things have contributed. In exaggeration in the BASF fight this shore was presented as an island of fat cats whose spendings promised easy pickings for thieves. Much has been made of the number of prominent people here, many listed in *Who's Who* and vouched for by Bradstreet. Maybe too little attention has been paid to the fact that in the increasing numbers some have arrived whose names would better decorate police blotters. The place has been advertised as a rich target for criminals. And to that has been added practically the advertisement that it is a safe place for criminals where more and more crimes occur but arrests and convictions are almost nonexistent.

There are said to be three resident deputies on the island, some increase over the recent past. But it is very doubtful that the increase in deputies even approximates the increase in people and the taxes paid by them to Beaufort County. After the double rape the sheriff dispatched three more deputies to the island, but from Beaufort —an hour's drive away. Clearly this island is inadequately staffed. And if the record of crime detection is the measure, it is ineptly guarded.

It will not be enough, however, to condemn the present protection provided by the law. Some of those who need protection are not without fault. There have been, it is said, cases in which injured persons refused to cooperate with officers out of fear—or cowardice. Two recent robberies provided a needed warning. Businessmen, whose big take is known, not only jeopardize themselves but others when they indicate a practice of taking money home instead of using the bank's night depository.

An advance story about the Fourth of July reported that, while crowds were expected, "most of the island's 11 miles of white ocean front sand offer comparative privacy." If those miles of beach are protected from invasion, so should there be no intrusion of outsiders upon those who customarily enjoy such a place as Burke's Beach, long popular with the blacks. Of course, strangers may stray out of ignorance, but respect for the privacy of others is the best protection for all.

The possibly sad truth is that we have got to give up the old notion that this is (was) a place of secluded serenity far away from all the ills which plague most of our city friends. Skull Creek is not a moat. Most of the time the drawbridge is down to let in lovely people, hard-working people, friends, and fair visitors. It is also down to let in every evil factor in our civilization and any and all hoodlums and criminals engaged in the service of malevolence.

The age of innocence is over on Hilton Head. The graybeards here can no longer act like children who can presume security. We have a duty to recognize our responsibilities as an inescapable part of life in an imperfect world. If we ran away, that world has run after us. Both Robinson Crusoe and Friday here are a long way from any desert island where only the wind in the palm trees murmurs in eternal peace.

July 8, 1971

Woodmason's Concern

There is nothing new about this as a country of contrasts between the rich and the poor, the old and the young, the orderly and the delinquent.

Perhaps the cry against the contrasts should be dismissed as interminable. Maybe after so long it should be harkened. Certainly it may be well to note that in all the generations well-to-do people in South Carolina have lifted their voices against human degradation, as Charles Woodmason did when in the 1700s he begged for schools in a colony "cover'd with Swarms of Orphans, and other Pauper vagrant vagabond Children to the Great Increase of all Manner of Vice and Wickedness."

He called for participation in his cry: "Speak O Ye Charlestown Gentry, who go in Scarlet and fine Linen and fare sumptuously ev'ry day. Speak O Ye overgrown Planters who wallow in Luxury, Ease, and Plenty. Would You, Could You Can You see or suffer Poor helpless, pretty Boys—Beautiful, unguarded, promising Young Girls, for want of Timely Care and Instructions to be united with a Crew of Profligate Wretches *Whose Mouth is full of Cun[n]ing Deceit and Lyes,* from whom they must unavoidably learn Idleness, Lewdness, Theft, Rapine Violence and it may be, Murder. . . ."

Mr. Woodmason, a planter who later became an Anglican clergyman, certainly indicated that not all early Americans were figures fit for a pageant. His description of some early South Carolinians hardly matches the conventional picture of the pioneers. He wrote: "Would we wish to see any of our own Complexion, Descendants of Freeborn Britons in such a State of Barbarism and Degeneracy? —And yet We began to be almost on the borders of it. Behold on ev'ry one of these Rivers, What Number of Idle, profligate, audacious Vagabonds! Lewd, impudent, abandon'd Prostitutes Gamblers Gamesters of all Sorts—Horse Theives [sic] Cattle Stealers, Hog Stealers—Branders and Markers Hunters going Naked as Indians. Women hardly more so. All in-a-manner useless to Society, but very pernicious in propagating Vice, Beggary, and Theft—Still more pernicious as We have frequently found, when United in Gangs and Combinations—Such bold and dangerous Offenders as contemn all Order and Decency—broke ev'ry Prison almost in America Whipp'd in ev'ry Province—and now set down here as Birds of Prey to live on the Industrious and Painstaking, Wretches, who have defy'd all Authority, and defeated the Laws of ev'ry Country. . . ."

There is a very modern sound about Mr. Woodmason's report. Those he described, of course, were not the Founding Fathers, but many of them were the Founding Children. Perhaps there should be no surprise in a descended nation. The probability is that the conditions to which he called attention in South Carolina were no surprise to "Ye Charlestown Gentry" or even to their fathers and grandfathers. Perhaps they were justified in shrugging their silken shoulders.

Furthermore, a lot has been done about providing the schools for which he pleaded. Much more has been provided. Still the problem remains. The appalling possibility is that it will always remain. The certain truth is that there is no telling how bad the situation might be or become without the succession in every generation of the Woodmasons. It may seem the strange thing about him that he was not merely a preacher crying "O Ye" to others in scarlet and fine linen. He was also, as scholars at the University of South Carolina today point out, "a large landholder in the Peedee River region and a respected 'Planter and Merchant,' prominent in affairs of church and state in Charleston."

He dressed well. He had his share of luxury, ease, and plenty. And perhaps he was a little naïve when he proposed that, in the schools, he wanted the louts he had described to be taught "to sing after the Parochial Manner that so they may be useful at Church on Sundays—to carry on that Noble Part of Divine Worship quite neglected in our Congregations. . . ."

Evidently, he was one of "us" but he did not lack concern for the eternal "them," who may have deserved his indignation but never lost his creative and conscientious concern.

July 15, 1971

The Gold Bug

What a homesick island this must have been in the days of its
military bustle during the Civil War occupation. The big graveyard
in Beaufort indicates the very many who never did get home again.
Certainly there were thousands more young boys here who ached,
and not merely with the fevers, during that period. But one of the
most tragic boys far from home on the South Carolina sea islands
was one who came here earlier—and really was homeless when he
came.

South Carolina, which has just published a fine anthology of its
literature from 1670 to 1970, makes no claim, of course, to this
young man. But in all the recollection here of things past and the
joyous development of things present, maybe some attention might
be given to this young soldier, enlisted under name of Edgar A.
Perry. He served briefly at Fort Moultrie on Sullivan's Island in
1827–28 and left much of the sea-island atmosphere in his work.

He was, of course, Edgar Allan Poe. Then aged eighteen, he had
been rather roughly treated by his foster father in Richmond,
though perhaps his student behavior at the University of Virginia
provided some excuse. The facts, however, are that the young fel-

161

low, after a violent quarrel with his foster parent, left home. In Boston he spent his last dollar getting a small volume of his verses printed. The book won little applause. He was not able to find work. So, on May 26, 1827, giving his age as twenty-two, he enlisted in the army. Military records described him as having gray eyes, brown hair, a fair complexion, and as being five feet and eight inches tall. Of course, no mention of his notions of himself as a poet was given. The army certainly could not have been concerned about the fact that he had lost his home, left his girl (whose parents sternly intercepted his letters), and was without money or friends.

So far as time is concerned, any South Carolina claim of influence on the young man would be strictly limited. His regiment was ordered south at the end of October 1827. From November 1827 to December 1828 he performed garrison duty at Fort Moultrie. Unexpectedly, he must have been a pretty good soldier. He was given clerical employment and when his unit was transferred to Fortress Monroe in Virginia, in January 1829, he was made a sergeant major.

Already in those days Sullivan's Island was a popular resort. In the year before Poe arrived, its village of Moultrieville was described as having "a handsome appearance . . . the greater part of the houses (for more than a mile) front the beach, which extends the whole length of the island, a distance of three miles." Summer residents included such well-known families as the Pinckneys, the Hugers, the Middletons, the Simones, the Prioleaus, the Petigrus, and the Ravenels. Apparently, they had some problems then. An ordinance was passed prohibiting the cutting of trees. There were expressions of regret that the ten-cent ferry fare brought "all sorts and conditions of people" to enjoy the island. All in all, though with residents of a more native character, the place of Poe's military exile then seems much like Hilton Head Island now.

Poe left no memories of participation in the gaiety of the belles and beaux of the place. Instead, while he was there, he gathered the material which he later worked into "The Gold Bug," his classic story of buried treasure. Also, apparently, it was on the island that he wrote his poem "Israfel." Possibly his sense of loneliness and lack of appreciation in South Carolina, as elsewhere, went into the poem:

In Heaven a spirit doth dwell
  "Whose heart-strings are a lute;"
None sing so wildly well
As the angel Israfel,
And the giddy stars (so legends tell),
Ceasing their hymns, attend the spell
  Of his voice, all mute.
....

If I could dwell
Where Israfel
  Hath dwelt, and he where I,
He might not sing so wildly well
  A mortal melody,
While a bolder note than this might swell
From my lyre within the sky.

Obviously, Sullivan's Island then, despite its beach-front houses
and the society which filled them, seemed a long way from heaven
to a boy stranger of nineteen. Parris Island today might seem far
from heaven, too, to a marine draftee. Even Hilton Head Island
could seem so to one of the long-haired visitors, who often seem
more brash than bewildered. We can probably be comfortably confi-
dent that there is no genius among them—but we never can be
absolutely sure.

                                             July 22, 1971

Village Service

Savannah is a city. Beaufort is a pretty big town. Ridgeland is only a quiet village even if it is the county seat of Jasper County. It may be natural then that most new Hilton Head Island residents headed for town aim at Savannah or Beaufort. Many would make no mistake if they tried Ridgeland. No military base has transformed it. It is not plumed with the smoke and smog of a great paper industry. Perhaps its greatest fame, as a South Carolina guidebook says, is that once it was a sort of Gretna Green for the young-in-love-and-in-a-hurry from Georgia, who sought the leniency then of South Carolina's marriage license laws.

It has more virtue for Hilton Headers than the fact that it is a good deal shorter distance from this island than the other two places. Its main street does give the appearance of the sun-beaten Southern town. Indeed, despite the signs of modern national advertisers on its stores and streets, it is just that. It is marked neither by the developer nor the restorer. So it remains typically and truly Southern and South Carolinian—maybe more so even than Charleston, which always held itself apart and aloof from the simpler state behind it and about it. Ridgeland is still a sweet village in a piney plain.

164

But let nobody be fooled by its appearance of somnolence. It is true that the Gullah speech of the blacks on its streets is more pervasive even than on Hilton Head Island, where old-time blacks, like old-time whites, have had to learn to communicate with the Yankees. But both blacks and whites there keep an antique politeness often lacking in larger and more invaded towns. The suggestion of slow pace there is belied by a readiness to serve promptly and to do a job well.

Undoubtedly this may be only the quick impression of one man on one visit, but one who expects to go back again. His journey was no adventure in exploration. He had an ailing automobile. He was accustomed to the long-line, couldn't-care-less of much service, particularly in Savannah. So he dared Ridgeland. And he is glad to make happy report. He told his troubles to a gray-haired gentleman with *Sims* embroidered on his work clothes. Sims recognized the trouble and reported that the owner could have the car in an hour and a half.

The Hilton Head Islander walked a little way around the corner and found a very pleasant restaurant with linen on its tables. There he was pleasantly served and did some homework over his coffee, with no sense of push on his table. Birds sang outside the window of the air-conditioned room. Leisurely, he finished. Across the street was an interesting antique shop, unfortunately closed but filled with items worth noting through the windows. The word *Browse* was prominently displayed, even if at the moment unavailing.

Back in the air-conditioned showroom of the garage, an affable young South Carolina manager by the name of Fickling introduced himself. He had thought of opening a branch on Hilton Head Island, but the prices for any highway-front property asked by Harold Depkin and Fred Hack gave him more than pause. In Ridgeland land is land, not gold. The same applies to other prices. Of course, he would take a check. Within an hour and a half from the time of the car's arrival, another competent-appearing mechanic brought the car to the door, and the visitor to Ridgeland drove home with his motor humming and in time for lunch on Calibogue Cay.

Also, he came home with the sense not exactly that Ridgeland tries harder, as Avis says to Hertz. Ridgeland has not lost the Southern pace. But, though maybe with a drawl, Ridgeland goes about its work pleasantly, promptly, and competently. The visit seemed to be an escape from bustling and bungling, brusqueness and boredom in many large cities and towns.

For him pleasantness was added to a chore. And that is something rare to find in South Carolina, Georgia, or the world.

July 29, 1971

Daniels Tower

A twenty-story residence tower to cost approximately $10 million was projected in a building permit issued to Jonathan Daniels and associates.

Mr. Daniels, who has been a sojourner and writer here for a decade, said that he could not now say when construction would begin; but his associates, builders and promoters from Nevada and Florida, were anxious to secure the permit under existing zoning and building laws.

"My function," he said, "will be largely to publicize this great facility. Planning and building will be under the direction of gentlemen who have had much experience in the expansion of resorts on Miami Beach and in Las Vegas."

Daniels, who in the past has opposed high-rise developments, explained his position.

"I know I will be charged with inconsistency," he declared. "When I first came to Hilton Head Island, land which my wife and I purchased contained a stipulation that no duplexes could be built on the property. Soon afterward, however, multiplexes—or condominiums—were begun in large numbers in the same area. As a writer with no other weapon than humorous verse, I opposed them in some doggerel called 'Condominium, the Gem of the Ocean!' Last year a reprinting of that verse was sharply criticized. I still opposed the multiplication of people in proportion to space or facilites upward or sprawling. But, obviously, I was no King Canute against this tide. Before I became a literary recluse on Hilton Head Island, I was not only an editor but also a politician. I learned the old piece of American wisdom: 'If you can't lick 'em, jine 'em.'

"So recently when some of my old friends in national Democratic politics approached me as to this venture, I agreed to join them. I know that they are excellently qualified in the fashion of American resort development today. Some of them have been active in the phenomenal resort growth in the West Indies. I am sure they will bring to our island all the varied recreational and pleasure facilities available in the Caribbean, but within the United States and in easy auto and plane access from all parts of it.

"They have plenty of capital and are not seeking any here. They ask no special privileges from the island or the state of South Carolina. They only wish to take advantage of the opportunities available now to every other builder and developer. Of course, their projected twenty-story tower would provide many jobs and attract other related businesses to this shore."

Mr. Daniels said he does not like the term "high rise."

"I prefer to think of the twenty-story tower as a beacon, one about which many thousands of people could gather on the shore and which would proclaim the charm of this island to mariners far at sea. Much as we older visitors here may regret it, I doubt that we can in good conscience deny the beauty and charm of this island to thousands more who might enjoy it as a result of such facilities as my associates plan."

Mr. Daniels denied that Charles Fraser, Fred Hack, or Daniel J. Donahoe III were involved in the project. He felt, however, that they would not find it competitive but an aid in their plans to appeal to more and more property buyers on the island. And, also, he said that, contrary to some rumors he understood were circulating, Howard Hughes was not in any way connected with the matter. "I have the greatest respect for Mr. Hughes," Daniels said, "but he has nothing to do with this enterprise." Neither, he added, do the builders of the new Disney World in Florida, though in connection with the tower some good, clean attractions would be provided having a somewhat similar appeal to those being built at the new Florida amusement area.

Mr. Daniels said that he had been flattered by the suggestion of some of his associates that the fine, high residential building be named the Daniels Tower. He thought that it would be wiser to give it a name more indigenous to the region, such as Coligny's Column. Or, to emphasize the concern of many, it could be called the Environmental Vision Inn.

"Anyhow," he exclaimed, "It's going to be high and handsome. It may have many imitators but will not soon be surpassed."

August 5, 1971

The Winebibbers

High over Harbour Town, at the invitation of Ruthven and Roberts, the small (and Oh, very select!) company gathered. In what would normally be a conference room for ecologists and entrepreneurs, a long table was spread with linen. Upon it sat smugly, presumably ready for tasting, bottles of imported wines.

A tall, handsome, talkative salesman of a company which sells high-proof American whiskeys and smooth wines of the vineyards of France took over. He was instructive, persuasive, and prolonged. He gave a lecture on what every Hilton Head Islander should know about the virtues in his bottles, the differences between domestic and foreign wines, the heritages of French vintners, and the taxes in American states. Back of all his talk was a feeling for the recently developed taste buds of connoisseurs of wines which now exist in Atlanta, Georgia.

He was tolerant, nevertheless, of people who drink cheaper American wines. He urged his listeners to buy and drink the wines which pleased their palates, regardless of the cost. But he mentioned wines selling for forty dollars a bottle. He recalled an Atlanta man who had built a new house and came to buy one order of six hundred dollars of choice vintage to begin the cellar of his establishment. (An impertinent lady spoke, in an aside of "instant culture.")

While the gentleman talked, the uncorked bottles sat more patiently on the table than the audience listening before it. Ruth looked restless. Roberts brought chairs for late arrivals. They were not too late. The talk went on. The people and the wine waited as clocks pushed toward the luncheon hour. Jayne Withers, looking pretty enough already, had to leave for a beauty parlor date. Others waiting lit cigarettes regardless of the damage to their taste buds. But at length the wines came, served in plastic glasses which could be discarded in a big plastic barrel between each tasting so that no trace of the first wine before could mar the perfect taste of the wine ahead. Old glasses were discarded as crystal goblets were once flung into fireplaces after toasts to the king and queen.

The rain had been pouring down when the talking and the belated tasting began. The sun shone over the yacht basin as the successive wines were poured. Booklets were distributed as to how to cook with Old Crow, which—it was learned—was a corporate cousin to the Beaujolais.

Someone recalled that there had not been another wine tasting here since Charles Fraser gathered a similar group to taste the wines and the food he and Franz Meier planned to serve at the Plantation Club. Then, that epicurean facility was still in the planning stage— before the population explosion in it and certainly before the explosion of any popping corks there.

Tasters expressed their preferences. And the wine master in the blue coat and the wide, white tie told of his own initiation at wine tasting. He had been given by his mentor a costly bottle. He wanted him to describe it after long, careful, leisurely tasting. The poetry of the wine came into his report. As he drank it, he felt himself in an ancient wine vault, rich with the bouquet of the vintage years which had filled its casks.

Good old wines grew in value, he said, more certainly than stocks and bonds—even Hilton Head land prices. But if you like a two-dollar bottle of wine, buy it and drink it. If you like a forty-dollar bottle of wine, likewise. The price is not the thing but the taste, foreign or domestic. Slowly, glowingly, the party dispersed, all late for lunch, but informed, enlightened, and illuminated.

Not all were sure just which wine, red or white, best satisfied their taste buds, but there was general agreement that the tasting of the wine was worth the long, long talk about it. One gentleman as he departed was heard murmuring, "What is it that the vintner buys half so precious as the stuff he sells."

He was seen later in the Calibogue Café adding a martini to the best imported wines in the world.

August 12, 1971

River Called Mendel

A garland of memorial addresses for a dead politician may not only honor the man but point the repetition of an irony in the story of an aristocratic citadel. Old Charleston has long felt that the elect should only be those born below Broad Street. Yet, anciently, it proudly followed in mourning the catafalque of John C. Calhoun, who was not to the city born. Now a small black-and-gold volume of congressional eulogies (none quite matching the eloquence of such Calhoun contemporaries as Clay and Webster) evokes in a minor key a similar tale. It is, of course, the story of the eager welcome of dead officials, onetime outsiders, into the elegant precincts of the patricians.

Once it was said that the Cooper and the Ashley rivers came together at Charleston to make the Atlantic Ocean. More recently it was said that the three rivers of Charleston were the Cooper, the Ashley, and the Mendel. And now, Charleston, grown fatter if not prouder as a result of Mendel Rivers' congressional position, is planning a second monument to him. That will put a capstone on the tale.

In his memorial address, Senator Strom Thurmond related the

173

fact that Rivers was born in Gumville, South Carolina, "situated in an area also known as Hell Hole Swamp." Gumville is neglected on the maps. Also, the official guide of South Carolina, published about the time Rivers first ran for Congress, says that the exact location of Hell Hole Swamp along the road between Charleston and Kingstree is "undetermined." It described the swamp as "an area of indefinite extent, its whereabouts always designated as 'just a little piece down the road.'" But it added, "During prohibition days when South Carolina was actively advertising the iodine content of its vegetables, the Hell Hole brand of 'liquid corn' was notorious with its waggish slogan, 'Not a Goiter in a Gallon.'"

That was a long way from the Battery. And when Mendel Rivers ran for Congress, the "Charleston machine" preferred another man, a banker and former athlete named Fritz Von Kolnitz. Early returns from Charleston County gave Von Kolnitz a big lead. Von Kolnitz carried the aristocratic county by four thousand votes. But the outlying-country counties gave Rivers so one-sided a margin that he won by three thousand votes.

Times change. Forty years later at a banquet in Rivers' honor, a somewhat kindred spirit, Vice-President Agnew, solemnly declared: "I would like to lay to rest the ugly, vicious, dastardly rumor that he is trying to move the Pentagon piecemeal to South Carolina. I have been to Charleston several times, and I have had it clearly explained to me that the military facilities so evident in that area are a testament of Mendel Rivers' unselfish willingness to allow his own First District of South Carolina to accept in the national interest military installations that just had to be put some place. . . .

"Even when it looked like Charleston might sink into the sea from the burden, Mendel Rivers' patriotic response was: 'I regret that I have but one Congressional District to give my country to—I mean to give to my country.'"

Finally, however, the vice-president, "on the serious side," declared that such reports of the congressman packing the military on his South Carolina shore were "of such stuff that myths are made." Maybe so. But Charleston, which first rejected the young man from Hell Hole Swamp, has raised its two pedestals for the chairman of the Armed Services Committee. The Ugly Duckling of Gumville had become the militant swan of old Charleston. Or maybe Vice Admiral Rickover, who in the navy has been something of an ugly duckling himself, best put the story into words. Charleston, which honors the past but loves federal appropriations, will clasp them as its own. Said Rickover: "Some people judge an eagle by noting how it walks on the ground. An eagle must be judged by its majestic flight in the sky."

An eagle out of Hell Hole Swamp, clasping golden arrows in its claws, was, as always, welcome in Charleston. Charlestonians make monuments to such birds there, not a song as once happened in less-lucky Mobile.

August 19, 1971

Tower Troubles

Evidently in the race upward on Hilton Head Island the proposed Coligny Tower suddenly faces serious competition. The height of the sign on the proposed Holiday Inn with three hundred rooms has not yet been determined by the architects. Height also remains a question in the plans of the McCloskey interests on their recently purchased mid-island site. However, in a preliminary announcement these builders point with pride to their tall structures now renting at Pompano Beach and soon to be finished in San Francisco.

The interest in the Coligny Tower remains unabated. Emerson Mulford applied for a position as rental agent. Herb Perkins not only expressed interest in becoming house detective but even suggested that a telescope mounted on the tower might cut the need for more cops on the island. Frank Schaefer hoped to be able to get the concession for a no-thumb-on-the-wheel casino in the penthouse. However, applications for the penthouse greatly exceed the building's possibilities unless it is built in the form of a T. Only a few, including Joseph T. Elvove, of sugar and Sea Pines, sounded sour notes. He threatened to sue for "visual pollution," a term on which his chief associate holds the patent.

Nothing daunted by competition and conservation, the builders of the Coligny Tower (colloquially and quite inaccurately sometimes referred to as the Daniels Tower) are moving forward with their plans. Already they have secured, as consultant on recreation, Milwaukee S. Obolanski, whose part in arranging for the recent visit of the American Ping-pong team to Red China was apparently covered by security considerations. Mr. Obolanski feels that in the expansion of American recreational interests the time is ripe for a step beyond the stereotyped sports such as golf and tennis. He thinks Hilton Head Island, with the proposed high residence tower, offers special advantages in the development of new and fresh sporting activities relating to current American interests.

"All of the world's sport and games," he said, as a visitor here for the Tournament of Tennis Champions at Sea Pines, "have grown from the folk customs of the people. Our games only refine folk habits in knocking and throwing things. Now obviously, a most spontaneous such activity in America today is the throwing of the beer can. In a very real sense it could be the modern equivalent of discus throwing, which the Greeks developed in their early games. I can think of no better place for the sublimation of this American activity into a world of sport than Hilton Head Island, certainly with such a facility available as Mr. Daniels' associates plan."

Great as is the demand for a penthouse, a casino, and perhaps a helicopter landing platform on the tower, he said, he hoped there might be room for a platform for the human projection of such a familiar object as the beer can from the roof. The flight path, or trajectory, of such missiles form a curve, due to the action of the force of gravity and the resistance of the atmosphere. Meteorological conditions here are ideal for magnificent trajectories by players who understand the laws of fluid dynamics, which are essentially the laws of conservation of mass, momentum, and energy.

The sport might be much more spectacular than discus throwing, he pointed out, since the objects to be used would be less cumbersome than the official discus used in the Olympics. Greater distance and accuracy, he thinks, could be obtained with the lighter objects than the Olympic distance record of 212 feet, 6½ inches, set by Al Oerter of the United States in the 1968 games. Just as women have taken part in the Olympic discus contests since 1928, using a lighter discus, they would be admirably suited, he thinks, to this sport. Men might use the fourteen-ounce cans, while women flung the twelve-ounce ones.

Certainly there will be arguments about the formalization of the sport, Mr. Obolanski admitted. Sports scholars are still divided as to whether the reconstruction of a statue of a Greek discus thrower in the British Museum truly represents the style of the ancient Greek athlete. Similar differences will undoubtedly occur in the development of beer-can throwing as a major sport. Already, Mr. Obolanski said, Japanese athletes are urging that saki bottles be substituted for beer cans. Some British sportsmen are holding out for pub mugs. Such differences, Mr. Obolanski thinks, are healthy signs of world-wide interest. However, he insists that nowhere is there so much evidence of interest in the throwing of beer cans as in the United States.

He looks forward to the day when a major tournament in the sport may give further evidences of Hilton Head's leadership as an American sports and recreational center. Such an event would not only attract the leading figures to the island and provide employment for many residents, it would also provide opportunity for well-heeled islanders to participate as marshals, scorekeepers, and can collectors. In other events residents of the island have shown themselves eager to volunteer to make tournament play possible. He believes they would gladly costume themselves to give color to a major gathering here of the world's first flingers and fans of the sport. The danger to them, he thinks, would be slight. All volunteers would be glad to equip themselves with sturdy parasols bearing the insignia of the promoters of the tournament. The parasols might even be sold to the volunteers at wholesale prices. As a reward, the happy helpers might, in proximity to the champions, be able to secure more easily their autographs on the parasols, which they could preserve as mementoes. Also, Obolanski thought that, just as Delta Airlines has joined in backing sports events here, support for such an event might be secured from both conservationists and brewers. After all, he noted, a cigarette manufacturer, whose money might once have gone on TV, recently sponsored a much-publicized golf tournament at Pinehurst. The possibilities, he thought, were limitless.

"Imagine," he exclaimed, "the spectacle of great athletes flinging these shining objects from the top of the Coligny Tower over pine and sand and sea! If only half of the Americans who have everywhere demonstrated their interest in throwing beer cans could be attracted to such an event on Hilton Head Island, it would be one of the golden isles, indeed."

He shook his head in admiration of the prospect. "I can hardly wait," he said.

August 26, 1971

"I Don't Understand. . . ."

"I don't understand," the deeply troubled black woman said in contemplation of crime on the island. "It didn't used to be this way." *

And it was not this way. The long-time, almost wholly black community of Hilton Head was known as a peaceful one. The centers of much of its people's lives were the praise houses. Negro churches on this island have tended their black flocks for more than a century. They were poor. Perhaps they were, by modern standard, ignorant. They had a reputation as a good folk.

Now they are as disturbed as the white community about the succession of violent criminal acts. Once it was confidently said that any major crimes committed on the island must have been the acts of visitors or intruders. And now both peaceful blacks and peaceful whites are inclined to attribute terroristic acts here to wild ideas that are imports, too. And, of course, Hilton Head Island is not immune to the furies which have prevailed in the cities.

But change on this island has not been chiefly wrought by altera-

* In the summer of 1971 the island experienced an unprecedented outbreak of robberies and assaults.

180

tions in the characters and the ideas of the black community. This place has been transformed. Its greatest alterations have been in the white community. The influx of such people brought many of the best Americans to the island. Fear exists that some of the worst may follow. Certainly, in this time of great mobility for people, change for both good and ill is inevitable.

Undoubtedly the spectacle here of much luxury where only the possibility of subsistence was seen before has altered attitudes. The contrast between wealth and poverty has been sharpened. Expectations have been lifted. And patience has seemed less a virtue. The boom growth of the island has set a pace for all sorts of new and strange ideas. It would be odd if there were not confusion, sometimes expressing itself in aberration.

It must not be forgotten, however, that the old island does remain. The quest here for serenity by new people from far away has been served by the many old-time black people who have helped in its growth under the hot sun and in its quick transformation in elegant air-conditioned houses and rooms. The great body of black people are as eager for peace and serenity on their old island as are those who came here from many blighted cities. Perhaps the greatest surprise to newcomers here lies in the fact that they find about them the very dangers and faults from which they expected to escape.

The truth, of course, is that no people can hope to secure serenity and safety as simply as they can buy a lot. Here as everywhere else the good life has to be built. It is never prefabricated. Much has been done by newcomers in terms of the building of such things as the library, the day care center, the provision of medical care on a shore where once such help could be secured only at a distance and often at an impossible price. While poverty remains, new opportunity has been provided.

Yet it should not be a surprise to the white middle class, which has spawned so many hippies in this generation, that in the black community here there are also some delinquents, even criminals. But parental pain is as poignant among blacks as among whites. The disclosure that in a particularly atrocious crime here the one charged was an overgrown thirteen-year-old-boy of an ancient, honorable, and respectable black family was both terrifying and tragic. Children can be monsters, too. But true adults will not charge a whole community with the guilt of a few malignant members. Only the retarded will react to violence with violent suggestions.

If the white community has been brought by crime to a state of trauma, the intelligent members in it will recognize that the good blacks share their unhappiness. The desire to keep this an island of tranquillity is not racial. Vigilance is needed with regard to crime, but so is a sense of white and black mourning together for the sins in this disturbed Eden. There are blacks as well as whites who "don't understand" quite what has happened. There are blacks as well as whites who long for the days which "used to be" before bridge and boom opened the island to both landscaped pleasantness and mounting, unsolved, hurting, and frightening problems. The good life for all is something all must make together. And there are no islands of escape from responsibility and concern.

September 2, 1971

Fiddlers in the Vines

There had been a lot of talk about the great number of crabs hereabouts this summer. There were complaints that toes were nibbled in the surf. The high percentage of females among the crabs was noted by some who saw a sign of future plenty in their presence. Less attention apparently has been paid to a sudden seeming movement of sand fiddlers, or fiddler crabs, from the "intertidal zone" to places high on the shore. On Calibogue Cay they have appeared far back from Broad Creek, joining the crickets, spiders, and beetles on the paved terraces of houses. Despite their agility, this would seem to be a long journey for a sand fiddler.

In some cases the movement has seemed like a predatory invasion. Helen Cork on Point Comfort had what appeared to be a beautiful stand of tomato plants opulent with fruit. But when she went to pick a particularly luscious-looking tomato, she found that she had instead a whole colony of sand fiddlers, which had slyly slipped through an imperceptible hole in the skin to take up residence and gorge themselves inside. Helen may have been exaggerating when she said that the creatures were "eating our food and invading our homes." But she didn't get a single tomato from her vines.

This may be no surprise to biologists or ecologists. But to ordinary observers of such small Crustacea, the whole movement seemed like a sort of "man from Mars" invasion seen through the wrong end of a telescope. Coming not from space but from the tide line, they seem agile, energetic, and earnest in occupancy of a realm generally unknown to them. Perhaps we have minimized these visitors. This writer, his curiosity aroused, looked them up in the *Encyclopaedia Britannica* and found the most interesting information about the personality of the sand fiddler in the article on "Courtship." An exact quotation from that dissertation is as follows: "Although almost all Crustacea have well-developed special sense organs and internal fertilization, pursuit and forcible capture is usually the only preliminary to mating. In the semiterrestrial fiddler crabs, however, the males have one enormously enlarged claw, often brilliantly colored, and this is employed in a primitive form of courtship—not at first surmised, in fights between rival males or forcibly carrying off females. In the breeding season, a mature female passes near a sexually eager male, he stands on tiptoe and brandishes his claw in the air. As A. S. Pearse says, 'the males appear to be proclaiming their maleness.' The fiddler crab reacts to three main types of situation—feeding, danger and reproduction. The brandishing of the male's claw is to the female the visible symbol of the reproductive situation." Another *Britannica* item states that fiddler crabs that live in the intertidal zone alter their colors as the tides rise and fall.

Certainly this does not picture the sand fiddler as an inconsequential creature on our wide shores. Indeed, this description seems remarkably like our own species might seem if observed by some enormous Brobdingnagian eye. "Feeding, danger and reproduction" may seem a very limited repertoire of reactions. Certainly, however, much self-expression is indicated in the description. A lot of humans brandish their claws. Certainly the goal of many is to find the plenty and security of such an environment as the inside of a big tomato must be to a sand fiddler escaped from necessary scurrying in the intertidal zone. More and more human males and females are brilliantly colored. And love—

Maybe the moral to this, if any, is: Never scorn a sand fiddler. He may also be contemplating you.

September 9, 1971

Signs on the Shore

Island architects who will share in the evaluation and approval of the exterior sign of the upcoming Holiday Inn near Coligny Circle may be taking on a task like that Paris assumed in the award of the golden apple to the fairest lady in the ancient world. Some will remember that his choice of Helen brought on the Trojan War.

Possibly any such conflict can be avoided here. Still, the addiction of the Holiday Inns throughout the world to their high-standing, flamboyant, illuminated insignia at least suggests that they may not be content with a tiny sign speaking "welcome" in moderated, even dulcet, tones.

Our architects and the architectural approval boards of the various developments have in general done a fine job here in maintaining a uniformity which still escapes the stereotype. There are some exceptions. One recently erected residence seemed to this writer to look like a voodoo version of a columned Southern mansion. Still, that may conform to parallel traditions on this island before the first wave of Yankees arrived in gunboats in 1861.

They have done well, too, with signs. Perhaps this is most notable in the insignia of Palmetto Dunes which, probably unintentionally,

is a sort of fertility emblem on a multipying population. Deftly, the
p and the *d* in a circle looks like two fetuses tucked in a womb. Other
signs are less symbolic, though the small teahouses on poles, which
Sea Pines has adopted as directional road signs, clearly point the
exotic in the ecology.

Fortunately or unfortunately, there is no law limiting imagination
on this island, in terms of the signs erected. Most islanders, however, have voluntarily shaped or reshaped their signs to match the
subdued air of serenity which seems in order here. "Miss Katie"
McElveen has substituted for the almost-billboard which once stood
before the Roadside Rest a quieter proclamation of its presence.
It is to be hoped that such modification will not result in the missing
of her excellent restaurant by visitors moving at the customary
breakneck speed of those seeking tranquillity.

The Golden Rose Park had bordered its sign with a cypress frame,
which conforms to much island architectural preference. Still,
though it may be aesthetic treason to say it, the bigger sign of
Stewart's Paradise indicates the continuing existence here of an
exuberant spirit which no ironclad norm of the architecturally and
aesthetically erudite will ever wholly subdue. Certainly a native appeal to escape from hard work and humdrum is implicit in this sign.
It rises far above the standardized blurbs of Pepsi-Cola which are
attached to the names of the little stores. And certainly it is at least
as indigenous to this shore as the great golden scrawl on the Calibogue Café.

But to get back to the fastidious task of the architects in helping
the Holiday Inn to lift its ubiquitous emblem without offense to the
environment: It is difficult to think of a Holiday Inn without its sign.
Thousands of Americans have been taught that they can get the
same service at Holiday Inns everywhere—even to the same spreads
on the beds and pictures on the walls. Under that sign the traveler
can be sure that he will be safe from the dangers of diversity in
Charlotte, Seattle, or Hilton Head. And that certainly is an asset
which the smart operators of the Holiday Inns will relinquish reluctantly, even if they approach this shore with an air of deference to
difference.

Our architects face a challenge. Those who know their skill will
not doubt that they will meet it. All will expectantly await their
artistry. They may modify the big signs that soar above so many

roads. But they will be wise if they are cautious. In this world of glaring signs, even a little sign loudly crying hail and welcome could be like being a little pregnant.

What's a-borning?

September 16, 1971

Horace the Mule

A good many islanders remember the hilarious occasion when Ralph and Martha Boggs brought Edmund Harding here to speak to the historical society. This humorist of the Low Country of North Carolina died soon after he spoke here, but laughter lingers around his recollection. Recently Vernon Sechriest of the *Rocky Mount North Carolina Telegram* published the story below, which he got from Harding. It has been reprinted in the *Chapel Hill Weekly* and the *Virginia Gazette* at Williamsburg. It should not be denied readers of *The Island Packet.* Here it is.

HORACE THE MULE

Mrs. George Wood, now deceased, of Chowan County, had a mule who was named Horace. One evening she called up Dr. Satterfield in Edenton and said to him, "Doctor, Horace is sick, and I wish you would come and take a look at him."

Dr. Satterfield said, "Oh, Fannie Lamb, it's after 6 o'clock, and I'm eating supper. Give him a dose of mineral oil, and if he isn't all right in the morning, phone me, and I'll come and take a look at him."

"How'll I give it to him?" she inquired.

"Through a funnel."

"But he might bite me," she protested.

"Oh, Fannie Lamb, you're a farm woman and you know about these things. Give it to him through the other end."

So Fannie Lamb went out to the barn, and there stood Horace, with his head held down, and moaning and groaning.

She looked around for a funnel but the nearest thing she could see to one was her Uncle Bill's fox hunting horn hanging on the wall. A beautiful gold-plated instrument with gold tassels hanging from it.

APPLICATION

She took the horn and affixed it properly. Horace paid no attention.

Then she reached up on the shelf where medicines for the farm animals were kept. But instead of picking up the mineral oil, she picked up a bottle of turpentine, and she poured a liberal dose of it into the horn.

Horace raised his head with a sudden jerk. He let out a yell that could have been heard a mile away. He reared up on his hind legs, brought his front legs down, knocked out the side of the barn, jumped a five-foot fence, and started down the road at a mad gallop.

Now Horace was in pain, so every few jumps he made, that horn would blow.

All the dogs in the neighborhood knew that when that horn was blowing, it meant that Uncle Bill was going fox hunting. So out on the highway they went, close behind Horace.

It was a marvelous sight. First, Horace—running at top speed, the hunting horn in a most unusual position, the mellow notes issuing therefrom, the tassels waving, and the dogs barking joyously.

They passed by the home of Old Man Harvey Hogan, who was sitting on his front porch. He hadn't drawn a sober breath in 15 years, and he gazed in fascinated amazement at the sight that unfolded itself before his eyes. He couldn't believe what he was seeing. Incidentally, he is now head man in Alcoholics Anonymous in the Albemarle section of the state.

By this time it was good and dark. Horace and the dogs were approaching the Inland Waterway. The bridge tender heard the horn blowing and figured that a boat was approaching. So he hurriedly went out and uncranked the bridge. Horace went overboard and was drowned. The dogs also went into the water, but they swam out without very much difficulty.

Now it so happened that the bridge tender was running for the office of sheriff of Chowan County, but he managed to poll only seven votes.

The people figured that any man who didn't know the difference between a mule with a horn up his rear and a boat coming down the Inland Waterway wasn't fit to hold any public office in Chowan County.

September 23, 1971

Long Forgotten

It is strange how or why Hilton Head Island was so long passed by, even by those who knew and celebrated the beauties of this coast. Sometimes it seemed kept in a case like an old cameo. There is a book, hard to come by, called *Glories of the Carolina Coast*, written by a man named James Henry Rice, Jr. It was published in 1925 by the R. L. Bryan Company of Columbia, which is still doing books about this region. In it Hilton Head hardly got a place in a parenthesis.

"If a man sticks to the coast with the determination to make a home and stay there," wrote its author, "he will in due time have his portion of the blessings of God."

Obviously Mr. Rice was an enthusiast about this region. He almost sang about it less than half a century ago, giving a sense of the natural beauty still known but somehow a little more fragile and threatened. He wrote: "A summer trip along one of the coastal rivers will show the giant yuccas in flower with the magnolia, 'the royal woman of the Southern wood,' with its creamy white blossoms laid on shining green leaves; the cypress clad in vivid green and 'lilies' floating on still waters, while the wampee shows forth its blossoms—everywhere bloom runs riot. On the uplands tall brooding pines sway in the wind and murmur things unutterable. Huge wood ibises stalk along the shore; redwings chatter and quarrel; rails cry in the reeds; coots and gallinules patter over the lily pads; the bald eagle soars, often a speck in the empyrean, while coppices are snow white with egrets; and nonpareils cling to grass stalks, eating seeds. All is life, life omnipresent—bird and beast, insect and flower, reptile and fish. What sane man can call so fruitful a region poor? It is opulent, prodigal, with a lure no soul may resist."

Well, today the bald eagle is not often seen. And some sane people do call the land poor for too many. But beauty does remain, though sometimes precariously.

Mr. Rice only mentioned Hilton Head by saying that the May River "turns into Calibogue Sound and passes out to sea between Hilton Head and Daufuskie Islands." Evidently there seemed no choice to him between these islands. He mentioned that Beaufort had been called "the most beautiful town on the Atlantic" and dissented only to point out that it is not on the Atlantic. He moved on from Beaufort toward this place: "Picturesqueness and variety . . . reach perfection at Bluffton on the May River, lauded by all travelers from Ribaut down . . . at Bluffton, the live oaks are uniformly larger and more symmetrical in the unfolding of their mighty crown. The limbspread is enormous, one limb measuring recently eighty-four feet two inches. . . . Bluffton retains enough flavor of old days to let one know he is within the pale, surrounded by the purple-born, through storm and stress, which through war and misfortune, have clung tenaciously to their birthright."

Yet less than a decade later, William Watts Ball, editor of *The News and Courier* of Charleston, whose love for the state gave him the right to chide it, cried in loud lament: "The State needs more white people . . . Nordics, Latins, Slavs, and if they should bring with them new religions, Roman Catholic, Jewish, Greek Orthodox, as well as Protestant, so much the better.

"We South Carolinians have been so insulated in ignorance that a horrible crust of vanity and self-righteousness has encased us, and anything that pierces it will help though it brings pain. The politicians boast of the State's 'homogeneous and Anglo-Saxon' population. That is what ails it. For two centuries the blood has been stagnant."

Of course, there is no collision implicit between the writing of Mr. Rice and Mr. Ball. They were not in basic disagreement. What one called stagnation seemed a precious preservation to the other. It was a sort of slow pace in a time that preserved the beauty and left to lushness the plants and creatures and some of the people, too. Newcomers of all kinds, who once seemed intruders, may enliven it now. And even the bald eagle may be spared in the process. The long-forgotten Hilton Head Island may now be the place where the experiment is being staged as to the possibility of retaining old varied charm with the arrival of new varied people.

The results will be interesting to those who live to see them. At the present rate that should not be too long even—or especially —on Hilton Head.

September 30, 1971

Oxford First

"Oxford First" somehow suggests a cry of announcement that the Oxford crew has beaten the oarsmen of Cambridge in the regatta on the beautiful stretch of river at Henley-on-Thames. Apparently that is not the derivation of the name of the Philadelphia company which has "merged" with the Hilton Head Company on the island. Still, the name carries the image of the strong shoulders of young sportsmen driving their shells along the straight, placid stream. That is a sort of symbol that would be most welcome here.

In many ways this is an island of strangers. Its many new residents come from a variety of places to make a remarkable homogeneity on an old island. Still, old strangers have a way of warily welcoming new strangers. Only a little while ago the background of all the developers here seemed to be Liberty and Long counties in Georgia. That area gave no reason to expect the imaginative treatment of this long-isolated island which its sons, Hack and Fraser, provided. Maybe the island's good luck as well as their good sense attended the blossoming of this shore.

Now many newcomers as companies are in command. The Greenwood, South Carolina, boys who first opened Palmetto Dunes have

been succeeded by gentlemen representing the vastly wealthy
Phipps interest. Some up-and-coming Georgia boys have acquired
Port Royal Plantation and have assumed the direction of its destiny.
The McCloskey interests of Philadelphia have plans for an impressive mid-island shore center. The Holiday Inn people of Memphis
are involved in the erection of a hostel of this great chain on the
beach front near Coligny Circle. Rumor reports that a similar inn
of the Ramada chain will rise in the same general area. And Oxford
First is the parent company of a subsidiary much involved in American recreational development.

All, as they join in the protective development of Hilton Head
Island for the pleasant recreational resources of America, should
be welcomed. They come for the same purposes which brought the
first developers here. Others long here join the procession. Joe
Jones, Pete McGinty, Tom Wamsley are building or designing new
projects. The Taj Mahal, which Bill Cork has built in place of his
Island Interiors establishment that was burned, seems designed to
serve more people wanting more furnishing to put inside more
buildings.

More and more, despite its length and breadth, Hilton Head
becomes a tight little island. But it remains an island on which most
of the old hands and newcomers are preoccupied with their own
multiplying and particular concerns. Indeed, sometimes the island
has been marked more by feuds among its promoters than by cooperation among them. And people just watching the process seem
impotent, if not entirely innocent, bystanders. Nothing but self-
defense, as in the BASF fight, has served to unite them.

Babel does not have to reach up into the sky. It can spread on
the ground. And obviously there is already a multiplicity of tongues
here, even among those who in varied accents speak what they think
is the same language. To benign dictatorship at hand has been
added absentee ownership by companies of multiple ownership.
Architects multiply, but social and civic planners are either absent
or unarmed. And often progress seems given to those who may buy
here, rather than to those who are here—notably the big black
population, which is just getting the promise of clean wells but little
reason to believe that proposed sewer lines may reach their houses
at reasonable costs.

Oxford First is as welcome as any other new developer to this island, but something in the nature of Hilton Head Island First seems long, long overdue. We've got new stores, new banks, new condominiums, new houses, new bars, and new bands. The one thing we haven't got—and show little sign of getting—is an enlightened community sense working for and watching over the welfare of everybody on this very definitely threatened shore of beauty, charm, order, and tranquillity—and don't ever forget it, fragility, too.

October 7, 1971

Warning in the West

Anne Blackman, who maybe loves Hilton Head Island more because she is one of those who cannot be here all the time, sends a lovely little book—and a sad one, too—from California. First published in 1920, it is called *Our Araby* and is about a then little village in the mountain and desert country.

"This little book," said its author, "is designed to invite people of the right kind—not too many—to a region that is meant for the discerning few." But he added confidently that "of the multitude of Californians and California tourists, not many, relatively, are likely to wish to visit the desert: and this is fortunate, for if too much peopled its charm would be lost."

Yet, he wrote, for so small a place, the number of people who had fallen under its charm even then was surprising. In winter and spring there was apt to be "a total of three hundred or more residents and visitors (the latter much the more numerous); in the hot summer months residents may number a dozen or two and visitors there are none."

He went on: "The village itself is a place of two or three score unpretentious cottages scattered along half palm-and-pepper-

197

shaded streets. We do not run much to lawns and formal gardens: we live in the desert because we like it, hence we don't care to shut ourselves away in little citified enclosures. But the two or three old places which formed the nucleus of the settlement are bowers of bloom and umbrageous greenery. . . . Wealth and fashion, as such, are not much attracted to our village. . . . The average of us is automatically raised by the total absence of any hoodlum element, such as is sometimes in evidence on the sands of the seashore."

In "a strange sun-bleached land of the pale, mysterious desert" those who praised it thus in the early twenties were "well content to remain far down the list of census returns." This pleasant, undefiled "village," of course, was named Palm Springs.

And in 1939, another California book—*A Guide to the Golden State* —gave another description of the scene where a few had hoped to hold content forever. It reported: "Palm Springs—one of the newest playgrounds of rich America . . . Today this ultrasmart winter resort for movie stars and for people who like and can afford to live where and as movie stars live, gleams as brightly as a new toy village. Its buildings are uniformly of California pseudo-Spanish architecture: the white, lemon, or buff-colored dwellings, entered by doors painted bright red, blue, or yellow, are surmounted by tile roofs and enclosed by wooden fences, bordered by rows of pink and white oleanders or the green feathery plumage of tamarisk trees. Here are branches of the most expensive New York and Los Angeles shops: golf courses and hotels that range from the palatial to the modestly magnificent . . . no lack of masseurs and masseuses; dude cowhands for atmosphere and branch brokerage offices for the bigger businessmen. . . .

"Here one finds the desert safely pushed to the borders of a transplanted section of Hollywood Blvd. Guests spring about town on bicycles, sip cocktails, play table tennis, explore the nearby desert on horseback, or, relaxing in some hotel garden, enjoy the lengthening shadow of the San Jacinto and the quiet of the land stretching out to the eastern hills. After dark they visit the night clubs, casinos. . . ."

It is difficult to decide on Hilton Head Island just exactly what music should accompany such lyrics—a jig or a dirge. Maybe, listening backward instead of looking ahead, we should turn to one or another of two titles: "California, Here I Come" or "Oh, Susannah, Don't You Cry for Me."

Some kind of a paean to Progress would certainly seem to be in order. It may be time to tune our instruments for accompaniment on this thickening shore.

October 14, 1971

Alligators with Affection

Long ago, before even we were young, Hilaire Belloc wrote a book of verses about beasts and children in which were the lines (as an old man remembers them):

> As a friend of the children
> Commend me the yak.
> You will find it exactly the thing.
> It will carry and fetch.
> You can ride on its back
> Or lead it about with a string.

Nobody ever so commended the alligator, though long ago (Hilton Head Island time) Charles Fraser gave much that impression. First newcomers here, maybe others, remember the picture in the late, lamented *Saturday Evening Post* of a younger, very debonair Charles and an evidently friendly alligator strolling together over terrain which might be purchased cheaper than it can be now. So the alligator went to work then as a sort of assistant salesman for Sea Pines Plantation. He was the creature who indicated the climate of this island as well as did the palm.

On the roadside by the lagoon, southeast of the present Plantation Club, a sign marked a good place for alligator watching. Then, over near the present Lake House in another lagoon (or is it lake to match the house?), there were other big lizards almost trained to wait for their dinners at the hands of happy men, women, and children who flung them fish or other food. Legend, possibly fact, said that one of them would answer to his name, which is now forgotten. Those, perhaps, were the good ole days for men and alligators. Certainly some now regard them as such.

But some irritants creep into the relationship. Marge Timberlake was startled to find one of the big creatures in her garden. She made, so the tale went, the classic remark that the alligators ought not to come on private property. Some other people became more seriously concerned about alligators as a menace to small shore creatures like dogs and children. Now, recently, the destruction of two small basset hounds—one in Sea Pines, one in Port Royal Plantation—has taken any humorous aspect out of the joint residence of people and alligators on the same island. Also, as Sonny Graham has pointed out, anger has moved somebody to the stealthy shooting of one alligator, perhaps not a guilty one, which had already been slated for removal to a refuge.

The big creatures (they get their name from *el lagarto*, Spanish for "lizard") present a puzzle on an island where people want the ecology to remain unchanged but their surroundings to be made as safe as a park. Maybe there is both reassurance and warning in the scientist's statement that "many a large mammal coming to drink at its accustomed place is dragged into the water by the lurking monster. Certainly there are occasional man-eaters among them. . . . As a rule, however, they are so wary and suspicious that they are very difficult to approach, and their haunts are so well stocked with fish and other game that they make off and hide rather than attack a man swimming in their waters. But if a dog is sent in there will be a sudden yelp, the splash from a big tail, and a widening eddy."

Here seems to be a case where some compromise between man and nature, alligators and people, is indicated. The best solution of this problem would be the removal of all sizable alligators from lagoons around which many dogs and children regularly play. On the margins of other lagoons signs should be prominently displayed warning people to be careful about their dogs and children.

Most of us came here because we like to live close to nature, understanding, of course, that that may mean snake bite as well as bird song. The alligator is a dramatic item in nature here. Any danger he presents can be more easily removed than that from the bite of a malarial mosquito. The log-like alligator is more often a comic creature than a dangerous one to man. It is not necessary to make dragons out of all alligators. Certainly we will not profit by making a Saint George out of anybody who shoots one in the dark. The alligator should not be lost from the sight of or the fantasies of children:

> "See you later, alligator."
> "Wait a while, crocodile."

We can keep the alligator and keep him as an unmenacing creature and we should not wait a while to do just that.

October 21, 1971

Guard That Gate

Hilton Head Island

If it is too early, as some seem to think, to consider the incorporation of Hilton Head Island, it is probably way too soon to talk about the provision of city parks here. That, of course, is what the whole place is in appearance. That is what it plans to be. That is what its purveyors offer in multicolored brochures to purchasers.

Golf courses, while designed for both play and profit, provide the great expanses of lawn which make any other open green spaces seem superfluous. And landscaped areas are laid out in and around all the developments. There are the circles at the Sea Pines end of the island. Fort Walker is preserved at the other. Still it might be nice if certain areas were forever set aside as places to present the personality of the whole island. It may not be too soon to think of that.

Certainly the first, delightful sight of Hilton Head Island, which comes suddenly, almost startlingly beautiful into view, is the rim of the island as the inhabitants or visitors cross the bridge coming this way. The two wide creeks, Jenkins Island, and the main shore of the island beyond make as lovely an entrance scene as any place could hope for. Our green shore is seen over blue water, broad marshes, with lazy boats moving in the picture below and white birds above.

Self-interest should preserve it. Clearly, despite the temporary piles of dirt along the highway, Joe Jones is carefully working to protect, for his purchasers and those who pass by it, the new condominium community he is building on the island shore. Still, some trees had to be cut to make room for the buildings. Any more thinning on this rim of small islands and marshes could mangle this beautiful green margin entrance to the whole island. And not all builders might be men like Jones, who is rooted in this place and devoted to its preservation.

Somehow the entrance to this island ought to belong to this whole island and to all those who come to it for serenity and beauty. Of course, the approach to this island—like that to any island —could be an ideal place for billboards reciting the merits of facilities to be found beyond it. Americans have a way of making the entrances to their communities as cluttered and hideous as possible.

Indications are already at hand to tell us that the road from Ware's Fruit Stand to the bridge cannot forever be expected to be a green lane between woodlands, orchards, and meadows, where cattle graze under pecan trees with white bug-eating egrets on their backs. Welcome as Herring's has sometimes been to islanders and others seeking everything from fish to firecrackers to bait to motorboats, a succession of Herring-like places might not be an avenue promising approach to perfection

Chief among the horrors of Florida are the environs of the still-guarded enclaves of palm and grass, white paint and black wrought iron. There and elsewhere many resorts seem almost in the ugly embrace of ragamuffin, tatterdemalion streets and roads. That may be a fate which awaits Hilton Head Island, too. Possibly it is inevitable—private property being so sacred and free enterprise sometimes so damn free. But there is nothing in either which prohibits public concern. An island with any community sense for its appearance should somehow be able to protect the face which it presents to the world. And Hilton Head's face is the beautiful picture it first shows after that long, long ride from Stuckey's to the bridge.

We can at least hope that it will not become just a memory on a more and more crowded road.

October 28, 1971

Epitaph to Murder

Naturally and properly, residents on Hilton Head Island are concerned about crime. They should not get the idea that law violation in the South Carolina Low Country is something new in a world which sometimes seems plagued with more ills than the past ever knew. The good old days were pretty bad sometimes on this shore. And crime is not only remembered but monumented in marble in—of all places—Saint Philip's Churchyard in Charleston.

Around 1947 the architect and historian Samuel Gaillard Stoney got down on his hands and knees and transcribed the worn inscription on an old stone above a man who was murdered in 1788, when the United States of America was just coming into being. In a now hard-to-come-by book called *Charleston Murders,* he gave the legend on the stone, which is to be found in the western part of the old graveyard near a low masonry wall surmounted by high iron pickets. It reads:

To The Memory Of

Nicholas John Wightman
Who was killed by a Footpad,

On the night of the 12th of March, 1788,
Aged 25 years,
Peaceably returning home
to his Brother's house
where he resided.
The Villain met and made an attempt
to rob him, which he resisted,
and was instantly shot dead on the spot.
His Brother, with but small assistance
the same night, secured the murderer
and six accomplices, being the whole of a gang
that then very much infested the peace of the City,
and by their frequent Robberies,
and attempts to set fire to houses,
kept the inhabitants in constant alarm.
They were shortly after tried, and upon the fullest conviction,
Condemned and Executed.
Divine Providence ordered it so that a single button,
belonging to the coat of the murderer,
found on the spot where the murder was committed,
by a child, a son of Mr. Edgar Wells, Mercht.,
served, with other proofs, to discover and convict him.
This Marble is erected, by an affectionate Brother & Sister,
in memory of the virtues of their dear Brother,
who was beloved by all who knew him.
He was mild and affable in his manners,
Just, Generous, and Humane.
He is loved with the sincerest affection.
His soul rests at the Mercy Seat of his Creator.

From the inscription, Stoney went back into the old newspapers of the day to gather information about the crime and the trial. Certainly a villainous crew was involved. But speaking well for the ideas of justice at the time, General Charles Cotesworth Pinckney was appointed to defend the criminals, who added slave stealing to robbery and murder. Clad all in velvet, General Pinckney undoubtedly did his best for the rogues. That did not save them from the gallows. And, sadly, the gallows did not save Charleston.

Stoney wrote: "Putting this gang out of circulation made no visible effect on the crime wave. Within a month of the murder, two men knocked down by footpads in Meeting Street had to save themselves by their own exertions, though they were within shouting distance of the Guard House. Nearer than that a house was set fire to. . . ." Crimes went on which kept Charleston in a "state of nerves."

It won't make us feel any safer now to remember that this period of crime coincided with the year when General Pinckney with other great Americans gathered in Philadelphia to shape the glorious Union. Philadelphia wasn't too safe then either.

November 4, 1971

The Ferryman

As many newcomers on this island count age, Tom Barnwell, who died in his early sixties last week, was too young to be a patriarch. Yet, he was just that as a strong man who saw much happen in little time on a native island swiftly altering about him. His chief possession, as a shrewdly humorous, impeccably polite man, was a universal respect. He was a citizen of dignity and wisdom. He will be much missed as the quiet and perceptive counselor he was in the life of this coastal community of white and black people living close together.

He lived long enough to count much change on the shore where he was born and died. In 1909, when he was born, the immediate day-by-day problem on this island was survival. Men worked at the basic tasks of farming and fishing. Unbridged waters cut them off from the shore, and across the waters there was limited opportunity. Few health facilities were available. There was an almost absolute separation of races on an island from which all whites, except occasional hunters and fishermen, had disappeared. The public schools provided were poor in quality for all South Carolinians, scandalously poor for the blacks. But aspiration was marked here by the fact that young Tom was sent by his parents to the Penn School at Frogmore, which had been set up by Northern people moved by a noble missionary spirit toward their less fortunate fellow men.

Education here meant no easy opening of doors to opportunity for a black man in a state still captive to the hard doctrines of Negrophobia behind such leaders as Cole Blease and "Cotton Ed" Smith. Barnwell came back to his island. He married young Hannah White. Together across the years they made their home a light in a clearing on a semitropical island. They did so in terms of leadership in religion, health, and virtue for the community to which they belonged. They set their own children's faces forward.

Former corporation executives and military chieftains now settled here in rich retirement may have regarded the tasks Barnwell performed, and in which he excelled, as humble. In his last years Barnwell served as a doorman and a messenger. In his life he not only tended a door at an inn but helped to open doors for his people. He was in the character of his life a messenger of the glad tidings of greater hope and opportunity.

In the symbolism of his place on earth perhaps the best work he performed was that of ferryman. Undaunted, he faced rough waters and high winds. He had to know his way between reefs and marshes. Sometimes his boat moved in darkness. And often the shore seemed distant. The lanterns at the landing were sometimes far from bright. To many the crossing seemed slow.

Perhaps, like some of the others of us older ones here, Tom Barnwell, as his days lengthened, seemed old-fashioned to some younger people around him. He had walked humbly but always with dignity. He had not grown rich, though he always settled his scores. Yet there seemed in the new world little room for the slow pace of the ferryman, little room for tolerance of the darkness.

He lived into the day of the bridge. Movement swiftened for everybody, and sometimes those moving at the new pace were still impatient because they could not hurry forward even more rapidly. That is understandable in a people who still have a great distance to go toward the goals of justice, equality, and opportunity which they properly seek.

Tom Barnwell's death not only provides the occasion to remember him as a lost patriarch who moved, loved and honored, among us. Also it serves as a time of reminder. Those able to move faster should hope for the fortitude, the devotion to duty, the reverence for eternal things which, as farmer-doorkeeper-ferryman, he possessed in bounteous measure. And he possessed them always in readiness to share with others.

All of us have many rivers to cross. We have reason, still, for praise of those who in less fair weather helped us across the dark, often turbulent, waters behind us. And high among us all, Thomas Barnwell is one who deserves such praise.

November 11, 1971

Village for Monkeys

Disney World has opened down the road near Orlando, and Charles Fraser has his Point South Monument standing beside the great new road south to prove that he is aware of it. As in California, Mr. Disney's new mecca expects to pack in those who require stage sets as a substitute for imagination. But too little attention has been paid even on this island to the new village opened at Harbour Town, where those who bring imagination along with their cash can live in an infinite world of make-believe.

Many have climbed the steps to the first sample of the Sealofts which are rising into the trees and rising also from a starting price of $42,000. But now across what must be a somewhat startled stream, a decorative humpbacked bridge leads into a closely packed village of such unusual dwellings. Roads twist gracefully between them. Deer, raccoon, and other animals are expected to romp beneath them. Birds, bats, and tree frogs may confidently be counted on around them.

Many are welcoming them. There are few of us who did not in our childhood construct tree houses in our backyards. From them we could look down upon a world no longer merely cluttered with the commonplace. We could be bold navigators on a high bridge at sea. We could be African tribesmen living high above the earth and any enemies who might come to assail us. In the same imaginative Africa we could be hunters in high blinds waiting for the chance to shoot the tiger. The possibilities were endless until Mama called us down to come into the house and take our baths before supper.

No such mundane termination of dreams will assail the happy dwellers in the Sealofts. They can be as permanently settled in their dreams as savages who once made their homes and even buried their dead in the treetops. Of course, even earlier tree dwellers must have realized that some labor was required in carrying babies up and down the steps or ladders to their dwellings. Carrying the groceries up now will be like carrying up the game that was killed on the hunt—possibly with the same sense of triumph. Such things will only add reality to happily purchased fantasy.

The Sealofts in the new village do look a little close together on the ground. But the very compactness of the body of identical Sealofts or tree houses may serve both neighborliness and defense. Certainly a tribal spirit may develop among the occupants, who come from everywhere to this village which promises everything.

On a once boggy islet near once unassailed marshes, place has been found to put more people on Hilton Head Island. That will soon require increasing ingenuity. Also, in these unique houses, settlers will not have to be bothered by any architectural approval of design, since every house will be like every other one. This should eliminate both jealousies and complaints. Equality will certainly be added to freedom under the skies. The Sealofts offer everything to everybody except to those who have become aware of rustiness in the hinges of the knees.

The monkeys never had it so good.

November 18, 1971

A Small Ball in a Small Hole

As a cat may look at a queen, so a non-golfer on a golfer's island may regard with awe and admiration the assemblage of the great ones of the sport and the widespread gallery of their devoted followers. But to the non-golfer, with the awe and admiration comes a sense of guilt. This character was not always filled with a feeling for the glory of golf which now enfolds even him. It might as well be confessed at the outset that he was not always impressed by the importance of propelling a small white ball across lawn and hazard toward and into a slightly larger hole. A small ball certainly could be put into a small hole with less ado.

The probability is that penury was part of his prejudice. Across the road from his house lived a golfing lady with a golfing man. And on the wall Tootie Watters had hung a small plaque bearing the legend: "The only difference between men and little boys is the cost of the toys."

That should not have been news in that house or in any others on this island. The golfer acquires with loving care and lavish outlay the toys of his sport. He is prepared to knock innumerable balls not only into the little hole but also into bushes and woods along the

213

way he travels in his expensive vehicle. So the wiser sportsman seemed to the non-golfer to be Bill Bullock—whose sport had about it the virtue of acquisitiveness, which made it possible for so many of us to be here, golfing or grumbling. The Bullock collection of retrieved golf balls grew until it could be piled into a crinkled white monument like a pyramid almost man-high. That, surely, was a game worth playing.

But to confess agian, the non-golfer was undoubtedly moved into his lack of movement across the links by a desire to escape responsibility. He had lived a long, scheduled life. He had to get to the office on time in the morning and had to keep an eye on his watch to be sure he would be promptly on hand for the important engagement or the ever-recurrring conference. He thought a part of retirement was escape from that, and he watched with some amazement his neighbors going to the course as regularly as they once went to the office. Starting time was as imperative as the schedule of the commuters' train. In his unreformed state of mind, he had the notion that the one thing to escape on Hilton Head Island was the clock —even the calendar.

Fortunately—or inescapably—on Hilton Head, a light at last dawned. He couldn't forever be puzzled when asking where somebody lived to be told that his address (though not recognized by the post office) was the thirteenth green. So reform set in. The non-golfer and the non-golfer's wife sought membership in Sea Pines Golf Club, Inc. Though made with some trepidation, their application to the exclusive club was approved after scrutiny by the board of governors.

"Inc." is certainly an organization that brings people together. With the help of Warren Vail, the club's quarters were measured. He now forgets how many square feet or square inches would be available for each member if all gathered at once. But on such an occasion the meticulous Vail figured that, if the bar was six feet long, six lines of drinkers before it would have to extend out into the Lake House, maybe beyond. That would certainly interfere with the pleasures of convention and other visitors. The lines might even get in the way of the salesmen of lots and condominiums, who can also sell at least the hope that the buyers may possibly be elected to membership in the snug organization.

So, though sometimes feeling as phony as a seventeen-dollar bill, the non-golfer is now an accredited member of a golf club and entitled to all its privileges. His old crusty character as a non-golfer slowly fades away. He thrills at the assemblage of the bright and happy Heritage crowds. And if his present inclinations further incline, Charles Fraser may be the only non-golfer on the island.

November 25, 1971

Faustian Bargain

Dick Kelsey reports on the Hilton Head Island weather, but, as Heritage Tournaments come and go, it seems evident that Charles Fraser orders the weather as a sort of Prospero of this island. There had been adverse forecasts about the quality of the weather during the days of play. People went to bed apprehensive on Friday evening. Then, when the sun slipped magnificently through the trees on Saturday morning, in at least two houses a man and a woman expressed a similar conviction.

"Charles Fraser has sold his soul to the devil."

Certainly at that point His Satanic Majesty seemed to be keeping his promise in a Faustian bargain. But Mary Fraser, when told of this comment, denied any such transaction and suggested that any supernatural interposition had been effected not downward but upward, possibly with the help of Parson Calvin Reid.

Then at noon that black, black cloud rose ominously in the sky over the mainland nearby. Prospero seemed to have gotten his signals mixed. There were obviously buckets up there full of downpour. Some drops fell. Then, miraculously, the sun came to drive

216

the clouds away. Alicia Hack best expressed the sentiment of those happily surprised when the storm signs disappeared.

"Charles Fraser," she said, "must have made a human sacrifice of John Gettys Smith."

As it turned out, not a hair of the well-coiffured Smith had been harmed. Either the devil kept his bargain for Charles, or, as one of the Presbyterian elect, he was predestined to have sunshine.

In perfect weather the galleries took their places as members of Jack's Pack with Jack Nicklaus, or Arnie's Army of Arnold Palmer, or the Lee's Fleas of Lee Trevino. With his vision unimpaired by mist or rain, Trevino took time out to christen the many snow-white latrines among the rising architecture of Harbour Town, calling them "Polish condominiums."

Golf did not quite command the attention of all. Joab Dowling and company sat in his car admiring his own private high rise overlooking Calibogue Sound, listening to the radio report of the Clemson-Carolina game, which at that point was not going to his liking. Jay McDonald in his new house nearby had won a race which recently seemed a long-shot sporting event. Promised occupancy by the time of the tournament, all his friends, neighbors, architectural critics, and some mere bystanders had taken a very negative position about the matter. Rain or shine, they predicted, he would still be without shelter. He seemed a sort of miracle maker, too. As the due date approached, the grounds around his house seemed almost like a tournament parking lot filled with workers' cars. They swarmed over the roof, through the halls, up the stairs, by the breakfast room, and beyond the bidet. With all his drapes up, his furniture placed and polished, the Admiral looked like a sailor who had just made a hole in one.

Off across the smooth green grass and beyond the line of spectators, golfers moved to triumph or disaster, hole or trap. One small marshal, hardly as tall as his long, knotty staff, looked a little weary in the bright afternoon sunshine. Off on Calibogue Cay, Hugh Fraser, watering his shrubbery, expressed the hope that now that the tournament was over Charles Fraser would let it rain.

December 2, 1971

McGowan Punch

The historic document arrived just in time for the Christmas season. The original's place now is in the archives of the Caroliniana Library, which, with its ancient store of valuable papers, escaped even the burning of Columbia on the occasion of the visit there of General Sherman. So it should be safe there now and forever.

The valuable paper reached its well-guarded destination by the beneficence of Mrs. Gordon (Ruth Hancock) Hunger, who—on her way to and from her place at Boca Grande, Florida—often stops with her friends the Chuck Carpenters on Calibogue Cay. Recently she perfomed the sad and filial duty of going through files of papers left by her father, John M. Hancock. She found a batch of items relating to the youth of Admiral Sam McGowan of South Carolina.

Hancock, who was a partner in Lehman Brothers, was a valuable businessman volunteer in both world wars. In World War I, he and McGowan, who was paymaster general of the navy, spent what then seemed vast sums in navy purchases. They were so efficient that the secretary of the navy called them "the Gold Dust Twins" from the old-time advertising slogan: "Let the Gold Dust Twins do your work." It would not have been surprising if the McGowan papers

Ruth Hancock Hunger found in her father's files had been related to the prodigious purchases they made.

Instead the papers dealt with McGowan's youth in South Carolina, where he was the merry and gifted son of a judge and general who had not hesitated to take on a noted duelist who had spoken slightingly of a lady. Young McGowan grew up in a society which was hotheaded, warmhearted, convivial, and gallant. Perhaps it was not surprising then to find the document in his papers, a photostat of which the archivists in Columbia sent back to the sender. It may help make an old-time celebration at this season on Hilton Head Island if bold spirits still remain in South Carolina on its shore. The document, which will be forever preserved, is a recipe for "William Aiken Kelly Punch." Here it is:

> 2/3 gal. Brandy—Cal. or French
> 1/3 gal. Rum—Jamaica or Bedford
> 1/2 pt. Peach Brandy
> 1/2 pt. Curacao
> 6 Doz. Lemons—strained—no pulp
> 6 lbs. "A" Sugar—dissolved in 1 pint of warm water
> 1/8 lb. Green tea makes a pint
> 1 can pineapple
> 1 can white cherries
> 1/2 Doz. Lemons—sliced
> 1/2 Doz. Oranges—sliced

Possibly the essential ingredient was written below the recipe in red ink: "N.B. Next morning—plenty of crushed ice!"

There is no indication in the document as to who William Aiken Kelly was (Lucy Daniels thinks he was her great-uncle). Also, fortunately, there is no suggestion that Hancock and McGowan concocted this punch for their personal use while defending the nation from the Kaiser. However, they left it to posterity, which is us, if we are bold enough to take up the torch—or the cup.

December 9, 1971

Homesick Shore

"Nostalgia is the opium of the quietly frightened."

So, in the *National Observer,* wrote Edwin A. Roberts, Jr., a man so young that his boyhood was not over until the end of World War II. He was writing about that time on a quiet, leisurely, summertime shore. He didn't name his place. It might be almost anywhere. But what he wrote was not merely homesickness for place and time gone but a warning that times and places can go away forever.

"I think I won't be going back there anymore. Each passing summer reduces those boyhood places—the grassy dunes, the damp and sagging cottages, the mud banked creek, the waving cattails in the marshes, the surf that parts itself upon the black and useless jetties. . . ."

But he had been back, though not quite to remembered boyhood. He wrote: "Today beach parties are prohibited by law because they pollute the air and leave ashes in the sand. Ballplaying on the beach is illegal because a long foul might break a motel window or kill somebody on the boardwalk. The boardwalk was rebuilt after the hurricane of 1944 and it is lined with snack stands, kiddy rides, pinball emporiums, and peculiar shops. It is impossible to smell the ocean unless there is a brisk wind. What you smell mostly is the smoke from greasy griddles, the wafting pungency of pizza innards, and the ubiquitous reek of the popcorn machines.

"Many of the old cottages are gone. There are motels now, and something worse. High-rise condominiums, blocking breezes and vistas, cast long shadows across the beaches in the afternoon. The builders of these great walls of glass and concrete have made their easy fortunes, and the well-to-do owners of the individual apartments have found them to be investments with gratifying tax advantages.

"The beaches are, of course, jammed. Superhighways lead directly from the congested suburbs of once-distant cities to the now congested seaside. The boats don't bother to come by with their tuna flags anymore. There are just too many boats on the water and too many people on the shore. All the boats look alike and all the people are strangers.

"The creek has long since been bulkheaded. The salt marshes have been filled and now support hundreds of little houses and stores. All the streets are paved with lumpy macadam. Real estate prices are sky high. Rental rates are so stiff that many families double up and for several weeks live in tenement-like propinquity—all for a sun tan and the privilege of being jostled on beach and boardwalk.

"Time marches on. Progress must be served."

Nostalgia may be more soothing than forebodings. But somehow homesickness for a better past ought to be arrayed in change to prevent the spoilage of a threatened future. Mr. Roberts does good work in that direction. What he reports is happening everywhere and could happen anywhere. The opium of nostalgia sometimes seems to have been cut by its pushers.

December 16, 1971

Happy Hypocrites

Once Hilton Head Island seemed to have only a decorative or speculative future. Now it firmly possesses a precious past. And the proximity of New Year is a good time to point it out. The story of the newcomers on the island may seem brief. It is, compared to the long history of the blacks here, who still own and occupy something like four thousand acres of the island. Other properties in the past year seemed to have been bandied about like a bouncing ball. But newcomers also hold history to their hearts—sometimes with trepidation about the future. We are not exactly sure where we are in terms of time and the island. We hope tenaciously that we are near the point Mr. Shakespeare was referring to when he wrote that "everything that grows / Holds in perfection but a little moment." The greatest assurance of that lies not in the ecology but in the inhabitants. We are palm- and pine-blessed and in many ways people-blessed, too.

A man with a typewriter here once planned to write an improbable masque about a magic island and the people newly congregating upon it. In terms of the cast and the scene he was ready to plagiarize outrageously Max Beerbohm's fable "The Happy Hypocrite." That was the story, as you may remember, about the profligate who fell deeply in love with a chaste and beautiful girl. So he put on a mask of innocence in his wooing, only to discover that, in his benign courtship, his own face behind the mask had become that of goodness, too.

Something like that may have happened on Hilton Head Island. All came wanting welcome, so they put their best faces forward. Indeed, any whose lives had been marked by greed, avarice, hard-handed aggressiveness, ruthless acquisition, and scrambling ambition wore as they came the masks of bland amiability.

Then, as happens even on a magic island, a great hurricane blew out of the south. Palm fronds were blown right and left, television aerials screamed, pines cracked. And, in the tempest, the masks were blown from all the faces. Some fled to their mirrors in terror of disclosure, fearful that old lines of ugliness were showing. But they discovered that in the assumption of goodness their own faces were now in truth what they had only pretended before.

That could have happened on this island. Not all here, of course, needed any such pretense to begin with. But the lines in some of our faces may have been shaped by snarls in lives in which there was not much time for gentleness. Some of us may have protected our own past sinning by a cynicism about the goodness of others. The children we loved had grown up and were gone. Old neighbors at home had died. It took less time to count our contemporary kin. It might have been easier to have left the dyspeptic spirit uncovered. But the miracle which happened on Hilton Head was not designed on a drafting board. It is good to look back at it across the dying year.

Much has been added to our past in that time—some good, some bad. We have faced the threats of real and imaginary high rises. We have been startled by new noxious roadside signs which point to a resort in a fashion like billboards on the highways pointing the way to Florida snake and monkey ranches. Death, who is always waiting in the wings at our festivals, touched a great lady and gentleman who had had much to do with the loveliness around us. A beautiful young woman died like a bright candle suddenly snuffed out. A stalwart black man moved in dignity to his reward. Of a great vintner who died after a busy life which kept him in the office, one who loved him said, "His heart was always in the vineyard." To the advertisers it may be a strange thing to say that mortality adds to love for this island and to our sense of its beauty, too. Perhaps the loveliest garden on the island recalls one of its saddest events.

Of course, this is not, as is generally advertised, merely the island of landscaped escape from the world and its troubles to pleasantness and play. This would only be a stage set for a masquerade if that were true. Men and women bring their troubles with them, though they debonairly hide them. And they discover that an island without troubles could be an island without tenderness. Gaily, they sometimes make it seem a sort of island of kissing cousins. But they carry cakes and casseroles, and bottles, too, to the houses of neighbors in troubles. All live on an island where an instant cemetery was gravely cut from the brush for a dead child. Growth does not erase the memory of a time soon after, when an older citizen died and a strong, young land salesman guided the hearse through hub-deep mud to the grave. Even death is more landscaped now, but the spirit around it has not changed.

More things warm us here than the sun. Developers do not stress such things, but the heart finds them. This is no mere moss-hung Shangri-la or wave-washed Camelot. It has been sweetened by tears as well as tournaments. We have more scores to count than at the eighteenth hole. Not all our handicaps are arrived at by computers. The charm of this island may best lie in the discovery of goodness in people and the possibility of goodness in ourselves. That, however, is certainly not a basis for solemnity. Men and women carrying neighbors to cobalt treatments in Savannah make each trip seem a jaunt, not a grave, good deed. It was a part of development plans that there be no fences, but their absence is more than adherence to a rule. Neighborliness is not flaunted, but there is a very special symbol where next-door people have put up an old-fashioned stile over a hedge for easy movement between them.

The warm heart is a greater asset to Hilton Head Island than the warm sun. Once a year, at least, we should be able to say without awkwardness that love here is more important than building lots. And hearts do not have to be worn on the sleeve to say that love out loud to the whole company of companions on this new shore on which we feel so many strong ties.

December 30, 1971 *

* The column for December 23, 1971, was a repeat, by request, of the Christmas column of 1970 (see pp. 70–73).

Preface to Princeton

The alligators of Hilton Head Island are in the national news again, this time as participants in a sort of proving ground for the new president of prestigious Princeton University. The *New York Times* revealed the alligators' and the island's role in its story of the selection of Dr. William Gordon Bowen to the university post.

He is "probably," wrote a *Times* writer with traditional *Times* caution, "the only provost of an Ivy League institution ever to rescue a woman from a pond full of live alligators." His emphasis of the fact that the alligators were "live" suggests that William K. Stevens, the reporter, was carefully ready to concede the possibility that some such educator might have rescued a woman from a pond full of stuffed alligators. To anybody but a *Times* reporter the latter would have seemed the more improbable event. However—

The story went on: "It happened last spring on Hilton Head Island off the coast of South Carolina where the lanky thirty-eight-year-old Dr. Bowen—still as trim as when he played championship tennis as a student at Denison University—was meeting with the heads of major foundations."

225

The woman, one of the erudite group, "fell into the pond by accident and landed squarely on top of an alligator. Dr. Bowen hustled to the water's edge and pulled her out."

As careful as a *Times* reporter not to sensationalize the event, Dr. Bowen reported that "the reptile was probably as scared as she was, but that seemed something you didn't want to leave to the alligator." This, concluded *Times* reporter Stevens, was characteristic of Dr. Bowen, "who has a reputation for being a sharp, precise analyst and systematic decision maker."

Never leave decisions to the alligators may be a Hilton Head–born doctrine which more college presidents need to learn these days. If more learn it, the result may well be worth the cost of the lady's plunking into the pond—or the lagoon, as environmentally precise islanders prefer to call such bodies of water. Indeed, the description of the provost hustling to the water's edge to rescue the woman whose bottom had bumped the alligator's snout may make a sort of picture parable of the precise educator in action in the modern world.

Not all screams, like those of a splashed female, may indicate great, real, and present danger. Even alligators may have reasons for resentment when unexpected bodies land on their noses. Certainly not even wise men on the margin of collision scenes can be sure how dangerous the results may be. But whatever may or may not be the dangers, a wise man will act promptly, even though he may get his feet wet. And such action will properly serve as a basis for a reputation for being a sharp, precise analyst and systematic decision maker.

Hilton Head Island should be grateful for the part it played in the story of Princeton's new president. Not all its lagoons are quite as full of "live alligators" as the Bowen story in the *Times* suggested. And only rarely do ladies land on top of any of them. Certainly there seems no great need of a mobilization of the erudite along the shores of lagoons to be the ready rescuers of any ladies from the reactions of any startled alligators. When any such accidental meeting of lady and reptile does occur, however, there are plenty of people here ready to pull the lady out and shoo the alligator away.

And not many such here would regard doing that as a basis for promotion to the presidency of Princeton, even to the unique position as rescuer among Ivy League presidents. Young Dr. Bowen would "probably" be the last to suggest that one incident on an island, involving "probably" equally dismayed lady and alligator, proved him to be the man Old Nassau needs. Still, it helped.

January 6, 1972

God's Mysterious Way

Savannah recalls with pride, and Methodists everywhere remember reverently, the stay of young John Wesley in Georgia in 1736–37. What is not generally proclaimed is that Wesley left Georgia like a man in flight. Indeed, early in 1738 when he returned to England, he wrote to George Whitefield, in some sense his successor in Georgia, urging him to turn back and not sail to the land of his own unhappy experience. Viewed back through the multiplication of Methodists in the world, the Reverend Mr. Wesley is difficult to contemplate with anything but solemnity. Actually, however, a girl's elopement from Savannah to Beaufort County then must have made him, though a man in pain, something of a comic character, too.

When John landed in Georgia in February 1736, he was a thirty-three-year-old young man full of zeal, faith, and fortitude. As the parson chosen to undertake the spiritual oversight of the colonists and to commend the faith to the Indians, too, he shepherded his flock with tenderness but with a good deal of strictness as well. Then his eyes, which he kept turned to heaven, soon saw Sophia Christiana Hopkey, generally referred to as Sophy.

228

This Sophy was no ordinary girl. Wesley himself wrote of her many ardent beaux. She was described as a "lady, who had improved understanding and elegant person and manner." Her uncle was the chief magistrate of Savannah. Evidently, soon after the young clergyman's arrival he caught her romantic fancy. As Willie Snow Ethridge reports in her new version of this story (*Strange Fires: The True Story of John Wesley's Love Affair in Georgia*, Vanguard Press), Sophy once consulted General Oglethorpe as to what dress he thought would be most agreeable to Mr. Wesley. With the General's advice, she always came to services in white. Also, though not all her friends were pious, she listened lovingly to John's religious instructions and his long readings to her from works of theology.

It is easy to understand that she was in love with him. He kept a diary which made it plain that he was in love with her but much torn as to whether he could share his love with both God and Sophy. Sophy, who had put aside one ardent lover to listen to John's religious readings and theological conversation, apparently waited a year for him to speak something which was much on both their minds. But evidently at last her patience came to an end. In March 1737, Wesley was asked to post the banns of her marriage to an apparently quite eligible young man named William Williamson.

John was stunned. He confided to his notes: "I doubted whether all this were not artifice, merely designed to quicken me." If it had begun with that purpose, Sophy was still ready to fulfill the design. A year after she and John had first met, Sophy and Williamson, accompanied by another couple, set out by boat for the long-lost village of Purrysburgh in this county. There they were married. John recorded his actual physical illness at the news. But he was also enraged and infuriated.

Then, as spiritual leader of Savannah's flock, he refused to recognize the marriage as valid. He planned a protest to the Church of England about the "carelessness" and "illegality" of the South Carolina minister of that church, who had married Sophy to Williamson before the banns were properly published. He made a trip to Charles Town to protest to the Bishop there (or the Bishop of London's Commissary, as he was called). The Bishop promised him that nothing of the sort would happen again. That was not much help to John's heart. He threatened to repel Sophy from the Holy Communion. Williamson threatened to sue if he did. Sophy suffered a miscarriage. She had hardly recovered when, on Sunday, August 1, as she knelt at the rail before the assembled congregation, John told her that he could not give her the cup. Now the affair grew into a colony-splitting scandal. Wesley was indicted. He was ordered to post bond for his appearance. His place became untenable. On his way to England, John left Savannah secretly in the dark.

If John had married Sophy, some historians have suggested, he might have led a quiet, happy life, but no movement such as Methodism would have flourished. Savannah and Sophy amounted to his trial in the wilderness, they felt. Certainly if he had married Sophy he would not have married, as he did later, a waspish widow with four children. Her scoldings and jealousies, it was said, effectively removed any danger that domesticity might impede his wide-ranging ministry. Before she deserted him, she made his home life so miserably unhappy that he readily became "the traveler-evangelist" instead of a "stay-at-home parson."

Certainly Sophy's elopement from Savannah to Beaufort County may well be catalogued under the heading "God moves in a mysterious way / His wonders to perform," on this shore as everywhere else.

January 13, 1972

Cabell's Coming *

I looked at my watch. It was 5:25 P.M. on the afternoon of Wednesday, January 5, 1972, as we crossed the Byrnes Bridge and touched down on Hilton Head Island.

"Well, by God, we made it," I said to the lady sitting next to me. "For better or for worse, here we are at last."

She looked out the window on her right. It was half a minute before she spoke. "Yes," she said. There was a certain far-off quality in her voice. "We've made it, and we had better like it. We won't be going back anytime soon." Then she turned, and there was a faint smile of reassurance on her lips.

This was, indeed, within our small private world, a moment of historic significance. Not of exaltation, and certainly not of dejection, but a moment of benign inevitability—of what has to be will be, and don't knock it until you've tried it. We had been pointing toward this moment for months, most intensively during the past few weeks. We had done all the requisite things—formal retirement from a job that had nourished us for most of a lifetime; checking

* This guest column was written by Jonathan Daniels' friend Cabell Phillips, of the *New York Times.*

231

out with Social Security, pension plans, Medicare, insurance policies; selling one house and acquiring another; tidying up the family debt structure; saying repeated farewells with a slightly faked insouciance; packing, packing, packing, and appalled at the monstrous accumulation of artifacts. ("Where in God's name will we put all this junk?")

And now, across the bridge and onto the island, the moment of truth was upon us, eyeball to eyeball.

I suppose that retirement, in varying degrees, is a traumatic experience for just about everyone. There is a certain terminal quality about it that is, at the least, disquieting. For a fortunate few, probably, it is a state to be approached expectantly. Isn't leisure, lots of leisure, what all the rat race is about? Maybe, but what about it as a steady diet, as a suddenly enforced pattern of life? You wonder how much golf or fishing or shuffleboard or rocking on the front porch can be absorbed before boredom sets in. That's the sort of thing that bugs many a freshman "retiree." But inexorably the clock strikes and the decision has to be made—or is made for you. Like it or not, you suddenly have become a different kind of digit in census tables.

Why Hilton Head as a retirement home? We had a modest number of options open to us and no really compelling attachment to any. Why not Florida, or the Gulf Coast, or the Blue Ridge, or New Mexico, or the Caribbean? Why, indeed, leave home base at all, with its familiar associates and manageable discomforts?

That one is easier to answer than the others. Retirement without moving is little more than finding yourself without a job; of knocking about in one's accustomed haunts in the dubious role of a refugee or hanger-on; of inviting the obloquy of "twice as much husband on half as much income." Retirement, like salvation, is a state of grace that needs to be taken in full dosage to be convincing.

Climate, atmosphere, and the presence of a number of friends who had preceded us here were among the factors that led us finally to Hilton Head. But more important was the prospect of a few years, at least, of a reasonably uncluttered serenity; of clean air, open vistas, people decently spaced out, and time that does not incessantly demand to be made use of. If that is a reality rather than a dream, it probably is a fragile and transient one; the recurrent statistics in the *Packet* on building permits and other indices of spiraling progress clearly suggest as much. So do those seductive full-page ads in magazines like *The New Yorker*. But we are maybe a little ahead of the game; the serenity is a fact of the moment at least, and—who knows?—maybe it can be preserved.

It was in this benevolent frame of mind that, shortly after our arrival, I called my old friend Jonathan Daniels—essayist, historian, and the *Grand Seigneur* of this province. His manner on the phone lacked some of the expansive hospitality I had expected.

"Where you been?" he barked. "I want a guest column for next week's *Packet*. Six or seven hundred words. Anything you want to write about, but make it good and make it fast." *Click!*

Well, damn, I said to myself; for an old newspaper hack, this is a hell of a way to begin a life of serene and leisurely retirement.

January 20, 1972

Welcome to Martins

I never saw a Purple Cow,
I never hope to see one;
But I can tell you, anyhow,
I'd rather see than be one.

Not counting vigilant bird watchers, that old verse might have expressed the views of some hereabouts concerning the purple martin. But if enthusiastic island Rotarians behind Colonel Jack White have their way, that will not long be expressive of the island attitude. The welcome sign is out—and will soon be up in many places—for this ornithological benefactor of mankind.

Obviously it should be enough recommendation for this bird to report the fact that each martin in the big flock Colonel White hopes to attract will every day eat its own weight in mosquitoes. Furthermore, now when we have all become almost instant ecologists, the martin's appetite for bugs which have an appetite for man may make unnecessary the use of pesticides which may kill us and other creatures along with the mosquitoes. And beyond all this, it is hoped that the sale of elaborate, high-rise apartments for the martins may provide funds for scholarships and other good works. Certainly, as a man in the housing business, Colonel White should know the possibilities of such profits for benefaction.

Beyond all this, the movement represents a landmark in the approach of islanders to maturity. There was a time before more brush had been cleared for building lots when realtors like Colonel White only mentioned the word *mosquito* in a whisper. Indeed, back in 1961, before the irresistible quality of Hilton Head Island had been spread across the land, it was not considered nice to suggest that there might be biting bugs here. However, one prospective lot buyer did boldly ask Wally Butler about it. Wally pooh-poohed. In dismissal, he replied that Charles Fraser had already gotten that fixed up. Development has come a long way when land dealers here can frankly admit the presence of pests in paradise and cry the need for calling in the martins to do something about it.

The purple martin's virtues in this regard have long been known. Before the white man came, Indians hung up gourds with holes in them to provide the martins with nests. Blacks emulated the Indians. Fields about some plantations of aristocrats were festooned with such gourds to attract the summer home–seeking martins. Housing for birds, like housing for man, has improved. A gentleman from Illinois has made a home industry for his town by manufacturing what amount to aluminum condominiums for martins, arranged for easy cleaning (though some admirers even say that the martins carefully carry their debris away and deposit it at a distance). The houses for martins even come equipped with doors to keep the sparrows and the starlings from usurping their nests during the martins' absence in the winter.

Progress like this, of course, does not come for free. Low-cost-housing days seem to be disappearing for martins as well as for men. Apparently, however, the martins have become picky and choosy, too. Their advance scouts show a preference for such apartments high on telescopic poles. Gourds today are apparently as inadequate in attracting the martins as un-air-conditioned beach cottages are in appealing to people. Soon, in the competition for this useful bird, residents and realtors may be adding inside plumbing to their mansions for martins.

To get our metaphors all mixed up, there seem to be no bugs in this plan. Still, there could possibly be a warning in the American stories of the martins' chief adversaries, the starlings and the English sparrows. Both were brought to America by persons with the noblest intentions. In 1850 eight pairs of the sparrows were brought to New York State by persons with high optimism that this species would control cankerworms and be a cheerful addition to the landscape. The first starlings were brought to America in 1890 by a group aesthetically determined to introduce here every species of bird mentioned by Shakespeare. No special inducements in housing were necessary to their multiplication.

Other historical matters may be noted. Back in the days when old Natchez was flowering with the wealth of the cotton snobs, one mansion owner was married into a large family of people named Martin. As was the old Southern custom, these in-law relations made frequent and prolonged visits. And one day as he sat on his piazza, watching birds in his garden, the master was heard to say, "What can we do to get rid of the martins?" To his outraged wife and relatives he insisted he was talking about the birds. It is just possible that he was.

Such historical details can be dismissed. But one serious question remains: Granted that each purple martin will eat two thousand mosquitoes a day, can assurance be given that they amplify their appetites to include the no-see-ums of Hilton Head Island?

January 27, 1972

Cobalt Sonata*

The whole business was cleared up only after he was sternly interrogated in a room in the basement of the police department and after, strapped to the couch, he had undergone soothing, suggestive psychiatric questioning.

A twinkling old man of sixty-nine, he had come almost jauntily to the biopsy. He had a vaguely humorous memory that as he lay on the table with his arm outstretched for the needle the anesthetist muttered, "Here comes the brand-name urologist." But the existence of the malady was established, and just before Christmas he began appearing daily at the outpatient clinic for cobalt. It was a fascinating experience at first. Daily he pulled off his pants and shoes and donned a hospital gown which made him look like a grinning wraith amid the holiday decorations.

A small brunette, all in nurse's white, summoned him to the cobalt chamber. Entering, he exchanged a cordial greeting with another nurse—large, with a gentle face. Then a merry, tall, gray, competent Englishwoman helped him mount the therathon. The

* Daniels wrote this whimsy after undergoing prolonged—and successful—cobalt treatment in Savannah.

237

young women called the machine the Jolly Green Giant, he learned.
It looked more like a sea monster and seemed that more so as it
revolved with a motion like a writhing.

Outstretched upon it he lay very still while the tall woman painted
a target on his lower abdomen with red ink. The lights were turned
up, brightly illuminating the room, which had a picture of mountains on the walls. "Be very still," he was enjoined. The nurses fled
the to-be-irradiated room. The machine clicked, and he lay very
quietly, though his nose itched, while piped-in music poured out
the notes of "Rudolph the Red-Nosed Reindeer."

Only the music changed in the New Year. The same process went
on daily, daily, daily. No pain, no heat, no sensation, but the same
interminable indignity of his drawers pulled down, the target re-
painted, the machine aimed by numbered dials. "Be very still."
Lights were turned brightly on. The girls fled. The machine clicked.
And the music poured in. Each day the procedure was brief and
almost identical. The target was changed. The machine revolved or
writhed around him. Once a doctor spilled a bottle of the belly
paint. Once, before the nurses departed, one asked another, "Is
Larry in cardiovascular married?" They laughed.

Daily, daily, daily. This is like the Chinese water torture, he told
the young doctor who came in. Drop, drop, drop. Daily, daily, daily.
The twinkle disappeared from his eyes. He came in his gown and
his stocking feet with more and more muted greeting to the girls.
And gradually an unreasoning resentment grew as he lay in the
brightly lighted room listening to the eternal music. Evidently it was
then that he planned the crime.

It was easy for him to hide the pistol in the awkward folds of the
robe. He wore like a mask the old merriment he had begun to lose
daily, daily, daily. There was nothing of the mask in the amazement
the girls showed when he ordered them into the far corner of the
room. He went out the door through which they had always fled
before they turned on the radiation. He locked it. Then he set the
machine at full blast. Somehow he got into his pants and out of the
clinic. No sounds came through the thick walls of the cobalt room.
He drove away, only stopping long enough at a street-side phone
booth to call the hospital and warn that two bombs had been set
in it to go off in two hours, just long enough to give time to evacuate

all the patients. Then he drove the miles home whistling, as if back at a beginning, "Rudolph the Red-Nosed Reindeer."

It was three days before the police found him on the golf course at Hilton Head Island. He had just made a beautiful drive. He turned to the three armed officers with a look of perfect recognition.

"I've been expecting you," he said.

His eyes were twinkling.

February 3, 1972

Bird Feeder

The Sojourner's home roost, as some may have heard, is *The News and Observer*, of Raleigh, North Carolina. He still receives spiritual and some other sustenance from it, though for some time he has been periodically sneaking into senility on Hilton Head Island. Younger men now staff its desks, watching and reporting the world. They take their jobs seriously in a very serious world but sometimes work in the knowledge that all things are so serious that nothing should be taken seriously. Such an understanding motivated an able staff writer, Jack Aulis, to write on a subject of transcendent importance to Hilton Headers. He called his piece "Something for the Birds." People hereabouts may find a few crumbs of wisdom in it. Here it is.

Everybody says you should feed the birds in the winter but nobody ever tells you exactly what is involved. For example, flickers eat ants and robins eat worms but the people who sell bags of wild birdfeed don't put ants and worms in the mixture. Not intentionally, anyway.
Another thing they don't tell you is that the expression "she eats like a bird" is perpetrated by people who have never invited feath-

ered friends for dinner. If a human ate like a bird, he would eat 100 pounds a day. Birds eat constantly, and complain every time their plate is empty. I think the fat goes to their heads.

But if you already have a string of polo ponies and are looking for a new expensive hobby, here are some of the things you should know:

WILD BIRDFEED—That's the stuff that comes in plastic bags in supermarkets. It is mostly cracked corn and small grains such as milo. And a few sunflower seeds just to get you hooked on the hard stuff. Sunflower seed eaters will eat the sunflower seeds and throw everything else on the ground where other things eat some and the rest sprouts, giving you a chance to apply for a federal grain allotment.

SUNFLOWER SEEDS—Cardinals, evening grosbeaks, blue jays, chickadees, titmice, finches and squirrels love this stuff. Probably because it is expensive. A grocer whose customers are hooked on feeding sunflower seeds need not make a profit on anything else.

CORN—The corn should be cracked because birds are too lazy to do any of the work. On the ground it will attract mourning doves, grackles and other blackbirds, squirrels, possums and—in season—frogs, toads and now and then a turtle. You do not have to throw it on the ground. Put it in your feeder. The sunflower seed eaters will throw it on the ground. In disgust.

SUET—Suet is slimy white meat fat. Birds who normally eat bugs will eat suet. And probably anything else. It will readily attract woodpeckers, nuthatches, chickadees. starlings and—if not too high off the ground—dogs and cats. Also, if the weather is warm and the suet gets ripe, it will attract worms. That might, in turn, attract robins, but I doubt it. Butchers used to give you suet. Until they discovered someone wanted it.

PEANUTS—Peanuts are sure-fire for blue jays and squirrels. Technically, squirrels are not birds. For one thing, they have no feathers. But you might as well know about them. They spend more time on bird feeders than birds do.

APPLES, ORANGES and PEANUT BUTTER—These will almost certainly attract orioles who will almost certainly be chased away by mockingbirds. Mockingbirds do not like anybody but they do like apples, oranges and peanut butter. However, after the mockingbirds have chased the orioles away, the squirrels will eat the apples, oranges and peanut butter.

WATER—Water is usually put out in birdbaths but any old pot will do. Water will attract everything: birds of all feathers, squirrels, dogs, cats, rabbits, raccoons, frogs, turtles, dead leaves, algae and small children. I suppose we are lucky there are no elephants or tigers in North Carolina.

SUGAR WATER—In season, which this isn't, sugar water will attract hummingbirds. Also flies and ants. It might also be a good way to attract flickers, who normally have to dig their ants out of the lawn. But I doubt it.

BREAD—Bread is the thing people fed birds before plastic bags of birdfeed were invented. Just break the bread up into pieces and cast it on the ground. The way it's made these days it doesn't do the wildlife much good, but it's cheaper than sunflower seeds.

Do not throw it in the birdbath. In the case of birdbaths, if you cast your bread upon the water all you get is soggy bread. And, of course, squirrels.

February 10, 1972

Pen in Hand

When Charles Fraser takes pen in hand one thing certain is that hand and pen will not be soon parted. This was demonstrated again in his long statement to *The Island Packet*. Logically and at length he proved that he and his antagonist Fred Hack have both been inconsistent about airport development for the island.

Time was when Sea Pines Plantation Company and the Hilton Head Company each wanted the island airstrip located within their domains. When, after some bristling negotiations, it was located in the Hilton Head Company's suzerainty, that company began, as Fraser says, to advertise the advantage of closer approach to its area. Then, as Fraser also says, "Sea Pines Plantation, not surprisingly, countered in its own guidebook for property owners with the suggestion that the airport was close enough to be convenient to Sea Pines (twelve miles) yet its residents would not suffer any noise from the airport, as would Port Royal residents. . . ."

Now in a turn-around, as Fraser points out, Fred Hack fears, as Charles once did, the noise and pollution of a greater airport on the island and proposes that the expanded airport be located on Victoria Bluff. Fraser's fears of noise, et cetera, are now abated. He is eager for longer runways to permit the quick and easy landing *on the island* of the corporate jets of "many large U.S. corporations, major foundations, and trade associations" whose disgorged personnel might fill villas, hotel rooms, and condominia (he sticks precisely to the Latin plural) during the "non-vacation months of the year." Fred, whose brother was honored for his anti-pollution work in the battle with BASF, now fears the noise and pollution which did not seem so threatening to him when the developments were younger and smaller.

So the feudal lords are, not surprisingly, locked in combative embrace. Both Fred and Charles, who are often approachable neighbors here, deserve to be considered as benevolent despots. Both love this island. And though Fraser only makes the point in Hack's direction, both have been "financially fortunate" in turning a jungle into a bonanza. Certainly nobody who knows Fred Hack will agree that, in his proposal to put the airport beyond the dangers of smell and clamor, he is insensitive to the needs of the less fortunate "resort workers" for whom, along with the jet planes of the corporates, Fraser makes his plea.

The one thing certain is that Fraser and Hack, elevated as they are, are not the only parties in interest in this matter. Possibly the first in interest are those who have already settled on this serene and hopefully never-to-be-overrun shore. Of course, high priority of consideration also belongs to the workers who have been blessed by the jobs of doubling and redoubling development. Few of them will come in corporate jets. They get here all right now, as the prodigious parking lot around the increasingly complex Sea Pines complex indicates.

One possible solution to this problem might be that both Fraser's and Hack's plans be discarded as threats to this island's content. What both are proposing on different sites are bigger airports for more planes, bigger planes, quick and easy inpouring of more and more people to buy more lots and condominia [*sic*], or merely to occupy a room for a night, or just to swim and fling a beer can on the beach beyond Coligny Circle. No one can blame the developer for wanting to develop. Progress—it's wonderful. But even at this distance we ought to be able to hear the screams against inpouring jets on Martha's Vineyard. With the help of jets Hawaii has become a haven of the hippies. Convenience is a wonderful thing, but there are some virtues still in at least a little isolation.

Maybe the time has come for that committee formed to blow up the bridge to get ready to plow up the runways.

February 17, 1972

Flight from the Island

This certainly must be one of the travelingest islands in the world. Sometimes the movements of the newly settled here make it seem almost a port of exit to all the other places of the earth. Aldine and Emerson Schroeder's day-by-day address book must resemble the log of Captain Cook in his first circumnavigation of the globe. Some, going to far places, will only follow their inclinations, and this spring others, shepherded by Calvin Reid, will follow in the footsteps of Saint Paul. Those certainly are footsteps to follow, for Paul the traveler was almost as prodigious as Paul the Apostle. Calvin's companions, however, will have better and faster travel facilities than Paul got.

Indeed, except for the facilities, there is nothing new about the exodus from the South Carolina Low Country. Today it is not quite the hegira it once was—*hegira* in this case not meaning the flight of Mohammed from Mecca (though some travel agency might make following that flight a tourist attraction, too). The hegira hereabouts in the old days carried the second meaning of the word: a journey undertaken to seek refuge away from a dangerous or undesirable environment.

Not even our local Pied Piper of tourism, Jim Gray, would suggest today that what he proffers is flight from an adverse environment on Hilton Head Island. But he probably does not realize that in promoting travel hereabouts he is the successor to the mosquito. And it is not to minimize Gray's talents to say that once the mosquito was more persuasive than he. White planters in the old days did not wait until they were enchanted by brochures. They skipped out early in the spring and returned to their plantations only after a hard frost in autumn. In the 1850s Joseph W. Barnwell's family left their Port Royal plantation on May 10. They came back at the end of October. They and others dispersed to such places as the High Hills of the Santee and far beyond to Cape May, Saratoga Springs, and Newport.

A packet ran regularly from Charleston to Newport. On at least one occasion, however, John C. Calhoun's mother-in-law drove from South Carolina to Rhode Island "in her family coach, drawn by four splendid gray horses, with the reins held by an English coachman in full livery."

As sectional differences mounted, not all South Carolinians approved of their planter plutocrats traipsing off to Northern resorts. As early as 1820 a Charleston gentleman wrote bitterly of the summer tourism of the time: "the idle, the gay, and the luxurious fly before our scorching sun-beams, in quest of cool and fashionable leisure." He added that "much of our Taste, Intelligence, Beauty and Fashion is lost to us from June to November."

By 1850 a South Carolina editor wrote in really righteous indignation. "How long," he demanded, "will our Southern people keep going North to the Springs to be insulted and pay a set of fanatics to vilify us?" The Charleston *Mercury* growled over "the spectacle which every summer exhibits, of Southerners and slave holders by thousands, with their families, hurrying away to the seething cities of the North, or to its crowded and snobbish watering places."

Only war gave effectiveness to this "stay home" crusade. And fortunately no such Southern flight is any longer necessary. Routes of travel are reversed. The icicle is a sharper prod than the mosquito ever was. Tourism takes its place beside Mother and apple pie. Nobody disapproves. Bankers whose glass eyes once would have popped at the suggestion of loans for high-life holidays now urge

people, by billboard ads, to borrow for travel, and credit cards are represented as flying carpets for everybody to everywhere.
All aboard!

February 24, 1972

Reaction to Assault

Who in hell is Hamrick, who wrote that piece which *The State* of Columbia flaunted under an eight-column streamer, "Plush Living Contrasts Poverty at Hilton Head"? Black Thomas Barnwell, as director, and white Charles Rousek, as president of the island Chamber of Commerce matched each other in resentment. They were unduly indignant. The article sounded like a stuck recording of the loud accusations and laments the BASF backers were voicing some months ago. And in more ways than one it was a stuck record which was not so much an imposition on Hilton Head Island as it was on *The State* newspaper. Apparently the only other injured parties were the copyright owners of the *Hilton Head Island Report,* prepared sometime ago by Harman Associates, well-known evaluators of resorts.

Best information is that Tom Hamrick (said to be no kin of General Halftrack of the funny papers) is a retired lieutenant colonel who lives at Mount Pleasant, near Charleston. He came here briefly to report for *The Charlotte Observer* the happy occasion of the visit here of Secretary of the Interior Walter J. Hickel. Then he peddled this piece to *The State.* Maybe he sensed a ready market for detraction of Hilton Head in Columbia, where some resentment existed after the threatened BASF invasion here was repulsed by a combination of Hilton Head blacks and whites.

Certainly, while Hamrick was here, he laid his hand heavily on the Harman report, which gave a balanced evaluation of the island, sometimes critical, but more often lyrical in praise. Without giving any credit, he took double handfuls of the adverse passages that small book contained. He added some shots of his own about the insensitive snobs who dwell beside the oppressed blacks. The developers, he said, would push all the blacks off the island if they could. And new white settlers here live in a state of envy of Fripp Island, where only palefaces may live. Oo-la-la!

This evident willingness to stir racial feelings here might have been a demagogic dagger thrust but for its absurdity on an island where blacks and whites depend upon each other for their welfare and happiness in so many things. This certainly was original, but in other phrases and passages, which he appropriated from the Harman report, he masked his manipulations. He never mentioned the Harman report by name, calling it, instead, "a realty prospectus," which it certainly was not.

At the beginning of his article he picked up the Harman descriptive phrase for the island. Later, without benefit of quotation marks, he wrote: "One land sale prospectus now being circulated remembers Mrs. Reuben Clark, of Savannah, Ga., very well. When she bought her lot in the early days, good beachfront property cost $10,200. 'It's enough to make a man eat his heart out,' a realty salesman now admits in the mirror of present prices 10 times greater."

The original passage, in the Harman report, read: "And to think that when Sea Pines sold its first lot in 1957 to Mrs. Reuben Clark, of the prominent Savannah Clark family, all beach fronting property cost $10,200 and the inland locations went for $3,500. It's enough to make a man eat his heart out."

In another place Hamrick does use quotation marks, but in allusion to "propaganda literature"—not to the Harman report from which the quotation was lifted. That was the almost complimentary passage in which it was noted that the new islanders "have seen and associated with a great number of well known people. Therefore, they will not be particularly impressed that you have been executive vice president of World Petroleum, Inc., or president of Busy Beaver Suits and Coats."

Similarly, Hilton Head should not be too impressed or concerned about anything this onetime lieutenant colonel, now wildly shooting with borrowed weapons, has to say about this shore. What he has produced is a comedy in which a generally responsible newspaper like *The State* is put in a ridiculous position. Hilton Head ought to get more fun than fury out of the antics displayed. Fortunately, nobody has been really hurt, even if the Harman pocket has been selectively picked.

March 2, 1972

Dear Old Beaufort

BASF differences or not, it was probably inevitable that there should have been a little standoffishness between the people of old Beaufort and those of the new Hilton Head. New islanders were suspect as strangers in a country where the newcomers best known before were those who came shooting in blue uniforms. Others, arrayed in frayed frock coats and celluloid collars, arrived carrying carpetbags which they hoped to fill. And it might as well be admitted that some of those city people who have recently settled on the shore came from areas which once looked down on the South as a stagnant province of backward people. It is not necessary that a nose be patrician to look down it. They regarded themselves as more sophisticated than simple Southerners. Sometimes the attitude remained even after they met Joab Dowling, who boisterously wears the surface of a guffawing country boy while he expands his law offices on the fees he collects from worldly-wise Yankees. Soon he will be able to look down on all from the tallest house in the county.

It is doubtful that the differences will be erased by guided tours or barbecues or Chamber of Commerce resolutions about hands across the creeks and rivers, estuaries and swamps. Actually, though neither natives nor newcomers seem to realize it, the explosively developing island and old, quiet, lovely Beaufort have much in common. They are places of similar origins. The truth of the matter is that Jean Ribaut, Admiral Gaspard Coligny, and even Captain William Hilton were just passers-by. Beaufort's growth was as a resort.

Without benefit of a Fraser or a Hack, the town before *that war* depended as much on summer visitors as on rice or sea-island cotton. The visitors were apt to be cotton or rice men who were the fat cats of that time. Many of them went to Beaufort and built the beautiful houses there "in order to enjoy its salubrious climate." The South Carolina architect and geographer Robert Mills wrote in 1826 that the town had "always been remarkable for the health and longevity of its inhabitants." Beaufort was comparatively free of the "country fever."

Another writer about this period said, "Not possessing the commercial and political activity of a metropolis, Beaufort, which in those days was not even a seat of justice, was chiefly important as a planter's resort." In summer the town's population numbered some two thousand persons, more than twice as many as in the winter. This author, Lawrence Fay Brewster, added: "The planters who resided in Beaufort in the summer are said to have vied with one another in building their town houses—'imposing mansions,' ornately decorated and handsomely furnished. The result, according to a visitor in the 1840's, was 'a picturesque town composed of an assemblage of villas,' each of which was 'shaded by beautiful live oaks and orange trees laden with fruit.' " Some of the most imposing houses in Beaufort were built on the plantations and moved bodily to town—which predated prefabs.

Populated as a resort by Bulls, Barnwells, Chisholms, Cuthberts, Elliots, Hamiltons, Rhetts, Verdiers, and Woodwards, it was certainly then the serene refuge of the plush and well-heeled. Later, of course, the time came when Beaufort residents were too poor to paint and too proud to whitewash. The first crop of more recent Northern newcomers bought up much of the arable lands for hunting preserves. Hurricanes destroyed the phosphate industry. But there was until recently a bright reflection of the town's old fame as resort in the widely patronized Gold Eagle Tavern. It was so named because it had been the house of Henry William Desaussure, who, as director of the United States Mint, had coined the first twenty-dollar gold pieces.

Beaufort might do well to recognize that the new carpetbaggers are bringing in—not taking out—the equivalents of those shining coins. And Hilton Head should understand Beaufort as its predecessor as a haven for those who can afford "town houses" and "villas," even such as now rear their crowns at Harbour Town. Certainly both should be concerned together to preserve the handsome houses and façades of history in Beaufort, now threatened by a progress which would turn graceful gardens about old houses into parking lots or the like. One day Hilton Head's rich, recent development will be antique, too. It can only hope that when that time comes, it will be as worthy of preservation as its beautiful old neighbor is now. Hilton Head Island can well serve that hope by helping Beaufort keep and cherish the best of its past.

March 9, 1972

Cash and Tranquillity

Now our esteemed contemporary in communications Vance Fowler puts himself forward as a successful speculator. But what he says he was betting on, and only on, was "peace and tranquillity." The gain he counts is in cash. Like the rest of us, he has no ready measure of "peace and tranquillity." To prove his financial point, he printed as a quaint document, in his folksy periodic letter from Sea Pines, the 1962 price list for Sea Pines lots. And in italics he added, *"In my opinion, investments in Sea Pines in January 1962 carried with it a greater risk than land selling many times higher in 1972."* He did not quite say that the lot he bought for $4,500 in 1962, now worth probably $27,500, might be worth $162,000 in the next ten years. It might be. Still, it may be wondered whether the chances in "peace and tranquillity" have advanced at a similar rate.

The amazing profits were not promised in 1962, but the "peace and tranquillity" certainly were. Indeed, as recently as 1969 it was proclaimed in bronze, on the marker to the resort founders on the lawn of the Bank of Beaufort, that Hilton Head Island was and would be "a place where man could commune with Nature and enjoy the Sea and the Sky, the good Earth and the Forest and all

255

things that dwell therein . . . where man could live in peace and solitude for a day or a lifetime."

"Solitude" says the sign before the bank building which has just doubled its size. "Peace" proclaims the new city-sized post office beside what was recently the "new" one, where now in cramped quarters the cry is pandemonium. Before the new building opens its doors, there are complaints that there will not be enough parking before it. "Tranquillity" marks the doubled medical center where the injured and ailing have multiplied. Now one developer wants the airport on the island to bring in bigger and bigger jets full of more and more people, and his antagonistic counterpart is appalled by the litter of the people who have already arrived. Even the little old *Packet*, while it laments some signs of change, is talking about erecting its own building. The condominiums multiply. Even names for them do—villas, cluster homes, cabanas. South Beach is a good example of urban sprawl, though it hasn't half begun to sprawl yet. There are now more than hoaxes or hints about high rises. There are more Sealofts than deer on Deer Island. The boundaries for wildlife refuges seem more and more fuzzy and better prepared for human inspection than for animal living. And even Vance Fowler is retreating from the proximity of roaring traffic on Sea Pines Drive to a location of possibly greater solitude.

As a former seagoing paymaster in the navy who traveled all over the world before he came here, he is undoubtedly a good time-keeper and bookkeeper in cash. The financial risk in buying land here may now be, as he says, less than it was when the island was just the beautiful place he found at the end of his journey. Hilton Head might then have turned out to be a troubled island like Fripp, which Hilton Headers were recently said to envy. But the risks, in terms of the "peace and tranquillity" Vance undertook to acquire in 1962, may very well not be less in this year of our Lord 1972.

> . . . everything that grows
> Holds in perfection but a little moment.

It is hard to tell whether that moment belongs to Vance Fowler's past, present, or future. Such difficulty in determination is shared by other long-settled persons here. Certainly it confronts those potential lot buyers to whom Vance gives financial assurances as well as invitation. On this island to which he gave "love at first sight," he now, as development executive, gives love in the long look, too. Capital gains can be quickly counted from an old price list, but serenity in solitude may be getting to be more and more words on a historical marker in the midst of the thickening traffic at Coligny Circle.

March 16, 1972

Instant Elysium

High upon the rock
The ugly houses stand;
Come and see my shining palace
Built upon the sand.

Miss Millay was certainly not specifically writing abut Hilton Head Island. Yet some in righteousness from upland houses and even public buildings have pictured this island as a sort of Instant Elysium populated by rootless plutocrats who have no concern about poverty beside them. Big houses by big poverty have not always seemed reprehensible in South Carolina. One of the first to make a tour of homes here was a man by the name of William Tecumseh Sherman. He was said to be a little careless with fire. But he made possible a legend of lamentation to the effect that all white South Carolinians once had mansions in front of the quarters of their slaves. No guilt sense has attended that legend. That version of the big house by the slave shanties has been sung to banjo music. It was a South perhaps unjustly typified by the quotation, "Hold my magnolia while I whup this slave."

258

But now a contrast on the South Carolina shore between the rich and the poor seems somehow scandalous to some on the other side of Skull Creek. New islanders were expected to cringe when the envious or the invidious cried "Plush!" in this direction. The occasion of the tour of homes here provides an excellent opportunity for the quick and loud answering cry, "So what?" This is a plush and beautiful island. The smallest houses in its developed plantations possess comforts the nabobs of Newport never knew—or the masters of the rice plantations, either. In a wide variety of shapes, sizes, and everything else, they possess together a unity of planning for pleasant living which other South Carolina communities often lack.

Come and see our shining palaces and simple dwellings, too, all kept with equal pride. Ride to them beside the smooth green golf courses on roads under a sort of cathedral nave of trees. And don't fail when you are on your way to see the greatly improved housing of the poor. The poor are here. But the new residents of South Carolina did not bring the poverty here. They found it and have done much to relieve it. With the possible exception of the military installations, the Hilton Head developments provide more jobs than any other employer in Beaufort County— vastly more than any automated chemical plant would have provided.

It is not easy to say whether the contemporary house tours, here and elsewhere, should be classified as social events, benevolent enterprises, or studies of shelter. The first is evident. Ladies—and some gentlemen—come properly attired (no spike heels, please). Certainly they are hospitably welcomed by plush people who are hostesses, guides, ticket takers, and chauffeurs for the day. It is, of course, a benevolent enterprise in which men and women of all denominations work in ecumenical unity. Basically, however, these tours must be studies of shelter. And Hilton Head Island is unparalleled as a place in which to contemplate high hopes in human habitation. But visitors should not expect perfection. The place and its people have their faults, which will not be paramounted. Any dirty linen will be kept in the driers. All skeletons will be securely locked in their closets. At the gates of one plantation the security guards in their Graustarkian uniforms will welcome all to the habitations of the blessed on this magic island.

Plush? You can bet your life it is and hopes to stay so. At the moment hard times are not knocking at the door—or the gate. Spring is here. Come one, come all.

March 23, 1972

Trash Is Trash

HELP...
KEEP BEACHES CLEAN

Sometimes the roadsides seem almost rimmed by the mess of motorists ready to foul their own nests. Cans and bottles, boxes, programs, and candy wrappers pile up along highways and lanes in a profusion which must have required the labors or the lapses of many hands. No wonder Fred Hack, who has loved the island so long, is appalled, ready to assume a big part of clean-up and calling for others to join in removing the mess and clutter steadily created. That is going to be a race between the cleaners and the clutterers, with odds probably on the side of the latter. The saddest thing is that the worst of this situation is not the mess they leave but the presence of such obscene individuals here.

Part of the trouble derives from the use of the word *litter* instead of the good rough word *trash* and the substitution of the cute little term *litterbug* for *trash*, too. Fortunately, the state of South Carolina sticks to the natural language of its people in putting the label TRASH on its roadside barrels. And in South Carolina, too, the word *trash* has long been applied to people who only cluttered up and soiled the human scene. There are such folk. "Po' white trash" is a familiar term in this area. And today it is a term often applicable to some

261

who think their inferiority is invisible, or undiscoverable, if their cars are moving fast enough. As applied to people, trash has no special relationship to poverty or wealth, color, even position. Certainly a lot of people who qualify as "po' white trash" would be appalled at the suggestion that they do.

The roadsides suggest that the trash in the population may be gaining on us. The automobile, which takes the blame for so many of our modern faults, may be guilty in this matter, too. Anonymity is not a very good companion to politeness. A man who would not spit on the sidewalk may not hestitate to throw his nastiness on the road. The Cadillac does not make the gentleman. The Mercedes does not guarantee a lady at its wheel. The power of any car may give its driver a regardless arrogance toward others. The certainty is that, in speeding, parking, and littering, many people act with a rudeness they would not think of showing in ordinary associations. Much of this auto ill-behavior may be attributed to the uncouth among us, but most of us have seen some very piggish parking at cocktail parties. Champagne bottles as well as beer cans have on occasion been found on lanes to the beaches.

Roadside signs proclaim that littering—or better, "trashing"—is a crime. Yet there is a sense of only mischievousness in misdemeanor. What it is basically is an evidence of bad manners, ill-breeding, boorishness, and vulgarity. Yet many who would grin at paying a fine for fouling the landscape would really not like to be recognized as the yahoos such behavior shows them to be. Pretty is as pretty does. So is gentility.

By this time it is to be hoped that Fred Hack's call for a cleaner island will have had results. We know that, as usual, the island was polished and shined for the tour of homes. Its face should be clean now unless perchance some of the ladies looking at lovely houses tossed out trash with gloved hands. The thing now is to keep the island clean—and clean on all days, not merely on ceremonial occasions. It really is not necessary for riders here to prove that they are also the riffraff. And that is exactly what the trash and trash makers do.

March 30, 1972

And the Young Came

"You're my winter, summer, spring, my everything!"

That old love song might well have been addresssed to the weather in this area in recent weeks. A brash, bold, doomed pear tree was in full bloom in Bluffton in February. Oleanders, which had been blooming almost till Christmas, stood brown and cold-killed before March was done. Cedar waxwings came on time like dive bombers ruthlessly descending upon the pyracantha berries. Yet on the first day of official spring not very far to the north a blooming redbud tree was more beautiful for snow that covered it like a transparent scarf, emphasizing rather than obliterating its purplish promise. Certainly the weather is not always as expected. Neither is anything else—retirement communities, for instance.

Though it sometimes seems too much true, Hilton Head Island is not for everybody. An aging Southern writer who once was much preoccupied with the agrarian South now prefers a town house in Manhattan, from which many of his contemporaries are fleeing. And the conventional refuges of the retired are changing. Ancient Pinehurst is getting its face lifted to improve its appeal, not to old and irritated settlers who will soon be dying, but to another generation which is aging to take their places in turn. Even the young Hilton Head resort alters. More young people are arriving to provide the services required by the old. Most of them here are apt to dress more conservatively than their elders, or at least during the daytime business hours. The elders here are apt to be the ones garishly costumed, in contrast with their fathers who were the elders once.

Though Hilton Head seems to its geriatric settlers to be the perfectly patterned place for the so-called golden years, some of the gilded or merely gray-headed have other preferences. As the young have come to Hilton Head to serve the retired, many of the elderly have chosen such places as the university communities of Charlottesville, Virginia, and Chapel Hill, North Carolina, to take advantage of resources provided for the young. Neither of these collegiate towns possesses the sea, but they provide libraries, medical centers, cheaper student golf courses, lectures, music, drama from which the old are not barred. The contrast between Hilton Head and such places presents almost a geographical generation gap.

As Easter approached on a chill, wet Good Friday, it was fascinating for one of the ancients of Hilton Head to observe it at Chapel Hill. Though resting or residing in numbers on the surrounding hills, the elderly seemed scarce on the campus. The throng was composed of bearded boys and of girls with their hair long and loose about their shoulders. They moved to classes unperturbed by the rain. They crowded the booths and tables in the student union. In appearance they seemed almost a hippie convention. But books were piled by their coffee cups. Decibels marked some lunchtime hilarity. Sex sparkled between some couples at some tables. But at one nearby a young man of the coiffure and costume expected of a supposedly disheveled generation was seriously checking formulae with a scholarly girl whose long, loose hair still sparkled with drops of rain. Near them others were reconstructing the points made in a lecture they had just heard in a classroom. Evidently most of those gathered in this lunchtime recess from the rain were as serious about their work as their elders had been when the dress and the hair of the young were more conventional.

Suddenly in their midst the old Hilton Header became aware of his own costume—a bright woolen shirt and yellow, almost golden, corduroy trousers. He tried hopelessly to think of the elders so arrayed that he had known when he was young. Instead he confronted the recollection of a professor, who then must have been younger than he is now, in a high stiff collar and a blue serge suit slick from many pressings. All generations had changed in the gap behind him.

He pushed back his plate of unchanging apple pie and posed a moral. The dress does not make the hippie any more than the date of the month makes the spring.

April 6, 1972

Old Men Notice

"Old men notice when old men die."

Ogden Nash wrote a line like that long before he began to notice any departure of his contemporaries. Now, even though he has joined the majority, I think of him as a young man on his knees, not in prayer, but in a crap game on Sutton Place long ago when the whole world was young. So old men notice how swiftly life goes almost like a roll of the dice to seven or snake eyes.

So I noticed with particular poignance last week when the second of a trio of which I was one crapped out of the game in Mississippi. To me, though he was sixty-five, he seemed much too young to die. I remember Hodding Carter first when, though possessing great talents for America in World War II, his quick patriotism had trapped him as a forgotten private in the Mississippi National Guard. He escaped from that, as every literate American should know, to become one of the most articulate advocates of what the world should be for all men—even in Mississippi. No mere do-gooder, he brought the qualities of an impeccable Southern duelist to his readiness to face the rednecks and the Ku Klux in his neighborhood and on his earth. I understood the need but not the wis-

266

dom of his going armed in an area where assassination was definitely not obsolete. He had confronted Huey Long; lesser adversaries did not frighten him. Neither did they rob him of the humor with which he was also armed, nor keep him from the writing of excellent books which carried his convictions far beyond the circulation area of his small Delta daily.

Ralph McGill, fat, jolly, deadly serious, and passionate in his purposes, had preceded Hodding to eternity. And he went as he had lived, merry from his birthday party, which a few of the so many who loved him had given him. Beyond toasts and quips, he died without time for perturbation as he came out of the room of celebration. So he was luckier than Hodding, whose great mind had been clogged for months by arteries unequal to the drive of his spirit.

So another old man does notice. But what he contemplates most is not the incident of death but the vitality of their lives. Undoubtedly some solemnity attended their obsequies. That was meet and right. Still, almost the central fact of their lives was that in them they were entirely divested of solemnity. Perhaps no new patterns of personality are created in any generation. Yet they seemed, freshly, figures who could bring intensity to their concern for the least men beside them without ever losing the debonair spirit of men who loved the world despite all the evils they saw and faced in it. They never lost gusto in their eagerness for reform. They declined sanctimoniousness in their uninterrupted service to the South and the world beyond it. All their lives they were ready for merriment, like that which had been in the room from which McGill came, undoubtedly still laughing, to his death. They were, to use a worn phrase in perhaps a strange place, "gay blades" in a world the sadness of which they never missed. Their always gleaming blades were their pens or their typewriters, the ribbons of which were often worn by their ardor.

More than old men should notice when such old men die. Such notice, however, should not include any notion that more men like them will not come again. There are certainly young men like them now, perhaps kneeling in games of chance more often than in their prayers. Maybe God will forgive them that. Certainly young men and old men may understand that solemnity is not an essential ingredient of concern. Sometimes, even in tension and trouble, a strong hold on hilarity may better serve than the constant crying of heartbreak. The tragic sense of life may be best understood by the debonair.

The best sunsets are always bright. Certainly that is so on Calibogue Cay.

April 13, 1972

Aaron Burr and Bathtubs

It is maybe strange that water should be so important a commodity on an island surrounded by it. It becomes more important with every plumbing connection. Some "old-timers" find the taste of the stuff that comes out of the spigots inferior to that which they drank with so much pleasure a few years ago. And water which makes rings in the commodes may be leaving its marks on kidneys, too.

Developers and promoters produce constantly rising figures on the number of houses, condominiums, et cetera, on this shore. Apparently, counting the number of new bathrooms is a task beyond the powers of the statisticians. Yet the number of bathing facilities here, not counting swimming pools and sauna baths, must be staggering. The bridge and the rural electric lines helped make possible the explosive developments here. But no one should miss the triumph of plumbing in the process. At a time of much talk of pollution, people hereabouts must be less polluted than ever before. The bathroom is a most significant symbol in the development of this new, well-washed Southern land.

It was not always so. In the so-called golden years of the plantation South, two critical visitors made diverse comments on the bathing facilities of the gentry. When Aaron Burr's lovely daughter

Theodosia married the rich South Carolina planter Joseph Alston, her father gave her advice which included comment on the situation.

"If you have no convenience for a warm bath in the house," he wrote her when she had moved to the elegant Alston household, "set a mason to work tomorrow and make one in each of your country houses. It is a high evidence of the barbarism of our Southern States that, in an extent of three hundred miles, filled with wealthy people, and in a hot climate, there should not be, in any one private family, a convenient bathing room."

Burr wrote in 1805 after a visit to a number of such dwellings, including the great plantation of Major Pierce Butler on Saint Simon's Island. Apparently conditions improved during the following years. Another Pierce Butler inherited the Saint Simon's estate and brought to it as his wife the famous, beautiful English actress Fanny Kemble. Fanny liked the coastal scenery; she described the flowers and butterflies. But her journal is chiefly remembered for her condemnation of slavery. She found, however, an item which aroused her admiration. Some years after Burr's adverse report on Southern bathrooms, she was almost ecstatic about a slave product, "fragrant bathtubs made of cedar," which she declared she preferred to "the finest Staffordshire porcelain."

The South has always been the subject of contrasting reports. Hilton Head Island is even now. Not all the bathrooms possess such items as the porcelain fixtures decorated with bright red birds in tub, basin, toilet, and bidet which Don Jones brought back from Paris for the house he and the Admiral built on East Beach Lagoon Drive. There are shanties here still without water connections. A project of high priority has been the provision of wells in the neighborhoods of some residents. But the water flows into splendid tiled chambers of a rich variety of colors from cerise to avocado. Possibly Fanny Kemble, accustomed to Staffordshire porcelain as well as to sweet-smelling cedar tubs, would not be unduly impressed. Certainly Aaron Burr would approve.

All can hope that the water will keep on flowing, for the poor as well as the rich. They can hope, also, that it will not taste worse as time goes on or make darker rings in the toilets and the tubs. Happiness here will depend more and more for more and more people on what comes out of the tap and goes down the drain.

April 20, 1972

The Indestructible Earth

In the profusion of foliage which remains on the island, despite the passage of the bulldozers and the conversion of forests into building lots, single plants seldom get personal attention and affection. This is, of course, not true of Chet Goddard's spoon-fed orchids. Others may attend special plants with special care. But even camellias and azaleas here are planted and bloom in companies, if not battalions. So one fellow was a little startled by a sudden sort of love affair with two small vines.

A year ago Greyton Taylor, a man whose "heart was always in the vineyard," came to Calibogue in his station wagon. He picked a place which would receive the proper sun. He clipped little tendrils from the plants. With slim, strong hands he put the roots into holes he had dug. He packed the earth about them with his boots. He gave the recipient of this two-vine vineyard elaborate instructions about the spraying and fertilization of the plants. Then he went away forever.

The instant vineyardist left behind was a man who had never really touched the earth. His thumbs were not green. Such tending as his yard received was performed with good earthy wisdom by Johnny White and company. But the new vines were left to his care,

271

Johnny White only erecting a little trellis with iron rods used to
support roadside newspaper boxes. Greyton Taylor's instructions
got lost in the clutter of a writer's desk. The insecticide, after one
application, sat undisturbed on a utility room shelf. Sure enough,
holes in the leaves indicated that the predators had taken advantage
of the neglect of the vines. With fall the leaves not only turned
brown. Also the plants seemed withered and dead. The good gift
had not received the care the giver had enjoined. Here was not a
case of the stony ground or the choking thorns. The ground was
good, but the grower had failed. That made a sad addition to the
parable of the sower.

Then suddenly with the spring the vines turned out imperturba-
bly in full green leaf. They climbed a little higher on the trellis.
There was promise of grapes from them, maybe even of wine. This
surprising spectacle seemed almost a miracle of resurrection and
also, in view of the neglect, a sort of demonstration of forgiveness
of sin. The good vines, put into the earth by the wise planter,
declined to die. And somehow the two little vines provide reassurance in a day in which lamentation mounts about the manner in
which man has neglected and almost destroyed his earth.

It seems at least possible that man exaggerates his aptitude as a
mauler of the good, green earth of his heritage. Some rivers are
rotten. Roadsides, which are themselves evidences of the mighty
manner in which man can cut the hills and fill the valleys, are littered
by neglect—even by a gross and savage carelessness. Maybe man
will succeed in cornering himself into a few good, green places in
which he cannot long survive for the encroaching desert of fume
and designed dilapidation of poisons and pavement.

The two little vines on the trellis suggest otherwise. Despite the
paw of the human species, the carelessness of the so-called Homo
sapiens, Nature remains a strong and determined adversary. There
is a poem about eventualities which contains the line: "I am the
grass; I cover all." Even the developers on Hilton Head Island may
only make a temporary stand against the jungle. Vines could grow
in the cracks of old condominiums. Little pines might creep again
across the golf courses. In the long time even the dragon-like earth-
moving equipment of builders may be no match for the yucca and
the thistle, the vine and the weed.

That new word *ecology* seems to mean something that belongs to man. The probability is that man belongs to ecology. Except in bits and pieces, Nature is indestructible. They only boast who claim that man might destroy the planet. Somehow it seems certain that it will be green when golfers have joined the dinosaurs.

All the same, this summer the unworthy guardian of Greyton Taylor's little vines is going to be more careful with spraying, watering, clipping, fertilizing. Between the desert and the jungle they are special friends entitled to affectionate care.

April 27, 1972

Ring the School Bells

Traditionally on Hilton Head Island summer has been the season of the young. From Georgia and South Carolina, school being out they poured in with their parents upon this shore where more sedate Yankees privately possessed the winter, spring, and fall. They were welcome, but some felt that they left an undue clutter behind them when the school bells began to ring in the fall. That invasion, of course, continues despite the escalation of summer rents. Indeed, the steeper cost of "cottages" may increase the crowding, since more people, young and old, must be packed into fewer rooms to keep the price per head down to a reasonable—or even unreasonable—figure.

The more significant thing that has happened on Hilton Head Island, however, is that this has become a young place all the year round. The process was inevitable. The old who came to retire required more and more young people to baby-sit for them in a variety of ways—from decorating to shopkeeping, from banking to barkeeping. Signs of their presence can best be seen in the packed parking lot around the Sea Pines offices. Charles Fraser has passed forty, but most of his immediate minions are young, They are, indeed, to use a statistical term, of "childbearing age." And they carry out its qualifications.

All around the year Sunday schools, which once were little knots of kids, are now the companies of Christendom. And talking and planning about education of the young have flourished like the flowering spring. Sea Pines Academy has been seeking the funds essential to the explosion of its pupil rolls. Another private school nearby talks loudly of its sudden growth.

All educational moves for the education of the island's multiplying young are welcome. But one thing which needs always to be remembered is the increasing number of childbearing baby-sitters here. Most of them are separated from the old settlers not only by age but also by the power of their pocketbooks. As everybody knows, one of this island's chief problems is the need for more low-, or at least lower-, cost housing. The lack of it is pointed by the stream of commuters every morning and evening from and to less expensive dwellings in nearby towns and villages.

Many, however, of the childbearing population have already made a beachhead in the inadequate number of moderately priced dwellings here. And beyond the rents they pay, most of them can hardly afford the tuition fees which the private schools require. With tuition fees pushing up toward a thousand dollars per child, many families, upon whom this island depends in a variety of ways, cannot stand the gaff. And that means that if Hilton Head Island is going to have healthy growth, the older residents with the money and the younger residents with the children must have a special concern for the adequacy and improvement of the elementary public school here.

Maybe the battle of Waterloo was won on the cricket fields of Eton. Certainly parents able to do so may privately provide, if they will, better and better educational facilities for those who may seem to them to be the elite of the young. But the battles of the future, probably, even the skirmishes on Hilton Head Island, are going to require the best possible education for the children of families of limited income as well as of those who can pay high fees without hurting.

And one of the things all children should be carefully taught is that they will not in maturity confront only an enviroment protected in terms of color and class. The elders among them should be aware of that already and already determined that here there must be not only excellent schools for some but true quality education for all.

A "plush" island like this one can afford the luxury of private schools. It cannot safely escape the necessity of good basic education for everybody.

Ring all the school bells!

May 4, 1972

The Keystone Cops

Despite the deadly seriousness of the disturbed crowds which gathered to hear about proposed zoning plans for the island, comedy could result in that best-loved American pattern: the deflation of the self-assured. From the beginnings of this country the risibilities of Americans have most steadily been aroused around the right of the people to hoot, holler, and laugh at those who regarded themselves as their betters. One early American was jailed under the Alien and Sedition Laws for saying that he hoped that a salute fired in honor of John Adams would hit the President in the seat of his pants. Planners are not Presidents, but the bottoms of their breeches are not immune.

Those of us old enough to remember the Mack Sennett comedies in the early movies recall how this folk feeling was developed into an art form. Slapstick it was called, but it was very serious stuff. Charlie Chaplin became the favorite clown of America, and the world, when he embodied the much-pestered little guy who in the end successfully and solemnly kicked the tails or smeared the custard pie in the faces of the Keystone cops representing the Establishment.

The resemblance to that well-loved situation may not at first be apparent in the zoning explosion here. Obviously the little guys are around. So, though possibly plush, are the new white residents of the so-called plantations anxious to preserve the charm and serenity they came here to get. Others are the long-established blacks, whose feeling for freedom is most precious because belatedly acquired. What both see, possibly with astigmatic vision, is a plan to let the big developers do as they please while denying the white residents aesthetic protections and imprisoning the blacks in the uses to which they may put their properties.

At this point in the scenario the little guys look beset. Who are they to confront the big Keystone cops on this scene, who seem as planners to favor the Establishment? The big developers move in an odor of sanctity. Did they not make this island the appealing place it is? Did not they bring "the fast money on 278"? Yet, suddenly, they, along with the planners, to their amazement find themselves, at least in the minds of many lesser persons, cast in the role of the Keystone cops. The uplifted brogans of the little guys seem close behind them. The situation provides a rare occasion for possible amusement and island improvement, too.

Of course, there are virtues in zoning. At last beyond protests —and to smiles if not laughter—a zoning pattern fair to all may be approved. But to be acceptable such a plan must be for the protection of all already here and not merely for the profit of those anxious to attract others to this place. The careless must be curbed. The ignorant must be persuaded. But nothing is so apparent now as that the greatest danger to assured serenity here comes from those who seem to many angry citizens to be most and unduly favored under the plan proposed.

Apparently the sky would be the limit on the developers. Possibly they do not need to be curbed. They are in the business of peddling perfection and surely would not dilute it. They win prizes for their performances. They are all, all honorable men. Yet like the rest of us, old developers and new developers, motel men, and even some of the most pious environmentalists may be captured in processes they do not control. Growth can be caught in its own acceleration. As the island grows, so does the vast indebtedness behind its developers. Interest charges must be met to pay insurance companies and pension fund investments, banks and other money lenders far away. Multiplying payrolls must be provided for. The result is that ecology must generally take a seat behind the economics of profit.

In many cases it has done so. Maybe this can best be demonstrated by what may be called the Manhole Rule. That does not involve covered holes in the pavement. It relates to the future of the island and the man-to-golf-course-hole ratio upon it. The number of golf courses is limited, but the number of people is not. The rule involves the ratio of people to other things, too. Already, in the building since 1952, the villas and apartments outnumber the separate houses. Now plans are made to pierce the sky. That means more people to the acre, and more lined up hoping for starting times. That not only creates impatience among players. It also arouses a perhaps unjustified black suspicion that such zoning as proposed might result in pushing black people off lands they have long held to make room for more golf courses and condominium sites.

Other problems are related to the Manhole Rule. At no place of congregation on the island is adequate parking provided. Traffic thickens on cracking roads. It is almost a rule that the worst-paved roads are those on which the lots have already been sold. There is no longer a question as to whether there will be high rises. They already exist or are in immediate prospect, even if they have not yet reached the towering crests of popular Miami Beach.

Of course, zoning is needed here. Some sensible regulation of land, water, and other resources is imperative. But the elderly lady watching the bird feeder in her garden is not the menace, even if she opposes Progress in the form of skyscraper condominiums. The black, patching his house with reused plywood and plowing with his tacky horse, does not present the threat of the Dollar Dreamer with the bulldozer, the mammoth earth-moving machine, and the soaring crane.

The scenario moves on. The bigger the land users are, the more regulation they require. It is improbable that the little guys—or sweet old ladies—can in this case soon startle the Keystone cops of the Establishment with the swing of their shoes in the direction of the bigger behinds. But it is time that all recognize that ludicrous possibility. The zoning situation has set the scene for a denouement in relaxing laughter. That might mean real, sudden, surprising regulation of the big guys. The alternative to that could be sullen resentment and tragic disenchantment with this island, too. And that would be no joke for anybody's amusement.

May 11, 1972

Amelia Island

"Our dreams for a second Sea Pines are about to become a reality," Charles Fraser wrote as of May 10. Hilton Head Island residents were invited to come look-see or look-buy or maybe just phone. Certainly now more and more people here will want to know more about this island on the Florida coast north of Jacksonville. There is a lot of fascinating stuff to know about it.

Fraser is not its first developer. A Spanish post stood there as early as 1686. Pious Spaniards named the island Santa Maria, after the Holy Mother. But there was fighting as well as piety on and around the island between the British and the Spaniards. Then General James Oglethorpe, in 1753, established a post there. And history vouched for by the Florida Department of Public Instruction reports that he found "the island so beautiful that he renamed it in honor of Princess Amelia, sister of George II."

No question has ever been raised about the beauty of the island, but apparently there has been a little confusion about the Amelia for whom it was named. George II didn't have any sister named Amelia. But he had a daughter by that name: Amelia Sophia Eleonora (1711–86), the aunt of George III. The Hanoverians liked the name Amelia. George III had a favorite child so christened, who died when she was only twenty-seven, in 1810. Her death brought on the final and permanent insanity of this George, whose remaining years were passed in blindness and aberration.

Some of the island's other history sounds incredibly romantic, though it was apparently true enough. Powers tugged and pulled for its possession. Once in its history the Mexican flag flew above it. And sometimes it seemed most dramatic because no power really possessed it. Early in the last century, lying just across the American border, it became a resort of pirates and smugglers. A lush illicit profit situation was created under the Embargo Act and the laws prohibiting any further importation of slaves into the United States. Smuggling sea captains with cargoes of slaves not only had to run the gauntlet of United States patrol boats. They also had to beware of hijackers along the marshy shore. The pirates Pierre and Jean Lafitte were said to be engaged in this racket. The Lafittes sold the Negroes at a standard price of a dollar a pound.

Charles Fraser will have much lore as well as land to sell his settlers today. In Old Town on the island a short street is called Pasco de las Damas because it was once occupied by the female camp followers of a Spanish garrison. In the old cemetery a grave holds the body of a sea captain. Legend is that his wife placed flowers on his grave every day, only to have them removed by another woman who put her flowers there. The widow, it is said, at last had to go to court to stop her competitor in mourning. In 1888 a Negro stranger arrived on a white horse, raised a flag, and organized a strike of black longshoremen. Whites regarded it as revolt. The militia was called in. But the real strikebreaker was yellow fever, which swept protest aside and protesters into their graves. When the pulp mills were built in the Depression years, so many people poured onto the island seeking jobs that lots were filled with tents and trailers, and authorities had to make a public appeal asking folks to stay away.

No such message will be sent to persons interested in the newly opened Sea Pines Company lands. All of the first group of lots, Charles reports to his first friends on Hilton Head Island, may soon be oversubscribed. Also, under complex land-registration requirements, at present only citizens of some states can buy.

Evidently Amelia is as beautiful as it seemed to Oglethorpe in 1735. And according to last reports there were no perfidious Spaniards or predatory pirates awaiting the settlers from Hilton Head or anywhere else—at least not in costume.

May 18, 1972

Mangers of Silver

Golfers on Hilton Head Island can trace their heritage back to the earliest of American golf clubs in Charleston. Something of the same sort should be available to those lovers of horseflesh here who recently put on an impressive horse show in the Lawton fields. Somehow credit for the early breeding of thoroughbreds is usually given to Virginia, New York, and Rhode Island. But new and old South Carolinians certainly should not forget the John's Island stud of Edward Fenwick (1720–75) which produced the swiftest racers in the period from 1750 to 1788. Fenwick was, according to scholars of the sport, one of four Americans who were the Founders of the Turf in America.

Certainly some recent exploring settlers on this island must have visited Fenwick Hall, between here and Charleston. If much of the glory of its stables is forgotten now, once it seemed impossible to exaggerate it. Slaves handed down stories that its stalls were made of mahogany and its mangers of silver. Ghost stories lingered about it. Two of the ghosts were said to be those of a handsome English groom and the daughter of the house, who eloped. Sternly, they

284

were brought back, and the girl was imprisoned in a room overlooking the courtyard where her lover was hanged.

Not all such tales of this era of galloping sport are so grim. Carolina smiled and sparkled at the race balls given by Low-County jockey clubs. Large sums passed in the betting. Since the sport was restricted to amateurs, prizes were not in money but in cups and plates of silver. Sometimes, however, skullduggery slipped into the sport of gentlemen. This happened in a race in February 1769 between William Allston's chestnut Tryal, Mr. Rogers' chestnut gelding got by Valiant, and a famous bay named Noble, owned by Morton Wilkinson.

In the first round of this race, spectators could see that Noble was not up to his expected form. A report of the event said: "But in the second round, every sportsman saw the cheat. It was soon discovered, that Robert Gay (who, ever since he came into the province, had kept Noble, and rode him that day) had received a bribe of 500 pounds currency, to lose the plate. Gay, being charged with it, after some hesitation, declared that he had received the bribe from Fenwick Bull, Esq., one of his Majesty's Justices of the Peace, Register of Mesne Conveyances, Notary Public, Agent to the contractors for victualling his Majesty's troops in the province, Clerk to the Board of Commissioners of the Pilotage, &c, &c. This worthy Magistrate and Placeman was soon found and denied the charge, with the most solemn protestations; nay, offered to take his oath, that he was altogether ignorant of the whole affair; but being confronted with Gay, and one Bettely (another groom who was in on the secret) he could no longer conceal his guilt. After receiving the usual and proper discipline of the horsewhip, his worship was carried into a room, by the gentlemen of the turf, to protect him from the mob who would otherwise have torn him to pieces."

The *South Carolina Gazette* took pains to point out that this man, despite his name, was not kin to the Carolina Fenwick or Bull families. Such incidents were rare. Troubles did mount, however, in the changed society after the Civil War. Finally, on December 29, 1899, the South Carolina Jockey Club resolved that "the prospect of restoring the amusement of horse racing on a respectable and financially safe footing has been proved to be hopeless." Its track, a farm adjoining, and securities of the value of $13,500 were given to the

Library Society of Charleston, "the largest gift ever made by living persons to any institution in this city," the papers said at the time.

Lovers of the racing horses with the flying manes may feel that the gentlemen of the Jockey Club were too easily discouraged. The beat of hooves and the cheers of crowds still resound at the races in Camden. Aiken long seemed almost dedicated to the horse. Anti-gambling laws, however, keep many of the greatest racers away. It's a long way to Hialeah, where the flamingoes fly above the pari-mutuel machines. Still, the number of devotees of horses and horsemanship grows here as elsewhere. The love of fine horseflesh demonstrated in the recent show here is indestructible. Hilton Head looks forward to more displays of the finest thoroughbreds in America on this South Carolina scene. They are a part of heritage here, too.

May 25, 1972

Frasier the Lion

Marge Brown, of Brown Pelican Road, has brought back from her former home in Cincinnati a story which she feels should be an inspiration for any on Hilton Head Island who worry about the decline of wildlife, including themselves. Under the heading of "Our Hero of the Month," the *Cincinnati Post* published the saga of the redoubtable Frasier the Lion.

The report may have appeared in some other papers, but in case any of the readers of *The Island Packet* may have missed it, it is reproduced here, though not with any injunction to retired readers to go thou and do likewise. Here it is.

LAGUNA HILLS, CAL. (UPI)—"One Lion's Family," the saga of Frasier the Magnificent, resumes today with a bigger cast—much bigger.

When last we left Frasier, the doddering old lion was in the process of becoming a celebrity, a symbol of hope for the aging Lotharios of the world. And his accomplishments keep growing.

To the astonishment even of his veterinarians, Frasier—although rheumatic of hip, trembling in the legs and with a coat like a much-used carpet—was carrying on a sex life that would have daunted most healthy male lions half his age.

287

Frasier is at least 17 years old—maybe 25—which puts him on a par with a human male of about 90 or 100. Yet, at last count, he has 33 offspring.

And that includes the quintuplets born yesterday.

Frasier, with about 100 other lions, lives at Lion Country Safari, where African animals roam uncaged around a large, fenced-in reservation for the benefit of sightseers who drive through in cars.

The Safari's veterinarians were having trouble finding a male lion who could take over as lord and master for 11 healthy, young lionesses the attraction purchased from Africa recently. Five virile young candidates were mauled and rejected by the lionesses as not up to their standards.

Almost as a joke, it was suggested a chance be given to Frasier, an ancient reject from a Mexican circus living out his sunset years at the Safari.

The next morning, there were 11 lionesses, purring contentedly in a circle around Frasier—who lay exhausted on his back, paws in the air Snoopy-style, his tongue lolling from his mouth.

Since then, the vets have been keeping Frasier going with raw-meat, health food diet and massive shots of vitamins, five times a day.

Frasier became a celebrity—buttons, bumper stickers, T-shirts, a "Frasier Fan Club" and television cameras attested his prowess.

At last report, another lioness was in labor, and Frasier—who has single handedly increased the Safari's lion population by a third —was reporting early for his vitamin shots.

A suggestion has been made that a reproduction of this piece be placed upon the bulletin boards of all the men's locker rooms of all the golf clubs on this island. And perhaps in the wildlife preserve.

June 1, 1972

Wrong Number

"Johnny can't read."

That was said about the young. Apparently, on Hilton Head Island, it applies to all ages. Demonstration of that came on and after Sunday, June 4, which was an important change-over date in communications on this island. The Hargray Telephone Company had gone to the most elaborate pains to ease the transition to two exchanges and many new phone numbers. The occasion should have been a memorable one, marking the wonderful growth of the company, the lines of which once had to take long jumps between widely separated houses and phones on a sparsely settled shore. Now the houses grow and so does the number of phones.

New phone books were distributed in advance of the move. Even the little round number stickers to go on the dials were provided in good time. The changes were fully and carefully described in *The Island Packet.* But a lot of Johnnies could not read and maybe wouldn't listen. This the Sojourner discovered to his grief on what might have been a quiet Sabbath morning. Along with all other residents of Sea Pines, he got the new exchange digits 671. But he also got as the other four digits 3391.

Hold your hats or hold the phone! With 785 before it, 3391 was, before Sunday, the number of the Plantation Club. And so far as many obtuse or illiterate phone users were concerned, that, with the alteration only of the exchange digits, had to be the Plantation Club number on Sunday, too. Generally the callers were apologetic, and to a point the Sojourner et al. were patient. Still, as the day passed with the ringing of the bells, he planned logical but drastic action. He decided to take the calls. Anybody who wanted a starting time should be given it in a clear and welcoming tone of voice.

"What time?"

"Any ole time."

About a reservation for dinner?

"Any number any time."

That should have made all the callers happy, at least until sometime after they hung up the phones. Of course, it might have caused a little puzzlement at the door of the dining room and a little confusion on the golf courses. But it would have provided some euphoria to the phoners until the moment of sudden and inexplicable frustration. It would have been no worse than keeping Johnny in after school because he hadn't done his reading lesson.

The situation at least demonstrated that any number can play at the business of wrong numbers. Also it demonstrated that man is still in command or in a state of profound confusion in our wonderful electronic age. The Hargray Telephone Company could work carefully and overtime, as it did, in preparing for the change. The new exchange was built in an architecture which better fits the pattern of Sea Pines than many of its condominiums. The connections were carefully made. Unfortunately, Hargray, like every other person, firm, and corporation, has to deal with people.

So let the bells ring! The hope is that even the most retarded will at last comprehend that they live in a changing world, including changing telephone numbers.

But if they don't, drastic measure may be necessary.

"Is this the Plantation Club?"

"Yes, sir!"

"This is Henry Jones. . . ."

"Oh, yes, Mr. Jones, I'm so glad you called. Captain Vance Fowler has been incessantly trying to get in touch with you. He said to tell you that he and Mr. Fraser wanted you to be their guest at the club whenever you can come for play or dinner or whatever."

"Who, me?"

"Yes, Mr. Jones, and they said be sure to bring all your friends."

The possibilities are limitless. Keep ringing.

June 8, 1972

Trip to the Island

People still go to islands, none more happily than to this one. Now to Hilton Head Island the traffic thickens, often with U-Hauls behind the cars. More and more come by plane—and the push is for more and bigger planes for more and more people. Problems of logistics remain in the trip to "the island." Nowadays it may be the trip in the compact to the condominium. It is interesting to recapture the pattern of moving to "the island" as recalled in a book of memoirs written for her children by Laura Witte Waring, of Charleston. Her son, Thomas Waring, now edits the *Charleston News and Courier.* She called her book *You Asked for It* (Charleston, 1941), and all of us should be grateful to have it.

Sullivan's Island was the place of her family's annual summer migration—only a little distance from the city, but a trip which called for elaborate planning and operations. Mrs. Waring described the move in the 1880s.

"When the day came around, activities started at daylight, with the drays and wagons drawn by horses coming into the yard.

"The chickens and ducks, already crated, were hoisted onto a wagon; the cow was led out, the horse and buggy hitched up and driven out; any other of the animals, such as a bear, or some

292

monkeys, and the dogs that were due to travel were lined up; the chicken, cow and horse feed were piled upon the drays, and thus the advance guard moved off to catch the early ferry boat.

"At about 8 o'clock, Philippe, the bird man, who was always in charge of the moving, having collected the trunks and baggage of the servants, assembled the barrels and boxes of food and wine, and superintended the loading of the wagons. Then he would appear with his assistants at the bedroom doors for the family trunks, tying up the sewing machine with crocus sacking and stout rope, and collecting the linen baskets and dolls' trunks from the halls and playroom. Those wagons, with Philippe along, caught the 10 o'clock trip of the ferry.

"Meanwhile, the completely furnished Island house had been strenuously cleaned from cupola to ground floor after Mr. Beasley, the Island carpenter, had done any necessary repairing; or perhaps the house may have been for weeks in the throes of painting and renovation. All beds, bureau drawers, wardrobes and cupboards had been washed and sunned, and everything was in readiness.

"Breakfast on that day was not as leisurely as usual, as the cook and one butler went off on the 10 o'clock ferry.

"The family had the morning to collect forgotten things, pack the silver basket to be taken with them, lock the book cases, cover the piano, oversee the cleaning and washing of ice boxes, bread and cake boxes.

"At half after 1 o'clock, they all sat down at the breakfast room table to dinner furnished by Barron, the famous Charleston negro caterer. The dinner seldom varied, consisting of steaks, broiled chickens, shrimp pâtés, rice, boiled potatoes, corn on the cob, fried egg plant (always called guinea squash in those days), sewee beans, string beans and stuffed tomatoes.

"From the dinner table we collected our books, dolls, bundles and the silver basket, and steel knives, and the family piled into the Island carriage, the rockaway, the landau being left in the stable in town. The servants went to the ferry wharf by horse car and we all reached the 'swift and elegant new side-wheel steamer *Sappho*' well in advance of her leaving at 3 o'clock.

"One butler was left behind to wash the dinner dishes and close the downstairs rooms, the upper floors having been attended to before dinner, and he came to the Island on the 5 o'clock boat trip.

"When the carriage reached the wharf, the family alighted and went on board the *Sappho,* sitting on the upper deck. The driver, with assistance of boat attendants, took the horses out of the shafts, led them on board, and then pulled the carriage aboard. The trip lasted three quarters of an hour; a stop at Mount Pleasant to leave or take on passengers or freight was only a delay of a few minutes on the 3 o'clock trip. The boat docked at the Island wharf at a quarter before 4, and was met by the mule drawn streetcars, carriages, buggies and wagons.

"The day of our move, our horses and carriage were brought off the boat and harnessed, the family climbed again into their places, the servants taking a mule car. Those street cars were large and open, with the row of seats running across the width of the car. Each was pulled by a pair of mules, driven by a colored driver, and a conductor, an Irishman named Batty Buckley, went from car to car during the ride collecting fares. Those cars stopped from door to door as a passenger alighted or got on.

"When the family arrived at their house, it was 4 o'clock; everything and everybody and all the animals were already at home; carts had met the various boat trips; trunks were in the right rooms, and the boxes, barrels, crates and bundles were waiting to be put into the store room, which was kept locked.

"With hardly a moment's wait, unpacking began. The silver was put in its rightful sideboard drawers, after they had been newly lined with fresh white paper; the groceries from the town house, as well as those ordered to be sent by freight from stores, were unpacked by the cook superintended by some of the family. The linen had to be put away by the maids; but each child, if old enough, unpacked for herself; the mosquito nets were hung, beds made and by supper time, the family was settled.

"Every detail had worked without a hitch; nothing had been forgotten; the Island windmill was turning; the Island tradesmen had delivered ice and bread; the foreign shells had been taken from the cupboard, dusted and arranged on the étagère, and summer life had started."

It was well they had so many strong black hands to help. Also, fortunately, they stayed from the end of June until the first of October. The business, still, must have been a remarkable mobilization by Mama.

June 15, 1972

Insiders and Outcasts

Some of those islanders outside the Sea Pines gate evidently feel as outcast as the penniless waif with his nose flattened against the candy-store window. Possibly they give an undue emphasis to the quality of the goodies inside. Yet, in proud South Carolina tradition, some feel locked out in a free land. Undoubtedly their sensibilities are bruised, as often happened on both sides in the old American "fence and no fence" controversy. That was set to music in the *Oklahoma* ballad to the effect that the farmer and the cowboy should be friends. So, somehow, those on the two sides of the Fraser fence should be more amiable.

A little objectivity will not hurt anybody in this matter. Clearly, the Sea Pines purpose is protective. There are some bums outside of Sea Pines. And despite the staff indicated by the size of its parking lot, Sea Pines lacks manpower to separate all the sheep from all the goats inside and outside. Evidently, however, much research has gone into its classification of mankind by bumper stickers. The right of some to enter is absolute; of some, limited. Some are classified by the clock. It was probably only an oversight that no special stickers are provided for those with an absolute right of entry based on the property rights in the graves of their fathers in the cemetery at Harbour Town.

The indisputable fact, however, is that Sea Pines acted clearly in conformity with an ancient South Carolina tradition. It goes at least as far back as 1846, when William Gregg established his cotton mill village at Graniteville, up the road near Branchville and Saint George. Gregg, whose purposes were certainly beneficent, made more rules to protect his private village than even Vance Fowler had done. He went further in his determination to protect his villagers even from themselves.

He laid it down, as Rule 1, that those who occupied houses in the village "will not be permitted to bring into the place any intoxicating liquors; and persons will not be permitted to continue in the service of the Company, who lend their aid directly or indirectly to the encouragement of those who vend liquors in the vicinity." He was concerned with the welfare of his villagers, old and young: "Parents will be held responsible for the orderly behavior of children. All *males* over 12 years of age will not be permitted to remain in idleness about the village." Also: "As the Sabbath is a day of rest and peace, no street sports, or disorderly conduct, either in the village or neighborhood will be permitted on that day." Finally: "All those occupying the Company's houses, who keep hogs, must have a convenient place for them in the back yard, and not allow them to run about the village of Graniteville."

Not all these rules may be necessary in Sea Pines. Perhaps some others should be added. Possibly adherence to them would make Sea Pines indeed worthy of protection from the contagions beyond its gates. All will do well to remember that "strait is the gate, and narrow is the way, which leadeth unto life, and few there be that find it." That could apply to the almost celestial south end of Hilton Head Island.

Still and but—perfection somehow should be shared. Not all outside the gates are such peasants as one of them has characterized himself as being or feeling. It is even possible that not all within the gates are the perfect plutocrats. Some adjustments might be possible despite present tensions. Certainly not all those within wish to stand siege against aroused adversaries. Not all without are ready to assail the battlements. Diplomacy is indicated, almost of an international character.

Who to effect it? Charles Fraser is too remote. Vance Fowler is too rigid in his often underlined declarations of principles. Possibly solutions might be found by Joseph T. Elvove, who is already recognized as the Kissinger of the first Fraser administration. If Kissinger could go to Tokyo to placate the Japanese, who felt sort of left out, Elvove ought to be able to make it to Coligny Circle.

June 22, 1972

Dalmatian Man

It seems certain that, among those who made plans for a barbecue to raise funds for the good cause of the volunteer firemen on Hilton Head Island, no one remembered a one-time reputed relation between roast pig and fire. Others may recall Charles Lamb's essay on the origin of roast pig. If memory serves, it related that once long ago pigs were kept only as house pets. Then one day the house burned down. Its pig was caught in the flames. The master of the porcine pet put his finger on the poor crisp piggy. As the finger was burned, he snatched it back, with a little meat upon it. Ruefully, he put it in his mouth to cool it. Then he got not merely relief but the taste of a delicacy unknown before. The relationship between burning house and roast pig was established. There followed a succession of houses burned down in order to get roast pig.

The volunteer firemen of Hilton Head Island know better than that. They have reached the state of enlightenment where they know that serving roast pig plus barbecue sauce may be helpful in helping them keep houses from burning down. This event will be in addition to the annual firemen's ball. Actually, there will be two stands at this barbecue event: one at Turtle Lane Cabana and the other outside the Golden Gate at the firehouse on Cordillo Parkway.

The success of this Fourth of July feast is certainly assured by the activity of the firemen's friend Colonel Fred W. Hallagan. He knows much more than that you don't have to burn down a house to get roast pig. Possibly, as promoter, he wasted talents in military service which would have been formidable in sales and the services of benevolent causes like this one. At the gala Firemen's Ball last winter, the number of tickets for sale related rigidly to the size of Planter's Hall. So they were limited to one hundred and fifty. Single-handedly Hallagan sold the equivalent of ninety-four. No wonder the grateful volunteers gave him a plaque attesting their praise. They knew him as the man who runs ahead of the volunteers, financially clearing their way.

Possibly out of oversight the volunteer firemen did not give the energetic colonel a title along with the plaque. One is clearly indicated. As the one who runs ahead, he could well be given a title drawn from the folklore of fire fighting. One thing the volunteer firemen here lack is the beautiful, white-and-black-spotted coach dog who once ran before the galloping horses on the way to conflagrations. Though horses are no longer used in these modern times, many firehouses still keep as symbols and pets beautiful, sleek Dalmatians. Nothing would seem more proper than that Hallagan be declared the Dalmatian of Hilton Head Island fire fighters.

Slim and swift-moving, with a bark that is never a bite, but with real qualities as a barker, as his prowess in ticket selling indicates, Hallagan fits into fire-fighting folklore as hand into glove. Or, perhaps better stated, as hand reaches for the funds for firemen. We can be sure that he will be present when the pigs roast on the Fourth of July. We can also be sure that more other people will be present than would be there if Hallagan had not run ahead with the leaps of a beautiful, graceful creature long known as the firemen's best friend.

Has anybody here seen Hallagan? You bet your life everybody has who might possibly have the price of a ticket to the barbecue. Come one, come all. The more roast pig consumed, the prospect is that fewer houses will be.

June 29, 1972

Shipyard Gate

> . . . Everything that grows
> Holds in perfection but a little moment.

Many Hilton Head lovers have contemplated that poetic dictum with increasing fearfulness. Some, indeed, feel that the little moment of perfection on Hilton Head Island is behind them, and that before them is a shore which could go the way of Nineveh and Tyre, Atlantic City and Myrtle Beach, even the obscenities of Florida.

Any item justifying release from such fears is welcome. It is nice to be able to cling to another quotation: "A thing of beauty is a joy forever."

Well, *forever* is a long word even in times of concrete and Cor-Ten steel. But it can be said and ought to be said that no work of art, architecture, or imagination on this island has excelled the entrance monuments—they can hardly be called signs—recently erected at the entrances to Shipyard Plantation. Certainly they deserve more than the flash of appreciation by persons passing in speeding automobiles. They are, to say it quietly, beautiful.

Bigger, taller signs and showpieces have been erected here. Certainly more costly ones have been even taller, bigger, and maybe more startling. But Joseph Sonderman, of Charlotte, who designed these markers, deserves recognition not merely as an industrial designer but as an artist. He has done other work here—much for Sea Pines. He is now planning the interiors for the River Club that Sea Pines is building at its River Hills Plantation near Charlotte. Also, Joe Sonderman has not been above designing the package for a nationally retailed bread. He has added his artistry to chairs and airplane interiors. As a man working on the fringes of both architecture and advertising, he might be regarded by some as more of a huckster than an aesthete. Certainly both advertising and architecture would be served by the creativeness he has shown in these entrance pieces he has made for Shipyard Plantation.

But wait a minute: One of the things he has rejected on these handsome standards is the word *plantation,* which has certainly been overworked on this shore as a euphemism for subdivision or development. Simplicity is the central element of these works of art in advertising. Their cores were cast on the sites in wooden forms. There is no attempt to conceal the lines where the concrete seeped into the cracks in the forms. Indeed, they provide a rugged finish which removes any suggestion of the slick in conception. The four-sided pieces bearing the single word *Shipyard* were cast elsewhere and cut by a skilled stonemason. The stylized anchors are made of Cor-Ten steel, which rusts to an exactly desirable patina, then keeps that color ever after.

One sign, of course, does not set a standard for the Island. But there are other evidences of awareness of the importance at the entry places of "plantations." While disclosed so far only in photographs, the Palmetto Dunes directive markers are being given the importance they are due—and in this case, overdue. They promise to add much to the charm of this lovely area interlaced by canals. And Gene Martin, at the bulging Red & White, is indicating understanding that even a parking lot need not be only a desert of pavement.

The possibility of perfection persists here beyond a little moment. The Chamber of Commerce, in its new location on Pope Avenue, is securing a new sign, fairer than the stark billboard which served its old location. People who love this island may still dream about its possibilities. They might even dream or hope that it will be spared from a rearing, garish, and vulgar star over a proposed hostelry of a chain which has produced a galaxy of gaudiness along the highways of America.

We can't count on dreams, but we can at least hope for deliverance from nightmares.

July 6, 1972

Handle with Care

On this island, supposedly the place of people retiring from practical, no-foolishness careers, it is well for everyone to be careful about quoting poetry. The gentleman selling mutual funds can recite in stirring tones the whole of Macaulay's "Horatius at the Bridge." And with a few highballs in him he will sonorously recite it if you don't stop him. In less strenuous vein Edward Lear's "The Owl and the Pussy-Cat" never was rendered by a more charming *cantatrice* than Katherine Derby. Virginia Howe recited "Spartacus the Gladiator" as she rippled through a wide-ranging repertoire. A former steel salesman will quickly correct anybody who stumbles over a line from Byron and himself will put a special local connotation into:

> The isles of Greece; the isles of Greece!
> Where burning Sappho loved and sung. . . .

The works of Dorothy Parker, Ogden Nash, even Robert W. Service must here be handled with care. And if you slip on anybody's favorite poet, you've had it—or you'll get it. The Sojourner knows.

Another sojourner, Mrs. Percival Bachelder, who often comes from Maine to visit her son Phil and his wife, Barbara, here, caught this writer putting a wrong word into a verse by Edna St. Vincent Millay. Promptly and politely she brought it to his attention. Also, when she got back to Maine, she reported the error to a friend in Portland. And that friend reported the sad story of the lapse back to the culprit here. *The Packet* gets around. So do its sins.

The people of Maine are on guard for this graceful poet who was born at 200 Broadway in Rockland eighty years ago. Somehow those eighty years seem incredible. Not only did Miss Millay begin her chorusing career when she was nineteen, she also seemed forever young, and ought not to be dead but dancing now. Mrs. Bachelder in affection spoke of her as spending much time on a tiny island near Portland, and that made her correctly quoted lines worthy of greater respect on this other island today.

Poets as well as stockbrokers have long been seeking serenity on islands and not always finding it. It is difficult to recall that some of the 365 islands in Casco Bay—one for every day in the year—were already crowding when Edna Millay was young. Characteristically, she chose one of the most isolated of them. Ragged Island, where she lived, was so remote from crowding that in pre-Millay days it had been the rendezvous of lawbreakers—notably a gang of counterfeiters. That must have added an element of drama not unwelcome later to a lady singing in the winds of solitude.

Now Miss Millay is dead, and sometimes all islands seem besieged. Indeed, as long ago as 1937, when Miss Millay was no longer quite young, an authoritative work on the state of Maine used words about that—familiar sounding here and now. The islands then, this book said, were "frequented by city folk who desire temporary retreat from the stress of modern living to the simplicity, privacy, and independence of insular life."

Evidently Miss Millay moved, seeking such serenity. For a while she lived in the Ring Island section of Massachusetts, where earlier, in the Merrimack River estuary, boats were built and fish were dried on racks in the sun. Perhaps discovering the vulnerability of islands, she moved to a farm in the Berkshires, where she died. There was change even then evident in the wide meadows, small lakes, and elm-bordered streams. The lovely area had attracted residents on spacious estates. But long before the 1930s ended the estates were broken up into realty developments. Old-timers lamented the swift cars which whirled upon the roads. And even then: "Nearly every owner of a car on the eastern seaboard and many from the Middle and Far West at some time or other tour the Berkshires." The air is not quite as fresh as it was on the many islands of Maine.

The words of poets may never be altered. The same thing cannot be said of their worlds.

July 13, 1972

Lightning Look

Certainly most presidents of most chambers of commerce would accept with unadulterated glee a prestigious listing of their communities as among the "world's top 125 resorts." Possibly Hilton Head Island's new, vigilant C of C leader is hard to please. Certainly Charlie Doughtie was somewhere between a grin and aghast with a copy of the July 1972 issue of *Town & Country* in his hands.

This magazine, which undertakes to maintain the mythology of High Society, took, as it says, a "lightning look" at resorts from Austria to Yugoslavia and flashed upon Hilton Head in the middle. However, *Town & Country*'s looker—one Ted Burke—must have been traveling in outer space when he evaluated and described this island.

Mr. Burke listed sixteen resorts in the United States, ranging from Aspen to White Sulphur Springs. To Hilton Head he gave two stars, along with six other places. Eight resorts were rated above it, only one of the sixteen below it—poor old Hobe Sound. Oddly enough, at the top of the list, in the company only of Palm Beach, he put Vail, in Colorado. He gave more words (fifty-three of them) to Hilton Head than to any other place, but his key sentence about it read, "Alligators snooze in the lagoons, rich retirees play canasta, and everyone's mad for pecans, fireworks and Ne-Hi."

Certainly there should be no revolution of resentment about this. Somewhere on this island, though as yet undiscovered by anybody but Mr. Burke, there may be a canasta player—maybe even players enough to make a game, however many that is. Certainly there are some with an addiction to pecans; some, even to peanuts. But fireworks are frowned upon. Ne-Hi was brought into the history of this island only by another lightning visitor, who in the midst of the BASF episode described Fred Hack as drinking vodka and Ne-Hi in the morning. Fred then said he could deny that categorically. He never had drunk any Ne-Hi.

To the stars Mr. Burke bestowed on resorts in his lightning look, he added letters: F for fashionable; J for *joie de vivre* and high spirits; Q for quiet; T for too many tourists at peak season; W for winter sports; Y for yachting—and a dollar sign for expensive. All Hilton Head Island got was a Q and a $. Perhaps the other letters can be relinquished without too much protest. But there certainly are many in residence here who feel that that T for too many visitors is more and more an accolade this Q place deserves.

Charlie Doughtie is entitled to his amused amazement at this Burke phantasmagoria of all the great resorts of the world as it pinpoints this shore. Still, high above the body of his misinformation Burke does blazon one lightning stroke of truth: "Today's enchanting fishing village can be tomorrow's skyscraping eyesore. Resorts change—sometimes for the better, more often for the worse."

This lightning line should be placed over the door of the Hilton Head Island Chamber of Commerce. And on this island canasta players, pecan addicts, pyrotechnicians, and Ne-Hi guzzlers should never forget it. There is some old line to the effect that out of the mouths of babes and sucklings cometh wisdom. We can carry that line forward to the realization that some truth may be found even in the writing of a "lightning look" reporter who obviously flashed through here with his eyes shut, if, indeed, he ever bolted by at all.

July 20, 1972

Ah Wilderness!

Ah Wilderness! There are, of course, other shores that seize and hold the affections of men and women fleeing "from the pinpricks and hammer blows of machined existence." Howard T. Walden, in his charming book *Anchorage Northeast* (Morrow), describes his happy haven on the Nova Scotian coast. Walden's retreat at Jordan Bay is at the end of an unpaved road, with no permanent neighbor within a mile. The only air-thickener there is fog. The only alien noise is the occasional flight of an airplane far overhead, so infrequent as to arouse curiosity. And "environmental peace, so brittle and circumscribed at home, has here a breadth and stability."

And yet, he writes, on arrival there, of "light, warmth and the lively purring of utilities . . . hot water is in the taps . . . ice cubes are ready for the opening day libation." Evidently some wire runs the mile from that house to its nearest neighbor. Man in his flight from "a national principle of uproar" still likes to hear the "purring of utilities." Air-conditioning machines are not essential in Nova Scotia, but in the search for serenity on Hilton Head Island some of us, if we had to choose, might prefer the purring of the utilities to the sounds of the wind in the palmettoes and the birds singing in the oaks. And particularly in July.

Incidental Intelligence:

At about 3:20 P.M., Wednesday, July 20, 1972, ten cars backed up at the Sea Pines Drive gate waiting for admittance.

A pile of empty soft-drink bottles at Heritage Farm suggests that to organic vegetables might be added nature's own old-fashioned persimmon and locust beers.

The new Sea Pines welcome station suggests that Charles Fraser's next project here might be a ski slope.

Ben-Hur never had it so good: Burton Block & Concrete Company has added eight new concrete mixer trucks for use on Hilton Head Island.

Sometimes it is hard to tell friend from foe. South Carolina BASF backers called this the island of the fat cats. Now Ralph Nader's report on the environmental crisis in the Savannah area refers to our island as "a retirement paradise for rich old Yankees." "Fat cats" at least had a sleek sound but "rich old Yankees" somehow sounds like senile, alien Scrooges.

This year the Roeslers of Calibogue Cay have the best crop of weeds in their yard that they have ever produced.

People talking indignantly now about litter may as well remember that more than five years ago our neighbor and early settler Henry Lawrence wrote a poem which he called "Dirge." It ran like this:

> Why, old Ocean, do you moan and cry
> And tug fog blanket close about your face?
> I think quite well I know the reason why
> You weep and try to hide in deep disgrace.
>
> Across your bosom beer cans rust and roll,
> Rubbish and whiskey bottles, human litter,
> Discarded garbage bipeds scatter as they stroll
> Would give me indigestion, make me bitter.

I weep with you Ocean, as each bite you take
Of dunes you cleanly built and man is buying
But adds to dirty meals, keeps you awake,
And restless, and ashamed—and crying.

July 27, 1972

Crowding the Vineyard

This is the season on Hilton Head Island when the cocktail circuit slows and the fat cats make peanut butter sandwiches for their grandchildren. It is also the season when, as the slices are spread —often with jelly added—the complaint grows about the summer crowding. To it the grandchildren—other people's grandchildren, of course—contribute, often teetering on bicycles while the thickened traffic roars beside them. Change and complaint, however, are certainly not limited to this island. Possibly the central stage of this summer's island irritation and congregation is the once staid and certainly venerable resort Martha's Vineyard.

Well-heeled Yankees and others had their summer estates there before most of us newcomers, Yankee or not, on Hilton Head Island began to make our money or start our Social Security payments. Poets and playwrights shared its wind-swept solitude before placards in the upheld hands of the bearded young became a notable form of literature. Now on the Vineyard, lines are drawn and voices raised. The strident debate is about a bill (of a U.S. Senator familiar with the terrain but once confused in it) to preserve and protect the lovely island by federal controls, plus a $20 million land-purchasing

311

fund. A first "island trust" would be created in a combination public recreation area and private preserve.

Party lines and political prejudices have been disregarded in the debate. The dither about Chappaquiddick Pond this year seems to center around the fact that three acres on its shore sold for $125,-000. Some old-timers are disturbed because half-acre building lots on the island, which contains a good deal less land than Hilton Head, now bring as much as $5,000. In comparison with Hilton Head prices, such costs indicate that the explosion has evidently not been in the pocketbook. But people—and especially summer people!

Such a long-time island guardian as Henry Beetle Hough (pronounced *Huff*), editor of the *Vineyard Gazette,* favors the "island trust" plan. He says, "The bill would give us protection at last by cutting the speculation and development." But Robert Carroll, real-estate dealer and hotel operator, wants no such application of federal brakes to local explosion. Says he, "This is a bill to protect a few people from ever having any neighbors."

In the good old summertime at least the Vineyarders are certainly not threatened with loneliness. *Time* magazine reports that the permanent population of Martha's Vineyard is about ten thousand. If so, that is quickly up from the figure fixed in an official census in 1966. Then, Dukes County, which contains the island, had only a total population of about six thousand. The summer population now, however, is about fifty thousand—nearly double the summer crowd of ten years ago. Also today, in the changing multitude, five hundred thousand passengers come each year by ferryboat. Martha's Vineyard is not blessed by a toll-free bridge. The airplane is not unknown on the Massachusetts shore.

Looking even further out to sea, Vineyarders note that on Nantucket Island, where there are now about three thousand gray-shingle houses, this spring 1,884 new house lots were being planned for development. Also, the water supply on that outer island is already endangered, it is reported, and Hummock Pond is rank with sewage overflow. In comparison Chappaquiddick is still pure. But planners on the Vineyard say that "once the ground water is polluted this place is finished." Such dire predictions do not seem to deter those building and buying the new clusters of homes on Martha's Vineyards's own South Beach.

Perhaps the prophets of doom should be disregarded. Martha's Vineyard may remain, as one of its literary residents described it long ago, "a land of old town, new cottages, high cliffs, white sails, green fairway, salt water, wild fowl and the steady pull of an ocean breeze."

It is also a land where more and more and more peanut butter sandwiches are being spread. And, please, put a little bit of jelly on the bread.

August 3, 1972

Forten to Fraser

The world do move. Even in South Carolina. Some elders here are old enough to remember when "Cotton Ed" Smith walked out of a Democratic national convention because a black minister had been asked to pray. Seeing red over a black question, Cole Blease in the Senate cried, "To hell with the Constitution." Now, in 1972, comes the news of a sort of joint venture of Sea Pines Plantation and the National Association for the Advancement of Colored People. The scene in which Charles Fraser watched the signing of an agreement by which Sea Pines provided $36,000 for an NAACP program of title clearance, planning, and land beautification in the black community seems an historic one. Actually, the NAACP has deeper roots on this South Carolina shore than Sea Pines.

Some Southerners long tried to make the NAACP seem an alien, intruding organization. In doing so, they conveniently forgot or historically overlooked the strange story of South Carolina's role in the cast of characters at the organization's inception. First, there was Charlotte Forten. She was, indeed, a stranger here. The mulatto daughter of a Philadelphia sailmaker, she was one of those Northern teachers who came here during the Civil War to help the recently

314

freed little black children. The journal she kept in this island region has become a classic of descriptive writing about the Low Country. She came here as a protégé of the poet John Greenleaf Whittier, who wrote a Christmas song for her shrill, young pupils to sing. She went north after the war, but others like her founded, on Saint Helena Island, the Penn School, which so long served as a light in the clearing of much black ignorance and poverty.

Then there were the Grimké boys. In South Carolina aristocracy the Grimkés ranked with the Ravenels, the Pinckneys, and the Prioleaus. Still, in the 1830s two daughters of this wealthy, aristocratic, and conservative Charleston family became ardent abolitionists, freed the slaves who had come to them as a part of the family estate, and moved north. However, they left behind a brother, Henry Grimké, who sired sons by a slave, Nancy Weston. When he died in 1852, Henry Grimké willed his slaves to his eldest son, E. Montague Grimké, specifying, however, that his slave children—the half brothers of their new owner—be freed. The injunction to free them was not carried out. Freedom came to the slave brothers only with the collapse of the Confederacy.

Then Francis and Archibald, half brothers of Montague, moved north and enrolled in Lincoln University, a college for Negroes in Oxford, Pennsylvania. Making a remarkable record there, the brothers came to the attention of their white aunts, who publicly recognized them and gave them financial aid as recognized members of the great Grimké family. Archibald graduated from the Harvard Law School with distinction. Francis entered the Princeton Theological Seminary. A man of uncompromising righteousness, he was known as the "Black Puritan." In 1878 Francis married Charlotte Forten, the keeper of the beautiful journal.

Both these brothers of slave and aristocratic South Carolina lineage were active in efforts to advance the black race. Charlotte Forten Grimké's journal has been described as revealing "undying belief in human decency and equality." Her husband preached that cause in Washington in the Fifteenth Street Presbyterian Church, of which he was long minister. As lawyer, speaker, and writer, Archibald Henry Grimké was more prominent in the organization of the NAACP, first as president of the Boston branch, then as vice-president of the national organization. In 1919 he was given the Spingarn medal, the highest honor annually bestowed by the NAACP upon an American citizen of African descent. It is interesting that he was also descended from the second landgrave of South Carolina, a title of nobility not lightly bestowed in that early day.

Charlotte Forten Grimké died in 1914, but her beautiful journal of residence on this shore was only published, to much acclaim, in 1953. Certainly blacks and whites now can appreciate her loving description of this land. To it, obviously, the NAACP comes to Charles Fraser's welcome and aid not as a stranger.

August 10, 1972

A Sentimental Plea

"A sentimental plea," Mrs. Walter Mingledorff said she wanted to make.

Mrs. Mingledorff owns Belvoir Plantation, across which the highway department proposes to run a new short route between Beaufort and Hilton Head Island. That may be the best way to speed the traffic between town and island. It may not be the best route. But one thing certain is that Mrs. Mingledorff's plea is not merely a "sentimental" one. Her late husband bought Belvoir to preserve its beautiful trees. And, like many of the rest of us, Mrs. Mingledorff has recently seen the spoilation of Bluffton by the destruction of so many of the trees which gave the town almost its only claim to distinction.

Perhaps this was not a wanton chopping. Possibly it seemed a very practical procedure to those who ordered the destruction in the name of Progress. Maybe it will help speed the traffic, which recently seemed almost too hell-bent to Bluffton. Safety may be served. But no one should be surprised that Mrs. Mingledorff, seeing the spoilation in the little town, may fear the results of new highway pushed headlong to divide her plantation with a paved swath where the

317

loveliest trees now grow, bearing veils of moss swinging in the sun.

Is the lady merely "sentimental"? Only a fool could think so. The truth of the matter is that the most "practical" possession this corner of South Carolina contains is beauty. It is the only real and substantial basis of its hope for progress. Indigo passed. Rice lapsed. Cotton fell before the boll weevil. Phosphates were more profitably mined elsewhere. But in recent years the loveliness of the land has attracted more people and money to the area than anything else at any time. And whether we like it or not, there are those who would destroy this gorgeousness which has produced the golden egg.

Undoubtedly, as business has grown as the result of new influx, there are a lot of us on Hilton Head and in Beaufort who would like to speed passage between the places. That would certainly be convenient. It would reduce, by dividing it, the traffic which now so often clogs a single lane. But certainly speed and convenience should not be the only considerations in planning a new road or anything else.

In a conflict which seemed almost to make Beaufort and Hilton Head feuding neighbors, the polluting progress which BASF would have meant was prevented. That seemed to be a big dragon against which all the Saint Georges of Hilton Head arrayed themselves. But big dragons are not always more dangerous than small snakes. And Beaufort County today is more threatened by many small bites at its beauty here at home than by any monster from far away.

Small wounds multiply. They could be fatal. As Mercutio in *Romeo and Juliet* reported of the wound he received from the sword of Tybalt: "No, 'tis not so deep as a well, nor so wide as a church-door; but 'tis enough, 'twill serve." As one such wound killed a man, so many could destroy the loveliest corner of a state. And anyone can see how the small wounds multiply here now. A greater injury, such as a highway built without the careful regard for the forested places it pierces, could do the most "practical" damage to the Low Country. New roads in this area should be recognized as only passages in the service of a land the one asset of which is its appearance.

Maybe Mrs. Mingledorff is just a woman of sentiment making a sentimental plea. Engineers may scoff at her ideas about road building. But even those whose only interest in the land is its exploitation may well take warning from her fears. The bulldozer is loose in the land. The honky-tonks are not far behind them. And one thing certain is that Beaufort County is not immune to mutilation.

August 17, 1972

Crape Myrtle Days

A man can get a message. And when the last petal of what had been magnificent deep red pompons falls from the crape myrtle tree, he knows that summer is over. Maybe school has not started. Some resort operators still wait for the bonanza of Labor Day. The temperature stays in the nineties. But just as the crape myrtle and others had marked the summit of summertime, so the falling petals bring the news of summer's end. There is nothing sad about it, though it signals the dispersal soon of children to their schools, the separation of young lovers whose casual coming together on the shore had seemed momentarily eternal. Some grandparents even add a chuckle to a sigh as clamor quiets in their houses. The medical center turns from pediatrics to geriatrics again.

The crape myrtle, of course, is not responsible for all that. But it deserves recognition of its place in the calendar along with the first jonquil and the much-more-often-mentioned last rose of summer. Yet somehow, in comparison with other no-more-lovely flowering things, recognition of its importance has been neglected. People set up deer fences to protect azaleas. Camellias—or ca-may'-yahs—are crowned with praise. Last spring people spoke softly, as in personal grief, when late frost blighted and browned the oleanders. Yet much as people obviously enjoy them, little public praise is given to the crape myrtle. The official South Carolina guidebook, which goes into ecstasies about old gardens and new ones and the flowers within them, passes the crape myrtle by without one printed word. Perhaps there is something snobbish about this. The crape myrtle, which can take its proud and flaming place in landscaped gardens beside tenderly cared for camellias and azaleas, is not averse to growing in brilliant color beside the unpainted shack and beside the cabbages and collards. It somehow seems tough and delicate at the same time—and approximately immortal. A hurricane seemed to uproot and totally demolish one particularly lovely tree. The site where it stood was raked over. Yet in the following spring a whole company of little tendrils began their growth there into the blossoming of the future.

Possibly its long familiarity is a reason for its lack of public praise. Both Alva Hines Cunningham and Nancy Butler testify to its antiquity hereabouts. It was, says Alva, commonplace in Carolina gardens in the 1700s, even then a long way from its Asian origins. Nancy hears that the crape myrtles around the air force base at Charleston are the descendants of those André Michaux planted in his famous gardens when he came to Charleston in 1787. He arrived after a botanical pilgrimage which led him from the Jardin des Plantes to England, the Auvergne, the Pyrenees, Persia, and along the Tigris and Euphrates rivers. Certainly when Dr. Alexander Garden, for whom the gardenia is named, came to South Carolina in 1753, he must have found the crape myrtle already glorifying the summer and marking its end.

The gorgeous flowering tree has always had its lovers here. One old Beaufort story is about the crape myrtle and the devotion of John Jeremiah Theus Pope and his wife Mary Frampton Townsend. Pope always called her "My Mary," as if that were one word. A frail woman, she planted many crape myrtles around the house he had built for her as her health failed. When she died he moved a large tree from her garden and planted it by her grave in the old Baptist churchyard on Saint Helena Island. When—with other Beaufort planters—he fled in the Civil War, he wrote back most worried about one thing. He was fearful that, while he was in exile, the transplanted tree would die with no one to water it. A practical historian has bluntly reported that it did die, as now "no crape myrtle grows beside her grave." Maybe not only ladies but also crape myrtles are subject to mortality. Certainly, however, other crape myrtles circle the countryside in which Mary Pope lies. Ladies die, petals fall, summers end. But beloved or neglected, the glory of the crape myrtle will not soon pass away in this so-much-festooned land.

August 24, 1972

Motorized Nightmare

Hardly audible above the roar of the motors is the whisper that there are no traffic lights at the busy and busier intersections on the island because developers do not wish to have here, hanging high for all to see, this symbol of urbanized America. After all, this is a quiet island, and don't you forget it! There are miles of golden beaches and green golf courses, and to other forms of recreation is now added the game of trying to get a parking place in Coligny Plaza. What the situation is going to be when Fraser, Roller, Don Peterson, et al. get their new inns, condominiums, and apartment buildings completed in this area is not any man's guess. It is every man's certainty and possible motorized nightmare. Even now, lives are taken in hands daily by those trying to get from the bank, medical center, and post office into Pope Avenue. The way to the mainland is certainly a narrow path. And the one bridge is a cork to an old bottle into which a hell of a lot of new wine has been poured.

It is no wonder that Wilton Graves, as member of the state highway commission from this district, often wears a harried look. There is fussing around him as to a shorter road to Beaufort. Of course,

Beaufort businesssmen want more people to come to their town
from Hilton Head by a quicker route. But it is natural, too, that Mrs.
Mingledorff does not much want traffic cutting her plantation in two
where now lovely trees stand.

As the man in the middle, Graves does not possess unlimited
millions for road building and has a right to be worried. So does
this island and this county. One day another highway commissioner
from another area will take Graves's place. And, as can be expected
in South Carolina and everywhere else in the world, he will see the
road needs of his own area with much more clarity than those of
this area.

All this new wine—or carbon monoxide—in the old bottle of
Hilton Head Island certainly needs attention—and now! As South
Beach grows, the question may be, not a shorter route to Beaufort,
but rather a better route to Coligny Circle. In this season of many
polls, Sea Pines—in helpful curiosity—has asked its residents questions about their preferences, their incomes, and other things. One
question was whether they were satisfied with the road maintenance. A clearer answer could be expected to that than to whether
Nixon is going to beat McGovern in November. (However, as this
was written, crews with big, yellow equipment were at work on
Plantation Drive, widening and smoothing the road and presumably
also removing the long-lasting, built-in booby trap of an overele-
vated manhole. By November, as drivers and Democrats here may
hope, the road vote, like the Presidential vote, might change.)

In all this, there is the tale of two cities and an island. As Hilton
Head grows, both Savannah and Beaufort will be more anxious for
island customers. Bargain hunters have discovered that it no longer
costs seventy-five cents to go to Savannah. You can buy tickets and
make the return trip for twenty cents. A shorter road to Beaufort
might cut costs in time and money. With its naval hospital and
commissary, Beaufort has a captive clientele in many of Hilton
Head's old soldiers and sailors. Savannah has more places to shop
and eat. The time might come when island residents might be
caught in indecision between the equal appeal of both places—like
the donkey that starved to death between two equally distant and
equally appealing bales of hay.

The main problem for islanders, however, is the island. They are in no danger of starving to death with restaurants equal to—or better than—those in any neighboring places. There is talk that people here won't have to go off forever to get their cars serviced. The number of shops increases. More people may soon be coming to Hilton Head from Savannah and Beaufort than came to those places from Hilton Head. Inadequate parking here could become more inadequate. Crowded roads here could become more crowded. Lower tolls and a shorter road may serve our neighbors. But what Hilton Head Island needs most is help in a hurry on this side of that one bottleneck bridge.

August 31, 1972

Nixon Didn't Sleep Here

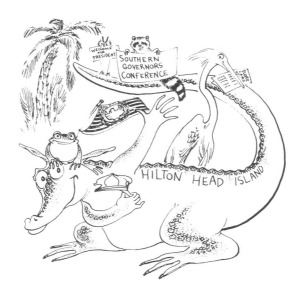

So Hilton Head Island will have to wait longer to entertain a President. Richard Nixon, involved in larger concerns on another island, won't be able to join the Southern governors here in their problems and play. It could be, of course, that history may count on at least a pre-Presidential visit in the persons of either Spiro Agnew or George McGovern. Both are willing to give history that right. But as of now Hilton Head is even behind Daufuskie in Presidential visitations.

George Washington was close enough to make a visit here when he passed through Beaufort in 1791. But the only American President who ever set foot on Hilton Head came here in May 1865, not to enjoy the island's charm and beauty but, it seems safe to say (reluctantly though, considering his dignity), not quite kicking and screaming. He was President Jefferson Davis of the recently defunct Confederate States of America. With him was his wife—the proud spitfire Varina. No social graces were offered her four children. Indeed, on a soldier-barracked shore there must have been few children except the newly freed black ones. In white society, the only women were the missionaries who had come to teach the black

babies. The amenities were largely those of a male variety on Robbers Row. It was, in much, a homesick shore on which the Davis visit
signaled for many the hope of going home. And there were boys
then as anxious to get out of South Carolina as some are now to
get out of Southeast Asia.

Even within the Confederate prison party, some relations were
stiff then. Vice-President Alexander H. Stephens, who was in it,
made no such amiable combination with his chief as the Nixon-
Agnew couple suggest. Indeed, in history the Davis-Stephens team
was more like a Nixon-McGovern or a McGovern-Nixon combination might be now. The diminutive Stephens, weighing less than
a hundred pounds, did not bend or bow to the rigid, militant Davis.
No fuss and feathers marked the occasion. Davis, Stephens, others
were sternly interrogated by a forgotten Union general named Brat-
ton. Then, little exposed to the curious who crowded about the
wharf near Fort Walker, the Hilton Head visitors were put aboard
the steamer *Clyde*, bound for Fortress Monroe, Virginia, and the
then uncertain ideas of Yankee justice which awaited them there.

After that, no more Presidents of any kind came to Hilton Head.
Legend that Theodore Roosevelt came here to hunt is apparently
baseless. There was hardly anybody here to be jealous when Daufuskie received the next Presidential visit to this area. No tenseness
marked that visit. The eminent guest this time was Calvin Coolidge,
who undoubtedly kept cool even on a hot island. He came, not to
meet Southern governors, but just to fish. Sheriff J. E. McTeer, chief
guardian of history hereabouts, suggests that his hosts were Gus
Ohman and Marion Dunning. Ohman, retired lighthouse keeper,
was, Sheriff McTeer says, "known as the King of Daufuskie, & entertained many distinguished Americans." Dunning came often on his
yacht to Daufuskie. He was collector of customs at Savannah and
Prohibition administrator for this district "but above all prominent
in the K.K.K. from which he derived considerable revenue." No
stenographic records of proceedings were made on that trip. Few
would have been necessary in the case of the laconic Coolidge.
There seems to be no record either as to the fishing luck Yankee
Cal had in such Southern company on the onetime secession shore.

In terms of Hilton Head's luck now, the inability of President
Nixon to come this time suggests the fish story about the biggest
one that got away. He will be missed by many. But maybe, as a man

seeking unity behind his candidacy, he is having better luck with the Japanese in Hawaii. There were rumors that while all wanted the President's presence there was some rivalry in hospitality. Joe Elvove's house on Beach Lagoon in Sea Pines was said to be being energetically swept in readiness for arrival. But there were at least whispers that a place was being prepared for him in Port Royal. The movements of advance agents caused some confusion in conjecture. Security, which must be tight to protect a President, may leave hospitable hopes in a state of suspension. Those most eager may be most sadly disappointed, and in an election year the purpose of politicians is not to disappoint anybody.

The island has enough to welcome in the distinguished array of governors, one or another of whom might become a President and leave us the memory of the time when he visited Hilton Head. Such chances exist also with Agnew and McGovern. Maybe, when history gets around to recording, we will have had a lot of Presidents visiting us this week. Hope doesn't hedge any bets, and there is hospitality enough here to go 'round. But the historical markers reading "RICHARD MILHOUS NIXON SLEPT HERE" can be put in storage for the time being. Still the beds may best be kept made and the front doorknob kept polished, As he travels everywhere, there is always the possibility that Kissinger may come.

September 3, 1972

Move to the Mountains

As remembered, it was a fantastic song of those years ago when most people only counted a single roof above them. It went like this:

> I've a shooting box in Scotland
> And a château in Touraine.
> I've a silly little chalet
> In the Interlaken Valley
> And a hacienda in Spain.
> I've a private fjord in Norway
> And a villa close to Rome.
> Oh, it's mighty nice to know,
> Wherever I go
> That I'm always close to home, sweet home.

Perhaps those lyrics are nearer to reality now than they were then. Hilton Head neighbors are now enjoying the mountain breezes at their other places at Hound Ears or Grandfather Mountain. Some may soon be securing second shelter in such places as Mushroom Park (honestly named for its treetop dwellings), High Meadows, and Uncity, now spreading like the rhododendron or the ginseng weed

329

all over the North Carolina mountains. Some are as plush as the big houses at Port Royal. And at Mill Ridge, between Linville and Boone in the skiing belt, one developer is offering a "second home" in round design for as little as $13,000, with only ten percent down. Maybe a revised version of the old song should go:

> It's no longer entirely out of my reach
> To have a Sealoft in Sea Pines, a chalet at Beech.

However, some prices also rise like Mount Mitchell and Clingmans Dome. A survey at Beech Mountain showed that more than fifty percent of the purchasers have family incomes of more than $26,000 a year and dwellings in the higher brackets also. Both might be even bigger at Hound Ears and the Grandfather Mountain Golf and Country Club.

Some of this may be news to those who are much aware of what has been going on here since Frank Schaefer confided to Charles Fraser the amazing facts about condominiums. Not all are aware of what is happening in the hills of Appalachia. Certainly that region can no longer be a label for a land of one-gallus mountaineers and their calico women. The cabins in the laurel are now totally electric, and the newcomers in the coves generally take their spirits from Scotland and not from the stills beside the creeks. Those creeks and the instant lakes into which they run are regularly resupplied with trout so that no fisherman need be long impatient. The winter-glistening ski slopes are beautiful in the summertime. In the new mountain story, the revenuers most feared these days are not the men after the moonshiners but the IRS agents possibly on the trail of putative millionaires. Maybe the multiplied security guards at the growing number of gates could keep even them out. The certainty is that the gates now are not to keep the cows in but the socially or financially unqualified out.

Maybe at last the mountains are moving to Mohammed or at least to those who feel that they can command what they wish for a price. Certainly the time when a man didn't want to live so close to his neighbor that he could hear his dog barking is behind us. Often now ladies and gentlemen are happy to live within the sound of their neighbors' air-conditioning machines. Beside them, ecologists and entrepreneurs are indistinguishable. The promises whisper through the thermal belt: "Escape from the tensions which are so character-istic of our times. . . . We are not building here what you are trying to get away from . . . solitude in a wilderness."

Every man a Daniel Boone. And in this at-least-two-home civiliza-tion it is good to know on Hilton Head and up the hills that a man can be a Boone and a beachcomber. Some here are, depending only on the season.

September 7, 1972

Mills of Marble

"Thar's gold in them hills"—and marble and also an old vision of perfect serenity.

So much can certainly be said of Big Canoe, the new North Georgia development planned after the Sea Pines–Hilton Head pattern. The nine thousand acres of this newest refuge for retirement and recreation lie, as Charles Fraser said, near Jasper and Dawsonville, amidst "the peace and grandeur of the Appalachians." They also lie in a region once occupied by the tragic Cherokees and later by rough, adventurous miners in the first American gold rush. In the same area are the Georgia marble beds from which came the stone for such buildings as the Corcoran Art Gallery and the Lincoln Memorial in Washington. Of possibly more interest to the golfing community is the fact that the grandfather of Bobby Jones was a power in nearby Canton, where he made his money in marble, banking, and a textile mill. Recently, a third of the people in Canton worked in cotton mills.

Not everybody flourished in the neighborhood. The Cherokees were driven out. The fifteen thousand prospectors, who once crowded the area along with the gamblers and saloonkeepers who attended them, left for the greater California gold rush in 1849. They hurried westward despite the fact that the assayer at the federal mint in Georgia protested against the emigration, crying "there's millions in it"—a phrase which Mark Twain used in *The Gilded Age*. Actually, the gold taken from Georgia dirt between 1830 and 1933 amounted to only $17,749,937—a good deal less than Fraser and his Atlanta associates plan to put into development now. Even the poorest people in the area made their steps and walks of marble, though many of them got little gold from the cotton mills in which they were employed.

Resort development here goes back almost as far as gold mining and marble quarrying. And certainly there has been no lapse of beauty in these hills. Long ago, near Jasper, tourists were attracted to Cove Mountain Cave ("dangerous without a local guide"). Near there also was developed a resort called Tate Mountain Estates. And thirty years ago Lake Sequoyah offered "golf course, tennis courts, shooting boxes, water sports and fishing, for lodge guests and residents only."

Certainly there is promise for development in the proximity of Atlanta and in the traffic pouring by on routes I-75 and I-85. If the place lacks the soaring majesty of the North Carolina mountains to which many Hilton Headers have been attracted, it will in autumn be rich in forest foliage and in other seasons will be fabulously colored by azalea, blood-red Indian paintbrush, rhododendron, laurel, and trailing arbutus. Such flowering in North Georgia provided the appeal which pulled such an island pioneer as Beanie Newhall to Tiger, northward and eastward from richly planned Big Canoe. Her place there seems a real piece of wilderness up a road landscaped only by nature. Yet, near her place is already in operation a plush establishment called Kingswood, which beckons well-heeled Atlantans. Beyond, in higher North Carolina, there seems scarcely a mountain without its old or newly aspiring resort—and some rise confidently now where forty years ago similar developments blossomed and faded.

Undoubtedly we live in a different day. Those earlier developers often only laid out their lots. Now more money is being poured in than all the gold ever taken out—and *that* before the first lots are sold to the apparently insatiable Americans seeking serenity, sport, and utility-attended seclusion. In their carefully planned purviews, the Grandfather Mountain Golf and Country Club, Hound Ears, and other such places have attracted wealthy and distinguished residents. Beech Mountain welcomes masses of the skiing young. In such waters, with such guidances as it possesses, Big Canoe should encounter few difficulties in the very real rapids of the mountains. It might provide for many a reality of perfection about which poor old mountaineers working in mines, quarries, and cotton mills only sadly sang. The content of the song suggests that it may have come from the old lands in which Big Canoe will be a new paradise. Its first verse pictured a happy land:

> Where the mills are made of marble
> And the looms are made out of gold
> Where nobody ever gets tired
> And nobody ever grows old.

The only trouble with that prospectus is that there is a security guard named Peter at the gate. And his many mansions—or condominiums—may be a long way from Atlanta.

September 14, 1972

Entrepreneurial Urge

"For some time I have felt the entrepreneurial urge. . . ."

So we were told by Dennie McCrary as he announced that he will form his own land development company, though continuing his relationship with Sea Pines. Of course, there was nothing else for him to do after the onset of the entrepreneurial urge. Nowhere can this condition be better observed than here. Some who have studied it at first hand associate it with the ecology-exploitation syndrome, which can sometimes turn the mildest servants of serenity into characters unable to control their hammering, nailing, bulldozing, and double-entry bookkeeping.

Fortunately, it is not usually fatal—except when associated with a national epidemic of the condition. Some persons are actually benefited by the stimulation which often attends the entrepreneurial urge. Indeed, one case which has been much observed on this island, that of Wilbert Roller, has seemed vastly more benign than malignant. Others have seemed to bear up under the malady, if it may be called that. One well-known case is that of Norris Richardson, who operates Coligny Plaza and the washing machines there. Another case, difficult of diagnosis, is that of Pete McGinty,

335

the well-known architect. Some, who have had plenty of time to observe his condition while waiting for their plans, have noted that he seemed more quiescent than infected with the entrepreneurial, or any other, urge. His case, complicated by quiet but obsessive acquisitiveness, indicates that it is not always easy to recognize those suffering from this temper—or distemper.

These are only a few cases to which more research might profitably be devoted. Even the public attitude toward the condition is difficult to assess. While there are some who regard entrepreneurial urge as a plague, many here would welcome the contagion. Some students of the condition have even suggested that it is endemic on Hilton Head Island.

The last report from Mr. McCrary's plat side was that he was suffering only from the fear that others might follow the urge before he did.

On islands, there are other urges more easily understandable. They involve vice-presidents who become ornithologists quickly. Apartment dwellers who become gardeners, even landscape architects. Certainly there are landlubber-lawyers. And generals who become cooks, though of course there is not enough cooking going on to accommodate all the retired generals. However, Alex Turner, who came to Planters Row from Toledo, shares with us the classic case of the retired warrior on Nantucket Island who rejoiced in his powers as a surfside chef.

According to a document passed on by Alex, the general acquired or sought quite a reputation as one who loved to cook shore dinners, replete with seaweed, sea grapes (Alex questioned that ingredient), beach plums, and other, unknown elements. One invited to share his feast made this report on the summer of 1972.

"Now, the general doesn't cook on a stove, like all of us common folks, Oh, no! He digs a big hole in the sand, right near the water's edge, and keeps a fire going in it all day. After a while he tosses in rocks and heats them up like you wouldn't believe. And then, when he thinks everything is all set, he tosses in the lobsters, the seaweed, and some other, secret ingredients, covers the whole thing with sand, and lets the dinner bake.

"While it's baking, he and his friends toss Frisbees back and forth on the sand and knock off a few martinis. Well, last year the general, it seems, miscalculated a bit, and by the time he tossed the lobsters into the pit, the fire wasn't as hot as it should have been.

"In a few minutes, while everybody was Frisbeeing and martini-ing, the lobsters pushed up through the covering of sand, scratched around a bit, and marched directly into the sea. No dinner that night. The general was most embarrassed!

"This year he vowed there'd be no such disaster. He dug a very deep hole, and he installed a fire big enough to stay hot for hours. At the proper moment, he tossed in the lobsters, garnished with seaweed, and covered the whole bit with plenty of sand.

"Then the Frisbeeing and martini-ing got going. Quite a battle with the Frisbees, surging up and down the beach. And the martini pitchers followed. Finally, darkness set in, and it was impossible to see the Frisbees flying through the air. The well-martinied Frisbee-ers took a sighting on their position (using the stars, real and imaginary) and discovered they'd drifted more than a mile from where they'd entombed their dinner.

"And you know something? What with the darkness, the martini-ing, and the Frisbee fatigue—they NEVER DID FIND WHERE THEY'D BURIED THE LOBSTERS!

"The general took everybody back to his cottage, broke open a couple of tins of sardines, and vowed that next year will be better!"

September 21, 1972

The Hilton Name

Governor John C. West, who cannot plead ignorance as an excuse, certainly seemed to put his foot in his mouth or on our neck the other day when he declared that the Myrtle Beach area has already become "a golf capital of the world." Fortunately, the governor hedged between Hilton Head Island and Myrtle Beach in using *a* instead of *the* in his description. The situation is still confusing, however. Some years ago, according to old-timers' tales, when Charles Fraser opened the then-called William Hilton Inn, he got a stiff letter from the Hilton Hotel people, in effect accusing him of infringement of trademark. It must have been a pleasure for Charles to be able to point out that Captain William Hilton predated Innkeeper Conrad Hilton by two hundred and fifty years plus.

The situation is turned around now. When Governor West made his golf-capital remark, he was in Myrtle Beach joining in the ground breaking for a Myrtle Beach Hilton-Resort Convention Motel fifteen stories high, with a three-level night club "suspended on the fourteenth floor." This use of the name Hilton even by Conrad on the South Carolina shore seems like a Johnny-come-lately Hilton appropriating the ancient South Carolina Hilton name.

This could lead to dire results. Some innocent people seeing the name Hilton attached to this seaside tower might easily come to the mistaken conclusion that it rose above the less-fetid shores of Hilton Head Island. Something of the real difference between these two places where the name Hilton is now hung high may be indicated by the fact that the ground breaking there, over which Governor West presided, was described as a "dune digging and pile driving" occasion. "Dune digging" is, or ought to be, a dirty word at this southern end of the shore.

The differences between the two seaside places is much more marked than feelings about a phrase. Thirty years ago, when Hilton Head Island was still a sleeping beauty yet to be awakened by the kiss of woodsmen from Hinesville, Georgia, Myrtle Beach was described accurately in the official guide to the Palmetto State vouched for then by Governor Burnet R. Maybank. It said of Myrtle Beach: "The northern end has attractive substantial houses in sodded lawns and bright gardens; the southern end, clustering around the pavilion, the village, stores, and the various concessions, is a miniature Coney Island."

Time has not greatly changed that picture, though the fifteen-story Hilton Motel with its skyscraping, three-deck night club may give that resort right to claim similarity, not merely with Coney Island, but with Miami Beach as well. True, like ladies carefully lifting their skirts to avoid a puddle, some Myrtle Beach area developers have—at a distance which they hope is safe—begun some resorts patterned after the Hilton Head Island plantations. Also, nearby—a true antique fitting the shore like the sea oats—is the authentic model among old Carolina resorts, Pawleys Island. Few landscape architects today would copy it, and fewer still would be able to duplicate its durable charm.

There is room for all sorts of resorts on this Southern shore. Certainly there is space and to spare for hope that each will maintain its already established individuality. Considering its crowds, Myrtle Beach cannot count on keeping such wide-open spaces as those here, to which some not-so-long-time old-timers cling tenaciously—sometimes, they feel, precariously. Hilton Head Island, of course, should not envy Myrtle Beach its fifteen-story tower with its high-rise night club, which almost seems designed after one erected in a solemn spoof here some months ago.

As a puzzled poet once noted with wonder, the same god made the lamb and the tiger. Each may be perfect of its kind. Let's keep it that way. Hilton Head and Myrtle Beach, each in its preferred fashion, may grow like the fine crops from rich Carolina coastal soil in the old Gullah legend. As real-estate prices rise and visiting crowds increase at both places, the tale may be worth repeating: "I know uh man who hab ground so *berry* rich, wen 'e plant corn de corn grow so high dey hab t' build ladder 500 yahd high t' brek out de year. An' wen she get t' tosselin'—well, wen she *did* ready t' shoot out—all de angel in Heaben, an' de sun, an' de moon, an' de star hab t' move. Dey hab t' back up out de way; an' t'ree day aftuh she grow up, dey hab de word from Heaben dat all de Missy angel eatin' roastin' years!"

Resorts can grow like this miracle corn. But if there is going to be any race between Hilton Head and Myrtle Beach, it is devoutly to be hoped that it will be on separate tracks.

September 28, 1972

Labor Statistics

Like a lot of the supposedly retired people on this island, Henry Lawrence is a regular working and a hardworking man. His escape from the frying pan in Anderson brought him straight into the fire-insurance business here. In the early days, he stood around waiting for houses to be built so that he could insure them. There are more houses now. That requires more work. But it could not have been evident to anybody how hard he worked until he provided the following array of labor statistics:

LABOR STATISTICS SHOW WHAT'S WRONG

Population of the U.S.A.	160,000,000
People 60 years of age or older	62,000,000
Balance left to do the work	98,000,000
People 21 years of age or younger	54,000,000
Balance left to do the work	44,000,000
People working for the government	21,000,000
Balance left to work	23,000,000
People in the armed services	10,000,000

Balance left to work	13,000,000
People in state and city government	12,800,000
Balance left to work	200,000
People in hospitals, asylums, etc.	126,000
Balance left to work	74,000
Those who won't work	62,000
Balance left to work	12,000
Persons in jail	11,998
BALANCE LEFT TO WORK	2

Two! Only two! You and I; and you'd better get to work 'cause I'm tired of running this place alone.

Well, at least two are working on the Scrapbook this week, though the Sojourner may be listed among the unworking. Hugh Fraser, fisherman of Calibogue Cay, provides the contending verses about our aristocratical neighbor, Charleston. The authors of these poems about the society around Saint Michael's Church are unknown but are equally entitled to praise. Here they are for the delectation of instant South Carolinians, proud patricians or scornful plebians, on Hilton Head Island:

The Holy City

I thank Thee, Lord, on bended knee,
    I'm half Porcher and half Huger;
With holy pride my heart doth beat,
    I live at nineteen Lamboll Street;
With grateful tears my eyes are wet,
    My uncle's J. LeBoutillier Rhett.

For other blessings thank Thee too,
    My mother was a Petigru.
Simons and Waring and Legaré,
    Appear upon my family tree.
Dear Lord, look down on those in pity
    Who dwell outside the Holy City,
And when I die save me from Hell—
    I go to church at St. Mich-a-el.

IN REPLY
(Apologies to an unknown author)

I thank Thee, Lord, on bended knee,
  I'm not half Porcher and half Huger;
With lowly pride my heart doth beat,
  That I do not live on Lamboll Street.

With grateful tears my eyes are wet,
  That I'm not kin to any Rhett.
For other blessings thank Thee too—
  My grandma was no Petigru.
Simons and Waring and Legaré
  Do not adorn my family tree.

My grandma, by the name of Brown,
  Was born on some street way up town;
My dad was a Smith of lowly rank,
  Who lost money in the People's Bank.

Dear Lord, look down on those in pity,
  Who think this is the Holy City—
And when I die, send me to Hell—
  So I won't meet the elite of St. Mich-a-el.

October 5, 1972

Conclave of Cats

A lady driving home at night to Calibogue Cay passed a big gathering of cats, like a conclave of witches, all staring boldly at her with big, blazing eyes. A newcomer to the scene, she learned from neighbors next day that this was a congregation of strays of long standing. There was no natural migration of cats to this island. So evidently these cats and kittens were originally abandoned here. Now, picking and choosing as they will, the sleek animals move from house to house on the supposedly secure small island for sustenance, shelter, sex, and multiplication. And they are pretty arrogant about it.

Some of them look like very nice pussies in the daytime, though a little scrawny in their independence—not fat cats by any criterion. Apparently the night belongs to the cats of Calibogue. Maybe they are not all vagabonds. Says one authority, "the house cat curled at this owner's feet, is still the hunter that follows his ancestral yearning when the night calls it out to pad soundlessly after prey." That might be particularly true here on an island of brush and birds, with more opportunities for hunting than in city alleys.

Stray dogs do not shun the day. They are often seen on the

beaches or the roadsides. The number of the collarless in this canine population indicates that there are a good many dogs operating in complete independence here. Maybe this is a good place to get rid of unwanted dogs. There were the people recently who undertook to sever the relationship between master and man's best friend by drowning two dogs in a channel here. Fortunately for the dogs, saviours were nearby. Happy ending!

All men and all dogs may make a beautiful friendship. As for cats, there are "ailurophiles" as well as "ailurophobes" everywhere. (Look them up and see which you are.) But people who have exhausted ecology as a subject and are rapidly wearying of pollution as a conversation piece are now turning to talk of animals (called "feral") running wild. Despite the fortunes that must be spent for the long rows of cat and dog food in the supermarkets, some people apparently don't want to endow these creatures. This is understandable when the statistic is rolled out that ten thousand puppies and kittens are born every hour in the United States. That could mean 87 million new pets—or pests—per year. The maximum life span of the cat is twenty-one years, of dogs thirty-four.

The argument as to what to do with all these creatures is not new. Long ago Thomas Jefferson aroused the ire of his cousin John Randolph of Roanoke when the sage of Monticello expressed the opinion that dogs were a pernicious, at least a useless, race, and that, to save food and put an end to hydrophobia, measures ought to be taken by law for their extermination.

Randolph let loose the high-pitched roar for which he was famous: "When a law is passed to exterminate dogs, I shall set *my dogs* on the officer who comes to execute it, and back them with my gun."

Jefferson survived the exchange. So did the dogs. It was sometimes said that in the South no family was so poor it couldn't keep a dog, and some were so poor that they could keep three or four. Cats have the hostility of bird lovers as well as of ordinary ailurophobes. Proposals have been made to curb their nocturnal roaming by law. And such suggestions have met with indignant opposition from ailurophiles. Perhaps the best-known instance of this cat and anti-cat collision was in Illinois, where a cat-control bill, passed by the legislature, was put for signature on the desk of Adlai Stevenson when he was governor. His veto message deserves the company of the famous, much-recited "Tribute to a Dog" by Senator George

G. Vest of Missouri. Governor Stevenson wrote: "I cannot agree that it should be the declared policy of Illinois that a cat visiting a neighbor's yard or crossing the highway is a public nuisance. It is in the nature of cats to do a certain amount of unescorted roaming. Many live with their owners in apartments or other restricted premises, and I doubt if we want to make their every brief foray an opportunity for a small game hunt by zealous citizens—with traps or otherwise. I am afraid this bill could only create discord, recrimination and enmity. Also consider the owner's dilemma; to escort a cat abroad on a leash is against the nature of the cat, or to permit it to venture forth for exercise unattended into a night of new dangers is against the nature of the owner. Moreover cats perform useful service, particularly in rural areas, in combatting rodents— work they necessarily perform alone and without regard for property lines. . . .

"The problems of cat versus bird is as old as time. If we attempt to resolve it by legislation, who knows but what we may be called upon to take sides as well in the age-old problems of dog versus cat, bird versus bird, even bird versus worm? In my opinion, the State of Illinois and its local governing bodies already have enough to do without trying to control feline delinquency."

Possibly thus spake wisdom, but "feral" statistics pile up. There could be some literal truth to the statement that the country is going to the dogs—and the cats.

October 12, 1972

Kitchen Artists

Almost as proudly as they speak of their golf and tennis stars in residence, the various resorts of Hilton Head Island point to the artists in their kitchens. The chefs of *haute cuisine* have been assembled here from one of the best restaurants in Chicago, from the famous tables of the Greenbrier at White Sulphur Springs, from Germany, from France, and a whole cooking family of them from Hungary. Properly, the plantations praise their cooks and their creations as bringing a whole world of delicious dining to their doors. Sometimes, casually—along with the palmettoes and the Spanish moss—they mention Southern cooking. One resort has even mentioned "soul food," but the best tradition of Southern cookery has received little or no attention here. That tradition was embodied or personified in the "very black and very heavily built" William Barron (or Baron), who emerged from slavery to become the cook and caterer for the most elegant Charleston society.

Memory has been very remiss concerning him. He might be entirely forgotten now except for the written recollections of two of the most literate and aristocratic ladies of the Low Country. Barron, as described by these ladies, was no mere ham hock and collards

347

man. Both ladies knew the best in their worlds. One of them was Elizabeth W. Allston Pringle, daughter of Governor Robert Francis Withers Allston (1801–64). Her mother was Adele Petigru, sister of the famous Unionist James Louis Petigru. The other was (and fortunately still is) Laura Witte Waring, whose son, a descendant of a long line of distinction, is today editor of the *Charleston News and Courier.* Both ladies remembered William Barron with gustatory delight.

First in recollection, Elizabeth Pringle knew Barron as the second house servant—or slave—in the big house of her father on his Chicora Wood plantation. Evidently the talents of this "excellent servant with very courteous manners" were not limited to the kitchen.

"He took the greatest delight," Mrs. Pringle wrote in *Chronicles of Chicora Wood,* "in arranging all the flowers in the house, which I also loved to do; and there was always a race between William and myself as to who should do it. I remember specially one yellow flat bowl on a stand with Greek figures in black chasing round it, a perfectly lovely thing for flowers; and it nearly broke my heart when I found that William had changed the flowers in it and arranged them to his mind."

The arrangement was undoubtedly no worse for the change. William was qualified for tougher tasks. He went through the whole Civil War as body servant to Elizabeth's brother, Colonel Benjamin Allston. After the war, in freedom, he became well known in Charleston "as a caterer, cook and provider of elegant entertainments." He took charge of the suppers for the Saint Cecilia Society, "which were always very handsome and elaborate and quite a feature." He maintained his affection for his former master and whenever Colonel Ben was in Charleston always sent him "a dish of delicious chicken salad or a shrimp pie, for which he was famous, or a Charlotte Russe, or some dish that he knew Mas' Ben specially liked."

A younger woman than Mrs. Pringle, Laura Witte Waring as a child knew Barron later. She wrote of the excellent restaurant he operated just off Broad Street. But in her memoir, *You Asked for It* (written for her children), she particularly recalled Barron as caterer in her father's great house, now Ashley Hall School for girls.

"When Barron did the catering at a private house," she wrote, "he would appear with a staff early in the afternoon, and the kitchen and pantry would be turned over to him. Standing by watching him make tongue and ham sandwiches, we would be given one or two not quite as pretty as the pattern he was turning out by the hundreds on to the silver trays. It was a treat to have Barron in the pantry and to know that those delicious boned turkeys would be saved, if any was left over, for the next day."

Both ladies agreed that he was an honest, enthusiastic, beaming, courteous man. "He had but one fault," Elizabeth Pringle wrote. That was one he shared with some of those he served. It was "to look upon the wine when it was red; he habitually took more than was good for him and lived too high, so that his health gave out before he was at all an old man."

Still there is something immortal about the scene in which Barron worked. Mrs. Waring remembered "the proverbial boned turkey with truffles in the stuffing, pâtés and sandwiches were being prepared, pâté de foie gras was turned out from the attractive yellow and brown jars it came in onto bed of lettuce . . . the labeled cut glass decanters filled with sherry and Madeira, the champagne was icing in big washtubs in the flagged back hall."

The master of the house joined Barron to make the punch: "A goodly array of bottles stood on the shelf in front of him, while on the table was the punch bowl of gigantic proportions. A strong tea and lemon juice and ginger ale acted as a base, peeled oranges and filberts were in bowls, and powdered sugar in reach, then the bottles of claret and whatever other liquor went into the making of the punch was put in. I think brandy was used. The nicest part was the pouring into the punch bowl of the cut up fruit and the nuts that went in with such a rush and fascinatingly squashy sound."

R.I.P. William Barron. After all, none of us can live forever. And it may be as well to die by the spoon as by the sword.

October 19, 1972

For the Ills of Man

In the early days, resorts grew where the health facilities were, not, as now, when a more elaborate health facility is proposed because of the existence of the resort. South Carolinians then, fleeing the miasmic summertimes of the Low Country, gathered at the springs from Old White in Virginia to Saratoga in New York. Dancing in such places was only an adjunct to the drinking of the waters. Health was the excuse for hilarity, not the other way around, as now seems to be the case.

So Dr. Peter LaMotte of New York, in planning a hospital for Hilton Head Island, may be, in a sort of reverse fashion, following the planning of other promoters, such as George Washington and Thomas Jefferson. They patronized the Virginia springs, though sometimes they seemed more interested in the real estate about them than in the therapeutic qualities of the springs—gushing and trickling, cool and sweet, hot and sulphurous, all guaranteed to ease the aches and ills of mankind. Mr. Jefferson in his last days was less than enthusiastic about the springs when he sought their curative aid. He had never been so bored, he said, as with the company around them. From the copious drinking of the water, he got, not cure for his old-age ills, but some boils on his buttocks.

Obviously, no substantial simile can be maintained about the old-time resort by the spa and the new plans for a very excellent hospital by the resort here. Yet something of the old and the new has been put together at the Greenbrier in White Sulphur Springs, West Virginia, where an excellent diagnostic facility has been created more for golfers than for guzzlers of the water. Certainly some such modern facility might not only attract some new visitors here but also provide close at hand a modern hospital for those already here who are as subject as the colonials were to the agues to which the flesh is heir.

Not everybody here has met Dr. LaMotte, but his enthusiasm is pervasive. The impression he has made as a person adds exuberance to his plans. By all reports, he is not only an excellent surgeon. Also, on an island much devoted to sport, his image is brightened by his participation in athletics as physician of one of the greatest American baseball teams. His preference for the ecology and atmosphere of this island over the clamor and crowding of practice in a great city will get him into no arguments here. It is easy to believe that he will be able to attract other practitioners as able as himself to this island once they are given hospital facilities equal to their skills.

Certainly his plans now seem hardly less audacious than Dr. Chet Goddard's move here less than a decade ago, when, though there was no doctor, there seemed doubt as to whether there were enough patients. That doubt has certainly disappeared. Now it seems incredible that there could be such an island as Hilton Head has become without the medical center's facilities, which have grown from Chet Goddard's first steps. The time for a hospital here may be at hand.

Without it our luck may not hold. Still, it may be well to remember how blessed we have been. Certainly many of our military neighbors would not have come here in the first place but for the naval hospital in Beaufort. And civilians here have found both tenderness and skill in the Beaufort Memorial Hospital, which has sometimes been able to avail itself of the ablest specialists, who happened to be on duty at the naval hospital. Many Hilton Head residents, recently from great cities, have found in Savannah, to their surprise, the highest quality of men and facilities in medicine. Men and women able to go anywhere they wish have found care and confidence they prefer to that they knew elsewhere. And they find it at a distance not greater than often existed in the great centers from which they came.

Of course, facilities for health care on Hilton Head Island must grow as the island grows. Already, where many are the elderly, the need for a convalescent home close to friends and relatives is being confronted. Perhaps an on-the-island hospital, staffed by full-time specialists, is approaching the point of requirement now. This may be so, though some residents now go the hundreds of miles to the Mayos in Minnesota and not merely the fifty miles to Beaufort or Savannah. Certainly, though Hilton Head need not plan to be an entirely self-sufficient island in health or anything else, an excellent hospital here could fit into the pattern of growth. But such an institution, if created, should be contemplated as a requirement of all people here, rich and poor, black and white, never as a refuge for physicians who would like to escape the hazards, hardships, and hurly-burly of big-city practice. Its staff should come to a challenge, not to any call of serenity on a shore landscaped in terms of human living as well as in shrub and tree.

That may be exactly what is contemplated as well as what is required. And so far as the island is concerned, anything else would be something in the nature of what Mr. Jefferson got when he went to the old Virginia springs to ease his ills and was afterwards not able to comfortably sit down.

November 2, 1972 *

* The column for October 26, 1972, was a repeat, by request, of the column of September 23, 1971 (see pp. 188–90).

In Glass Houses

Hardly anywhere else can there be more glass employed in the architecture of habitation than on Hilton Head Island. Certainly that is proper in a place where at least half the joy of existence lies in the mere viewing of sea and shore, chameleon marshes, great oaks and arrays of erect palmettoes. It marks us as people who live in glass houses all the same, and as such, people who should exercise a certain amount of care in the trajectory of any thrown stones. And that may be particularly true in the direction of Victoria Bluff.

A beautifully designed place for living was developed here. To an almost unique degree the needs of living were related to the preservation of a much-more-than-newly-picturesque island. And, properly, people who settled upon it opposed any such massive threat of pollution as was presented by what seemed the proposed arrogant intrusion of BASF. It appeared as a stranger, but certainly there was nothing mysterious about it. Its reputation as a despoiler had been clearly established on its own once beautiful river Rhine. Almost to perfection it embodied the kind of careless capitalism which in so many parts of the world has shown almost contemptuous disregard for clear sky, clean earth, unsoiled waters. Properly, it was rebuffed and rejected by the protectors of a lost, sweet shore in a nation where so many rivers pour only poison into the sea. That seemed here a victory for the mobilized angels over the monsters of pluto-politicians and devil-take-the-hindmost developers. That victory, however, hardly justified any assumption of arrogance by the angels. And that could be what seems almost an opposition to any industrialization at all of the potentially great harbor of Port Royal.

Undoubtedly, in Port Royal's development, good clean industries might be followed hereabouts by others of the careless kind ready to foul any nest and much less concerned with dirt than with dollars. Being a little industrialized may be like being a little pregnant. A monstrosity might be delivered on this shore. But a people who still believe in the possibility of planned development for gracious living ought not to dismiss the possibility of decent development for creative industry, too.

Man cannot live, we are often told, by bread alone. He would have a hard time living without it, and there are many in Beaufort County who lack it—and have long lacked it. Perhaps the landscaped resorts here were only possible because this area was for a long time not developed. A sort of last chance for shore uncluttered by honky-tonk sprawl was found here. And if men have shown here the imagination essential to tranquillity in living, it ought not to be impossible to design in this area a place where men might work and earn in decent plants as well as live in a plate-glass-vistaed tranquillity.

Maybe in the long run both are improbable. Certainly, as it grows, Hilton Head faces the dangers of self-pollution. Certainly, more and more carbon monoxide is loosed by more and more cars. Every condominium brings with it the flushing of more toilets. Some of the businesses most concerned with the architectural grace of the place have been quickest to pull in trailers to house their hustling. Apartments sneak skyward. Monkey houses multiply more rapidly than the wildlife beneath them. The alligator may turn out to be less a menace than the bulldozer. Old plans sometimes seem to be less important than new profits.

Of course, the ultimate threat of any new industry in Beaufort County must be confronted. But so must the ultimate threat of more and more people on the inelastic acres of an old island. A limited water supply may be consumed and soiled by people as well as by industries. A deeper channel might do no more harm than higher and wider havens for the purchasers of tranquillity. Certainly, the dwellers in the glass houses on Hilton Head Island and those who preserve colonial mansions in Beaufort should both be concerned with the present, limited chance this area has for a new American design in both living and working. Inevitably, despite many who have retired—and, as they think, escaped from the American rat race—living and working go together.

Real planning for industry as well as for serenity ought to be possible here. And something more than an exchange of stones will be necessary for real performance. A BASF may be grown at home—even on an island—and need not necessarily be imported from the Rhine. That danger might be lessened if we looked more often at our mirrors and not merely out of our windows, wide as they may seem to be.

November 9, 1972

Tranquillity for Everybody

Incredible as it may seem, the stream of those Americans moving in eagerness to places for themselves in the multiplying number of beautiful, planned resorts on shores, mountains, and lakes may be slowing. Or at least there is a suggestion that new incentives must be provided for them by competitive compounds of serenity and escape from the much emphasized tensions in the cities and towns of a land increasingly aware of both its prosperity and its pollution. More appears to be required than the laying out of lots and the opening of gates. Possibly, however, this is just a step in the provision of tranquillity for everybody.

First, there were just the lots plotted out on this or that old wilderness, with all utilities available and ready access to ski slope or shore. Then the great discovery was made that by the process of condominiums more people could be packed into the acre. Now from the West—and inevitably headed east—comes the new great idea. Now on Lake Tahoe and in Hawaii people no longer have to buy a whole condominium. In swank resorts developed by subsidiaries of the Hyatt hotels (which have plans for Hilton Head Island, too) you can buy a one-month interest in a luxury apartment "with-

out the burden of owning it the rest of the time." Plans for similar
part-time sales are in process in Arizona and at Acapulco. For a
minimum of four thousand dollars a buyer will be able to own an
apartment for one month of the year and to have it financed over
a ten-year period with only 25 percent down. Prices, however, will
vary, depending upon the time of the year the purchaser "owns"
the apartment. The first two weeks in July, a three-bedroom unit
will sell for eight thousand dollars. Two November weeks in the
same apartment will cost three thousand dollars.

Obviously, the possibilities in this part-time-ownership plan are
prodigious. And with high rises thrown in, it may certainly be said
that the sky is the limit. Only the reactionary will see in the arrangement any resemblance to the old-time "hot flops" where successive
people slept in the same bed.

Maybe a more instant incentive has been provided at Beech
Mountain, where some Hilton Headers have second places. Jack
Aulis of *The News and Observer* of Raleigh described it.

"It may be that you have never drunk a 10-ounce, blue martini.
If not, you have never drunk the fearsome 'Blue Max,' which is just
one of the inventions of the Red Baron Room—the most attractive
saloon in the state.

"The original part of the expanded room opened in late 1969 on
the bottom floor of Beech Mountain's Beech Tree Inn. It was designed as a 1916 French bistro, the kind of place where World War
I aviators might have gathered between sundown and the dawn
patrol.

"It looks old and wooden and the candles drip over the wine
bottles that hold them and everywhere in the place there are exact
replicas or actual mementoes of the world's first air war.

"Hanging from the ceiling, for example, is the bullet-shattered
wing of a German plane, red with a black cross, the kind of wing
that might have helped lift the Fokker triplane flown by Rittmeister
Manfred von Richthofen, the famed Red Baron.

"There are paintings of aerial combat scenes, and more than 100
period photographs of planes and pilots, including American ace
Eddie Rickenbacker. There are medals and uniforms and propellers
and engines. And period recruiting posters: 'Join the Air Service.
Be an American Eagle!'

"In the 'operations room' there is a large poster-photo of, I think,

Theda Bara in harem costume. It has been used with varying accuracy as an alternate dart board.

"Technically, the place is a private club for residents of the mountain, but those who rent rooms in the hillside motels become temporary members. And, thus, eligible to contend for the Order of the Blue Max.

"The Blue Max, as movie-watchers know, is the nickname for the top military honor awarded Germany's World War I aviators. It is a blue Maltese cross on a silk neck ribbon. . . .

"If you drink one of the Red Baron Room's inventions ($4.50 each), you get to keep the special decorative glass it came in and you get a small gold-colored coin. Once you acquire 20 of the coins, you are awarded the Order of the Blue Max, for which you get a replica of the medal itself. And, almost certainly, a medical discharge.

"The order's membership, I am told, totals 'under 10.' I didn't ask how many are missing in action."

There is no telling how many part-time chalets a purchaser might buy or require after that.

November 16, 1972

Mad Dogs and Englishmen

"The battle of Waterloo was won on the cricket fields of Eton."
Apparently no such statement has been made about any other battles and the golf courses of Scotland, England, the United States, and now parts worldwide. At the time of the Heritage Tournament here, this seems an oversight that ought to be corrected. There must have been comparatively few Eton boys fighting under Wellington—certainly a lot fewer than the golfers who have fought in battles since and may fight in battles ahead. We live in less aristocratical times, when the fate of the world can hardly be ascribed to players of cricket, or of any other sport, from any one exclusive school.

But the place of golf beside the battles was evident as long ago as 1898 when, in a more romantic time, wars and battles put the diamonds in the diadem of Queen Victoria. In his memoir, Frank Doubleday, founder of the big publishing company which bears his name, put golf and battles together sixty years ago and almost at the end of the world. Combining business and pleasure, Doubleday had gone to Egypt in 1913 on a trip with Mr. and Mrs. Rudyard Kipling. (Rud and Carrie, he called them in a familiarity supposed to be more common now than then, on golf courses and in other places.) They sailed up the Nile, but the Kiplings tarried when Doubleday went deeper into Africa to Omdurman, at the junction of the Blue Nile and the White Nile. There in September 1898 Lord Kitchener had won a great battle against the Sudanese, slaughtering many Arabs. It was not Waterloo, but it seemed almost an equal turning point in Britain's then imperial designs. Oddly enough, it was followed in the Sudan by the introduction to the world of a word which has grown familiar around many golf courses: the "Anglo-Egyptian condominium agreements of 1899," providing for joint occupation of the area.

In 1913 Doubleday wrote of his visit to this historic place deep in Africa: ". . . we went over to Omdurman, and a little further up the White Nile, and saw the site of the Battle of Omdurman, It was as hot as blazes and required a lot of effort to go over these places, but it was one of the most interesting experiences I have ever had. I was sorry that the Kiplings did not decide to go with us, because Khartoum itself has a perfectly good hotel and is an interesting place to see. I even went to the golf course which these English soldiers have laid out in the desert. Although there was not a blade of green grass, every shot had to be teed up in the sand. The temperature in the sun, I should think, was something like 130 degrees, but they diligently kept at it and played every day. No people in the world are like the English for sticking to precedent; I suppose they laid out the course and began playing the second day after the Battle of Omdurman was won."

Certainly they were still playing when Doubleday retraced his steps and joined the Kiplings again. He said nothing about playing himself. He did not mention any play by Kipling. Indeed, he rather suggested that the writer could perfectly describe the most strenuous activities without ever participating in them. Nobody could better describe a tiger hunt than Kipling, Doubleday thought, though he had never shot a cat. He evidently preferred night sails on the Nile to golf in the sun.

But the English officers were playing then on the desert course at Omdurman, where the temperature soared well over one hundred degrees. Of course, they were not the same men and boys who, on the cricket fields of Eton, won the Battle of Waterloo. But 1914, and World War I, was just ahead of them. Maybe they helped win that war on the golf course in the African heat, where no blade of grass survived. Nobody—not even Kipling, who felt very violently about that war—suggested any phrase similar to the one about Waterloo and the Eton boys. If he had, maybe he could have revised another famous line.

> Only mad dogs, Englishmen, and golfers
> go out in the mid-day sun.

No such line is needed here or will be needed here even when the Heritage next year is played in South Carolina's not-always-cool September. Charles Fraser has demonstrated his command of the weather in past tournaments and need not be doubted now. Despite a dry fall, the fairways are green. Condominiums here do not relate to a land deal by Egyptians and the British Empire. Maybe all the Doubleday memoir indicates is that golf is ancient, honorable, and ubiquitous, and that nature has not invented any conditions yet where it cannot and will not be played. Its relationship to battles Waterloo or Omdurman appears to be entirely incidental.

November 23, 1972

Poverty as Preservative

Captain Vance Fowler, in his current epistle to the residents and property owners of Sea Pines, reports that another of his company's developments, River Hills Plantation in the South Carolina Up Country, is "progressing <u>on schedule</u>." The last two words are characteristically underlined. And from another letter comes the news that the builders of River Hills will have native support there in the defense of ecology, which is, of course, a first developmental concern.

This news came round about from Dante S. Caputo, who, though he has his office as a certified life underwriter in the miasmas of Manhattan, is a Hilton Head friend and visitor. He forwarded, evidently with some approval, a letter to the editor of *The New York Times,* written with the gusto of indignation by Allan D. Charles of Union, South Carolina, which is just a piece down the road from River Hills. Under a heading "Despoiling the South," Mr. Charles avowed: "A new movement is afoot in the South of which the North must be made aware. Most of this nation is hopelessly overcrowded and polluted, but there exist formerly 'remote' sections which may yet be ecologically saved from the 'silent spring.' One of these sections is the South.

"Unfortunately, the political and industrial leadership in the South (both Republican and Democrat) is of one mind—a mind bent on the 'New Jerseyfication' of the South in as short a space of time as possible. The people who would pave over the South rule here absolutely, unchallenged by ecological action groups. Apparently such groups can only spring up where the environment has already been rendered uninhabitable by humans, and since the South is still salvable no one here is very interested. Southerners seem unable to learn from the miserable example so glaringly furnished by the North.

"The call then is going out: Northern industrialists, you find your non-union labor and lax pollution laws somewhere else: Stay up North and smoke up your own back yards.

"Northern environmentalists, please come down here and help us. Help us before we, too, succumb."

The help is on the way and _on schedule_. At least at River Hills, an area will be environmentally preserved to the taste of the most fastidious. But despite the fears of Mr. Charles, _improved_ might be a better word than preserved. Not all the ecology of the once "saved" South was perfect. Change is inevitable and not always evil. As a certified life underwriter, Mr. Caputo is aware of risks here as elsewhere. Premiums must be paid. But sometimes risks in the future are reckoned in disregard of the actuarial experience of the past. That could be the case with Mr. Charles and his town of Union, South Carolina, and even with Mr. Caputo in Manhattan. It is quite true, as Mr. Charles cries in anguish, that the South may be one of the last places which may be saved from the "Silent Spring." It is not quite true, however, that perfection always marked its earlier seasons.

It was certainly not true of Union, South Carolina, from which Mr. Charles wrote and from which Mr. Caputo got the message. The town was described in detail thirty years ago in a South Carolina guide officially sponsored by the late Senator Burnet R. Maybank, who was then governor of the state. That work reported Union as lying in a section marked by "old mansions, few of them painted, most of them run-down, and all of them weather-beaten. These big

structures, relics of the ante-bellum gentry that established large
estates here, exemplify early Up Country architecture at its best.
Farm tenants, assigned to the mansions by the landlords financially unable to restore them, are surrounded by carved woodwork, wrought iron, and delicately molded plaster ornamentation."

The book reported that, as of 1941, the town of Union itself "is
pervaded by a sort of lazy atmosphere that belies the bustling activity of its factories and mills. The plain-faced shops on both sides
of the narrow main street draw farmers and mill villagers for trade.
The ponderous brick courthouse serves a typical South Carolina
custom as a gathering place for farmers and mill workers when they
come to town. In warm weather small groups bask along the knee-
high wall that borders the terrace, their lethargy only slightly shaken
by the soapbox sermons of local and visiting evangelists—carpenters, mill operatives, and mechanics by trade, but long-winded
preachers by avocation. In winter the gatherings move inside the
courthouse, where spittoons and benches conveniently scattered
through the corridors are dragged closer to steaming radiators,
each the center of an open forum on crops, wages, weather, and
politics." Nearby was a section of the town then still called "Poverty
Flat."

Union has more than tripled in population since then. Maybe
some of the newcomers are Yankees. Undoubtedly, some Yankees
have spotted the carved woodwork in the dilapidated mansions, or
local antique dealers have put the old wrought iron in their shops.
Local idlers gather about national TV broadcasts now instead of
around the spittoons. But evidently leisure (now so much attended)
is not something recently invented there. It was possessed as the
hinges gave way on the doors of old mansions and as the loafers
were more numerous in courthouse squares. Maybe the ecology—
"pattern of relations between organisms and their environment"
—was better for people in those old days. Possibly wits were
sharpened in courthouse arguments by such folk as now, before TV
sets, only soften their minds with a variety of soap operas.

Mr. Charles gives the Yankees too much credit for both good and
evil. Of course, they did not discover leisure, which the South has
long enjoyed or endured. Too many men with only one gallus to
hold up their breeches long had leisure in the South. And the

spittoons in the courthouse suggest that at least some basic defenses against pollution were necessary in South Carolina long ago. Those mills around Union didn't pay munificent wages before Northern industrialists arrived. And now, as some of the best Southern developments, such as River Hills, are showing, the South is not entirely dependent on "Northern environmentalists" to point the possibilities of the best patterns for living. Both newcomers and Southerners with similar interests might point better environments for working. And they will find beside them, of course, Southern and Northern despoilers.

The sad thing in the problem Mr. Charles points out is that poverty can often be the best preservative of the environment. It is not generally regarded as the best fare. Mr. Charles should have marked his letter, "Southern papers please copy." *The Packet,* unasked, is glad to oblige. The saints and the sinners come from everywhere and confront or compound the same problems in every place. Mr. Charles and Mr. Caputo together cannot alter that.

November 30, 1972

Half Pint Flask

The coming of the mini-bottle is not expected to be attended by any such supernatural phenomena as DuBose Heyward described in his minor classic "The Half Pint Flask." In that tale a determined bottle collector who took "a first issue, half pint flask of the old South Carolina state dispensary" from a grave in a Negro cemetery brought upon himself implacable destruction by Plat-eye. Hilton Head, however, is not the Ediwander Island of Heyward's imagination. And superstition, of course, has long been dispensed with here except in such minor matters as copper bracelets. Still the mini-bottles will have a factual, if not a fantastic, effect on this shore.

Certainly the mini-bottle will steady the hand that pours the drink. Out of one of these small bottles, every glass will now receive exactly 1.6 ounces. With bourbon now selling at retail for around seven dollars a quart, that will mean thirty-five cents worth of liquor in each glass. All charges above that amount will be for ice, mixer, service, and decor. That will mean that for a dollar highball (if you can find one) the customer at the mini-bottle bar will be paying seven dollars for 11.2 ounces of liquor. That's a trifle more than a third of the liquor he would get for the same price from his own quart bottle in his own house. Outside it, he can't always do so well. Brown-bagging has not always been so cheap. At one high-rise restaurant recently, the system involved a very snazzy waitress who took the bottle in the bag and brought back the drinks with a stiff setup charge. The waitress was more economical with the liquor in the customer's bottle than she would have been with her own. The less she put in the glasses, the more setups seemed required.

On Hilton Head Island, perhaps the greatest change in the economics of potation may come, not from alteration in the liquor laws, but from the increase in Social Security payments. Elsewhere, that increase may have seemed essential to lawmakers on the basis of the rise in the cost of living for the poor (some of whom, we have been scandalized to hear, spend the money for liquor). On the plantations of Hilton Head, many of the retired have debonairly announced that their Social Security checks amounted to their liquor allowances. Now, with the 20 percent increase, most such senior citizens in their golden years get $259.40 a month. That would take care of a little over thirty-seven quarts of bourbon a month, or 740 drinks of 1.6 ounces each. That would amount to about twenty-four drinks a day—or the contents of a quart plus almost a half pint flask, like the one from the graveyard. Under such circumstances, Plat-eye could be dispensed with.

Fortunately, for the sake of both health and finances, this is not the general rule. Overt intoxication is rarely seen here, at least by the time the elders go to bed. Sometimes a very rigid standard is stated about drinking, as when, in the last issue of the *Islander*, Charles Price flatly referred to the sometimes bibulous novelist William Faulkner as "a drunk." He also said, however, that Faulkner was "probably the finest writer of the English language this country has ever produced." This recalls Abraham Lincoln's statement—when the charge of drunkenness was made against Grant—that he would like to find out Grant's brand so that he could furnish it to his other generals. And Lincoln evidently was not thinking about the mini-bottle but more probably about the demijohn, which those at the lower level of the generation gap may not know was "a narrow-necked bottle of glass or stoneware enclosed in wickerwork and holding from one to ten gallons."

The cocktail circuit spins. Possibly someday this resort may yet be worthy of the name "Cirrhosis Shores." But as the little-bottle business comes along, it may be that the author of the Book of Daniel was making a predated pun when he broke up Belshazzar's party with the line: MENE, MENE, TEKEL, UPHARSIN.

Roller and Ruthven, Mrs. Mac, and the plantations may take warning. But it should be remembered that there is a rule against unpleasant signs on this island.

December 7, 1972

Marengo to the Sea

A letter comes from Bob McGowan in Marengo, Illinois, in what we learned in geography or travel was the clean and open grain and dairy country of the Middle West. Brother McGowan is a photographer, and after visiting Hilton Head Island, he found it exactly the scene he wanted in his lens. Already he is planning to come and share our tranquillity. But certainly Marengo would not seem a place from which a man needs to move to satisfy his spirit. Escape from snow, yes! But from a sweet village in a rolling country of red barns, tall silos, and fat dairy herds, why?

The *Illinois State Guide* published in 1939 described Marengo. It lay seventy-seven miles from Chicago and twenty-three miles beyond Elgin, which then "marked the border of the Chicago urban area." At an altitude of 818 feet, the town had a population of 1,948 people. It was, said the guide, "noteworthy for its elm-arched roadway and the McGill Metal Products Plant, 127 E. Prairie Street, one of the world's largest manufactories of mousetraps. Marengo is the birthplace of Egbert Van Alstyne, composer of 'In the Shade of the Old Apple Tree.'" Certainly that sounds like a nostalgic picture of American tranquillity, though, of course, there may have been some

369

warning in the old line about the better mousetrap and the world beating a path to the door.

Apparently, though not necessarily impelled by the mousetrap, that is exactly what has happened. Bob McGowan reports with some anguish: "I moved to this sleepy little community ten years ago to escape the crush of humanity in suburbia (having already been crushed out of Chicago) and I've witnessed a horrible rape of a beautiful 'midwestern main street' town—not by carpetbaggers who ran out of room for their 'developments' but by second, third, and fourth generation grain and dairy farmers who wanted to climb out of the hollow and live on the hill. It wasn't progress that changed this town. It was greed that overtook inadequate planning. Their big-city cousins told them of the sucker that's born every second, and in ten years I've seen pasture land go from $300 to $3500. There's nothing wrong with making money. I do it every day. But there's been a loss in this exchange of dollars by both buyer and seller. A loss the government won't let you write off."

This cry of both pain and hope is not unfamiliar on Hilton Head Island. Our neighbors have fled from pressures, pollution, and progress in little towns as well as big ones across the American map. To them Hilton Head Island held up the promise, and nothing is more important here than keeping that promise high. And certainly it is important here to keep bright the dreams or the illusions of the Bob McGowans, wherever they may be.

This remains a beautiful island. Those of us who gripe at change still cling to our conviction that there is no more charming shore. Still, there are occasional forebodings. Old Hilton Headers never go to South Beach except as a means of doing penance for sin. Now, around the lovely man-made yacht basin, with its lighthouse pointing through the Quarter Deck to heaven, Harbourtropolis soars. It contains probably the most delightful playground for children anywhere. Its shops are excellent. So are many in Coligny Plaza, which apparently—and not too soon—is becoming self-conscious about its appearance.

Certainly something should be done to improve Coligny Circle, which will soon be so surrounded by inns, apartments, and villas that it may be the only green spot remaining in the neighborhood. But other improvements abound. There may soon be that second bridge to the mainland, which will let more people in as well as out.

A shorter route, preferably not at the sacrifice of Mrs. Mingledorff's trees, may take us to Beaufort more quickly, and we may find things there worth the quicker trip.

We may soon have our own hospital, which could become a diagnostic center like that of the Mayos in Minnesota (which is west of McGowan's Marengo). Perhaps the facility should put Dr. Jim Brawner on its staff or should bring in other psychiatrists of his high character, for there certainly is a diagnostic job to be done here in that field. The doctors will have to test it and treat it, but in advance and all for free is offered here the name of the disease from which this island chiefly suffers:

CONDOMINIMANIA.

There may be a cure for it. But some research scientists are already of the opinion that it could be as virulent as that German infection from which the area barely escaped. Certainly it is doubtful that Bob McGowan, even after his exposure in Marengo, is immune.

December 14, 1972

Santa Claus Is Dead

The rumor spread, maybe from Baygall, possibly from South Beach. Some wearing copper bracelets against arthritis gave credence to it at the medical center and the health spa.

"Santa Claus is dead."

The report is entirely improbable. It is as incredible as the supposedly scholarly statement (see *Encyclopaedia Britannica*, volume 16, page 477) that there is no evidence that he ever existed, even under his earlier name of Saint Nicholas. No such spurious scholarship will be accepted on this island about the beloved personage who for centuries has been adored as the patron of children and sailors. This can be asserted with more confidence since many new residents here come from the New York area. There, when English settlers in New Amsterdam began to borrow the customs and legends surrounding the Dutch Saint Nicholas *(Sinterclaes),* he became a kind of benevolent magician, and Santa Claus got the name by which we generally call him. In the face of reports that he is dead, however, it may be stated that it is true that his health and life depend upon the faith of children—and maybe of sailors and other elders.

That faith has lapsed on occasion. Sailors are notably skeptical, and some juveniles have taken a sort of perverse pride in the disillusionment of themselves and their companions. Some people retire from magic as well as from money-grubbing. Fortunately, some other elders, odd characters for the task, have wrought minor miracles in the rehabilitation of faith. Two of them, whose names are little remembered, were Clement Clarke Moore and Francis Pharcellus Church.

Moore was a rich and serious young man, possibly intolerant in his religious views. When he was hardly beyond the years of hanging up his own stocking, he expressed his regret that some of his associates did "not devote their leisure hours to useful learning rather than to frivolous amusements." Later he placed his basis for fame on his scholarship in the Hebrew language. In 1821 he became professor of biblical learning in the General Theological Seminary, which he had helped establish, and in 1823, he became professor of Oriental and Greek literature.

He must have been a very respectable and solemn personage. Yet in 1822, between these two professorial dates, he may have seemed to some of his clerical colleagues a little frivolous himself. Then, he wrote as a gift for his own children the ballad which has been a gift to all children ever since. It began, as all of us who were ever children recall, " 'Twas the night before Christmas, when all through the house. . . ." That's all for which today Clement Moore is remembered, and that's enough to be remembered for. It has done much to sustain the faith in Santa Claus, upon which Santa Claus's whole existence depends.

(Lucy Daniels on the island remembers that, as a child in Hackensack, she was taken annually to the big house of Moore's grandson, at the corner of Euclid and Grand avenues. There at every Christmastime this rich descendant of the rich old poet read the ballad to successive juvenile assemblies. So Lucy came close to a bright place in this Christmas tradition. Still, her chief memory of those occasions is that the son of the reader, Perry Moore, was a stinker. Possibly his crime was that he pulled her curls.)

The second great one of the strong in Santa Claus faith was Church, with the odd middle name of Pharcellus. He was an editorial writer on the *New York Sun*. At that time, the *Sun* was regarded as often cynical in its opinions, sometimes cruel, even— some said—malicious. But in 1897 a scrawled letter came into its editorial sanctum from a little girl named Virginia. Some of her friends had been telling her things that disturbed her. Was there really a Santa Claus? Eloquently, this newspaperman, generally engaged in tough exchanges on public affairs, answered her with the strong, affirmative "Yes, Virginia." He told her not to listen to such negative heresy. She was, he wrote, threatened by the skepticism of a skeptical age—as so many of us, young and old, are today. Of course there was a Santa Claus. There always will be, he wrote, as long as the blessed old saint gladdens the heart of childhood, and warms the hearts of elders, too.

Virginia was reassured. All of us should be. Santa Claus is not dead. He is not even ailing. He will cross the skies and gladden Christmas mornings as long as he receives the faith of little children. He needs also the belief of all those of all ages who keep the wonder and glory of childhood in their hearts.

Santa Claus has long known his way to Baygall. He will not be lost in the new maze of South Beach. He will always be as real as the expectation to which he comes. The only question is whether all of us, young and old, keep the capability of wonder and gladness where the stockings hang.

Listen carefully and you will hear him on Christmas Eve, "Happy Christmas to all, and to all a good-night."

The saint is as real as the sugarplum. Only dullards deny him. We need to mourn only those who dismiss his magic as they have lost their own.

December 21, 1972

A Little Pregnant

Tomorrow will be better.

Days that I have loved I close your eyes.

Either view may be appropriate as a new year comes. Pessimists and optimists may argue about the matter. The certain thing is that on Hilton Head Island the year comes to an argumentative close. Some of our most distinguished friends and neighbors took varying views about such things as the industrialization of the great Port Royal estuary and where to build, or whether to build, a shorter route to Beaufort. Their arguments, may serve us all. But it need not have been sharpened as good Chuck Carpenter did when, as a paper-company convert to ecology and a onetime champion discus thrower at Harvard, he really threw the javelin toward Henry Haskell's hide.

There are, of course, arguments on both sides of the question about the industrialization of the Victoria Bluff area. Some industry and industrial jobs may be essential to the improvement of the living standards of many people in Beaufort County, as Henry Haskell thinks. A little pollution and a little threat to the water supply hereabouts might be like being a little pregnant, as Carpenter and

George Dibert believe. Acrimony will not serve their debate. Also, in the discussion of the shorter route to Beaufort, general happiness will not be served by any skeptical Hilton Head inquiries as to who wants to go to Beaufort, fast or slow.

The new year might be a good time to begin the elimination of anything resembling invective from debate. Certainly Hilton Head has had enough of feuding. Maybe antagonism is the natural product of people cooped up on an island. Long before most of us came here, it was indigenous in the Montague-Capulet relations of the old Hinesville, Georgia, associates Fraser and Hack. Now a suit for defamation (the Atlantis Company versus the Hilton Head Company) arrays some old islanders against each other plus some new absentee investors who feel they have interests to defend. Some Atlantis stockholders seem to be being sued by themselves, which may be natural on a complicated island.

Still, somehow, serenity—which is universally presented as the chief product of this island—might be served by more attention to the amenities than the animosities. As charity begins at home, maybe the writer of this column should mollify his tilting at condominiums as Don Quixote tilted at windmills (with approximately the same results). The nicest people live in condominiums—even in Sealofts, which in delicacy should not be referred to as monkey houses. Certainly they have the rest of us outnumbered and, looking at the sales figures, outpriced. Certainly no fury should be enlisted in the cause of futility. Despite this writer's protest, the movable latrines still gleam like white monuments at the roadsides. He can take little satisfaction from the news that the protest here may have had some effect abroad. Lynn Bitner reports that at the new Sea Pines venture at Las Palmas on Puerto Rico these necessaries are "light green, very attractive, and blend into the landscape."

Possibly little is to be gained by any snarls from this island that South Carolina promoters and politicians, including some in Beaufort, are ready to destroy this lovely corner of South Carolina by industries of uncertain menace—even more determined in pique as a result of their rebuke in the BASF case. They may be all, all honorable gentlemen, not entirely intent upon fouling their own nest.

And here on the island old divisions might be modified. It would save six letters on the typewriter if, as Tom Howard suggested,

"Island" were eliminated from the name of this beloved shore. Perhaps Roller and McKibben were just men ahead of their time when they proposed a city here even before Charles Fraser made Harbour Town a metropolis and South Beach an apartmented suburb. The security gates should not divide a peaceful people, though Cabell Phillips, founder of the Peasant Freeholders' Party, will be wise in not trying to pet any of those carnivorous canines Vance Fowler is introducing to protect his people. Even the Cable Vision entrepreneurs—who recently, in bringing us a brighter image, disrupted water, electric, and phone communications—should be forgiven. Possibly Tim Doughtie, in dramatizing visual pollution here, as elsewhere, is overwrought. It is about time a calm people realized that, as the island grows, trailers must be accepted as a continuing item in island architecture. Maybe we should recognize that the speeders on the roads are rushing on errands to make us happy. At any rate, that seems to be the general impression.

A truce on gripes. A pox on defamation, legal or otherwise. All is for the best in the best of possible worlds. Anyhow that was what such a wise man as Voltaire had his Candide saying, come what might.

December 28, 1972

Our Vigilantes

One of Hilton Head Island's most precious possessions is a self-appointed and public-devoted vigilance committee. Excellent as were the purposes in stemming the population explosion here, the old Committee to Blow Up the Bridge was probably doomed to futility. Now with the possibility of two bridges to blow up, its chances of success would be even more remote. Among its members today there is a growing demand for two bridges for escape, even if one seemed too much for entrance.

The vigilantes may be more successful in keeping the populace here warned as to what it may face. Two of the most active members are Bob Whitney, who brings to his observations the talents of a long-time newspaper reporter, and Elizabeth Grant, who as artist never forgets the aesthetics of ecology. What both report and document by clippings is that coastal America is in clear and evident danger of despoilation. Bob brings the news of California coastal communities now up in arms against any more growth. And Elizabeth arrays the findings of two *Washington Star* reporters who write with alarm of the present possibility of a new American super city fifteen hundred miles long and about six blocks wide from Maine to Florida. "Its street system will be a profusion of country roads and former highways, lined with telephone poles, stop lights, gas stations, motels, cottages, pizza parlors. Its sewer system will consist mainly of hundreds of thousands of septic tanks. Its water will come from wells beside the septic tanks. . . . Its civic leaders will be mostly politicians and businessmen from small towns and rural counties who thrive off of higgledy-piggledy growth."

Though it lies in that fifteen-hundred-mile-long line of butchered shore and beach erosion, Hilton Head Island may be made relatively secure by the wide waters of Port Royal and Calibogue Sounds. Skull and Mackay's creeks may protect it despite more and bigger bridges across them. But the image of possible despoilation ought to be kept before us like the warning of hellfire between sinners and sin.

Islands better insulated by more water have not always been more secure. The latest word about such security comes from Guam. It lies in the Pacific, 6,300 miles from California and 1,690 from Tokyo. Once it was a place to which the Navy Department sent officers it couldn't get rid of but did not want around. There in super isolation they bore the title of Governor and languished in exile. Then World War II made the island a torn and contested base. Rusty old tanks and other war relics were left there with the peace. After the war one Japanese veteran was able to hide out there for more than twoscore years in a cave. Now the Japanese require condominiums. And they are getting them!

One press report states that Guam is "bursting with construction . . . land prices are soaring." One Japanese group is spending more than $20 million to push aside jungle and rusted wartime remains to build a hotel, a thirty-six-hole golf course, a country club, a marina, and an apartment complex. This is only part of the $78.5 million worth of hotel projects in the works. Building permits this year will total over $92 million—twice those of last year. Responsible estimates are that $200 million in resort investment is coming in. Already there is a five-counter McDonald's—called the world's biggest hamburger stand. Most of the customers and investors are Japanese and Nationalist Chinese. Other money is coming from South Korea. The earth may be divided by Communism, but it begins to seem truly one world in terms of the condominium.

Historians will recall that this generation brought atomic energy, flight into outer space, and the condominium. They should not forget pizza parlors and septic tanks, one-piece plastic bathrooms, the hamburger chain, and the beer can. Present occupants of islands better not forget them either. We need Bob and Elizabeth to keep us always reminded.

January 4, 1973

The Iron in the Velvet

Into his excellent article about our island as it faces its future in 1973 and after, Charles Fraser packed a great deal of good sense and splendid reassurance. Also, and perhaps characteristic of Charles, he slipped the iron into the velvet.

Future generations here, he said, may be the losers "because of the timidity of our polite Hilton Head society." All it would take to prevent such loss, he suggests, would be "five fired-up, impolite, unreasonable, opinionated old men and women in hiking boots and with a typewriter at their desks, and a willingness to spend a little time at the Beaufort County Courthouse to check to see if any conservation easements have been recorded in the various Plantations of Hilton Head Island, in order to prepare a map showing exactly where the permanently protected easement areas are to be. . . ."

There is a good deal to be said for the earlier statement by Charles that many conservationists here, including this writer, are "strictly concrete sidewalk people." This one certainly hasn't walked a beach before breakfast. Sometimes he finds it difficult to make it from the bed to the coffee cup. And, to be perfectly frank about it, he is sometimes more personally irritated by the lack of parking than by the limit on parks. He can, however, make some claim to being sometimes "a fired-up, impolite, unreasonable, opinionated" old man. Probably not even Charles Fraser would disagree about that.

Charles has made an excellent suggestion in his proposal that each development "set aside 20% to 25% of its space as parks (not golf course), woods, and open spaces." His suggestion is excellent even if it carries the implication that Sea Pines has done that and others have not. So the Sojourner has taken up the matters with that truer conservationist—his editor, Ralph Hilton. *The Island Packet* will be happy to print such a map. It will save a lot of trouble, however, if the developers will cooperate in this enterprise. Not even "fired-up, impolite, unreasonable, opinionated old men and women" should be required to search for these open spaces like needles in the haystack of Beaufort County Courthouse's records. Unless "impolite, unreasonable, and opinionated," the developers ought to be willing to help these old men and women. Each could provide *The Packet* with a full list of the plats they have made inviolately open. Then they can count on it that in a "fired-up, impolite, unreasonable, opinionated" manner *The Island Packet* will check their claims and make that map.

Certainly, as Charles says, we may all have been too polite. Our organizations may have clung too closely to the amenities in dealing with the developers and with others as well.

Now is the time, and by invitation, to put the chips on the table or, maybe better said, the claims of conservation on the map. Publicly, Charles has bared his own breast. He will undoubtedly be ready with the first list of "the woodland areas set aside now, in 1973, by permanent deed covenants which can't be changed by future changes of stock ownership, etc." Other developers should be glad to do likewise. They have told the world that they are fired-up.

Some of their brochures almost look like flame. All are polite gentlemen. There is no good reason to believe that they are unreasonable or unduly opinionated. None of them, however, qualify as old men or women. All look to the future.

So let's have that map. And once we have it, we should keep it up to date. Thank you, Charles. *The Packet* is prepared. Heigh-ho, to the courthouse with the lists! The map they bring back will be suitable for framing in appreciation of paradise or at least a guide to tell us whether hopes of continuing paradise should go up or down.

January 11, 1973

Lawyers Chose Hearses

Lands developed from the wilderness have similar problems. Captain John Rains, one of the long hunters in early Tennessee, described some. He welcomed settlers as strengthening the encampments that had grown into villages on the Cumberland River. But he scowled at some newcomers.

"We used to think we had the devil to pay (and a heavy debt, too, running on long installments) before the doctors and the lawyers came," he said, "but the doctors introduced diseases, and the lawyers instituted suits, and now we have all to pay."

The situation is not quite like that on Hilton Head Island. More doctors have come and more are needed. The old folks brought along their own ailments. And there were disputes before the lawyers arrived. Indeed, some of the island's energy in development may have come from the friction generated between the Hack and Fraser fiefdoms when most residents of the building lots were only songbirds and snakes.

Defamation in those days was just an ordinary element of conversation. Indeed, ripe rhetoric about some neighbors—even cousins—was an art form in this Georgia–South Carolina region before antagonisms advanced from the code duello to competitive brochures.

384

But now the brochures seem almost less numerous than the briefs. And defamation has become the subject of a $2.5 million damage suit in which the clients on both sides are so mixed up that some of those involved seem to be plaintiffs and defendants at the same time.

No mere layman should express any opinion about the merits of cases which the courts will have to decide. But a layman may note the proliferation of attorneys along the fairways and the lagoons. The Hilton Head phone book, which is already out of date in terms of new arrivals, lists a score of attorneys, and there are others just waiting for office space.

Certainly the number of lawyers must be counted as a sign of progress, along with the number of condominiums built and building. The lighthouse at Harbour Town is no more evidence of the island's growth than the almost-high-rise house of Joab Dowling, which sits between the cemetery and the sound. Also, in measuring its growth, Hilton Head can boast of more lawyers than are actually here. Some with offices in two places may best represent the need for a shorter, quicker route between the island and Beaufort— where the courthouse is, even if the best clients are really here. Lawyers from Columbia and more distant places, engaged in Hilton Head causes, help indicate the litigious advance of which any community counting its growth should be proud.

And, bless the boys, they are not always disputatious; there are deeds to be drawn, contracts to be made, estates to be settled, taxes to be avoided. Tax shelter and cabana are, sometimes with their aid, said to be synonymous. Where lawyers multiply, perhaps there should be greater confidence that justice is secure.

Anyhow, the time is long passed since Zack Van Landingham, as a man who had come for retirement or refuge from Mississippi, alone practically constituted the bar of Hilton Head Island. More lawyers came. More will be coming. One was waiting impatiently for *The Island Packet* to move out of its old quarters so that, in them, he could compose documents where just copy was written.

Old Captain Rains of Tennessee must have been just a sourpuss in his comment on the barristers. Long ago, a wiser man said that nothing is certain except death and taxes. He might have added that another certainty is that, in both cases, a lawyer will be at hand. Anyhow, that's so in the growing good fortune of Hilton Head.

January 18, 1973

The Lesson of Atlantis

One of the nicest things about the opening of the new office of *The Island Packet* is that it comes at a time when fabulously greater façades are being projected toward the skies. Risk rides as high as hopes. The scholarly incorporators of the Atlantis Company boldly took its name from the mythological island of the blest which sank into the sea, perhaps under the weight of its own virtues.

There is nothing mythical, however, about that company's plans to begin the spending of millions in May, more thereafter. Indeed, in its ultimate soaring prospects it proposes even to raze the Adventure Inn, which so recently seemed so substantial a monument on this shore. In its place, the company will erect greater edifices for more and more residents and visitors. And as the company soars, it does not take wing alone! Beside its precious properties and behind them, others are already raising buildings, the very mention of which a short time ago would have been regarded as a hoax.

So *The Island Packet* opens its doors with all due deference to its biggers. Our building will certainly not add such weight as might sink an island into the sea. But sometimes in its tabby story-and-a-half building mirrored in a lagoon, those who built it and love it have an uneasy sort of Cinderella feeling. Less than three years ago, as its voyagers frankly stated at the time, it was launched with a shoestring for a sail. Not a penny of profit has been taken out of it since. And now its dazzling new quarters look almost like the magic clothing provided Cinderella by a fairy godmother, which might disappear abruptly at the stroke of midnight—or maybe the dawn of April Fools' Day—leaving not even a glass slipper behind.

Such an event by the lagoon in the light of the moon is not apprehended. *The Island Packet* has only seen two calendar years, 1971 and 1972. Possibly that gives it the right to smirk with pride at the statement made by Charles Fraser coincident with the opening of the new building. Fraser wrote with some forebodings but much faith about "the excessive surge of building in 1971 and 1972." Well, Chanticleer was under the delusion that his crowing brought the sunrise. *The Packet* might be pardoned or laughed at if it had some similar notion. But Charles, as a romantic with his moments of realism, also called upon all to face the alternatives "delight or blight."

That confrontation may be a sign of island maturity. It could also be a sign that the first unblemished faith in perfection here has been slightly shaken. Not all growth has been good since those first days of the island's reawakening when Sea Pines promised one acre of wilderness forever to every acre of development. And if some fault has attended the island's expansion, or explosion, since, Charles and Fred Hack—as the original builders of the dream—might seem to be the men hurt most by it. It is easy to think of them as men crying all the way to the bank.

But no tears are evident. And if the growth has been excessive, as Charles says, he also sees the need for more restaurants and other facilities. If he has any feelings of guilt about "excessive" expansion, *The Packet* shares them. Since it began to publish, it has been muttering about that possible "blight." The Sojourner has even given aid and comfort to that company of fantasy—the Committee to Blow Up the Bridge. And yet, as Charles has sold more and more properties to the excessive buyers, *The Packet* has gladly taken the advertisements of possibly excessively hopeful vendors of goods and services. So while it has sometimes assumed the attitude of Horatius at the bridge holding back the hordes of hopeful sharers in paradise, it has also joined in the hospitalities. *Ambivalence* may be a good word for many Hilton Headers. Many are moved by that condition involving attraction toward and repulsion from any and all newcomers. Sometimes, indeed, this island seems to be wholly occupied by those who want to have their cake and eat it too.

And why not? So far that system has worked pretty well. Those already settled here don't want any more people to come, but Sea Pines reports that a great part of its sales result from the beckoning by residents to others to join them here. Certainly, as they might be expected to do in view of their aversion to more crowding here, islanders do not fill their letters or their mouths with reports about the island designed to discourage other possible settlers.

So beneath the topless towers of its neighbors, *The Packet* opens its doors with the island's neat combination of hostility and hospitality. Please don't crowd us but "Y'all come." Maybe that was the trouble with the island of Atlantis. It became, according to Plato, the ideal commonwealth. People seeking the ideal thronged to it. And so, at last overloaded, it sank into the sea. That does not seem immediately threatened here except in some of the erosion on North Forest Beach. But those South Carolina investors who named their company after great, glamorous, lost Atlantis may have known exactly what they were doing in terms of both classic knowledge and the profit motive.

January 25, 1973

Evacuation or Invasion

During the recent rough weather in the South, which sent icy chills even to Hilton Head Island, the professor and his wife drove this way from the North. Winter was no worse than expected in New Jersey, but Virginia and North Carolina were swamped with snow, and South Carolina was menacing with ice. Then they ran into that long, chill, rainy spell in Beaufort County. Almost warily they moved along the road from Ware's Fruit Stand to the Byrnes crossing. They seemed lonely on their side of the road, heading island-ward, but besides them coming away from the bridge was an almost uninterrupted, bumper-to-bumper stream of cars, trucks, and other vehicles.

"They're evacuating the island," the professor's lady said.

She had no way of knowing that it looks that way every afternoon, rain, shine, or storm—even in the very rare flurry of snow. The spectacle in the morning is that of an invasion. And to use a term learned from warfare in recent years, that is a real escalation.

Back in 1961 Editor Thomas R. Waring of the *Charleston News and Courier* wrote an appreciative piece about the possibilities of the island. He noted among other things that construction on the island in 1958 "reached a total value of $450,000 according to the chamber of commerce." Lots in Sea Pines then ranged in price from $2,400 to $12,000, and the best lot on the island had recently brought $16,000. But he used the bridge as chief instrument for measurement.

"During the first full year of operation (1956–57) when the toll was $2.50 a round trip, 48,000 vehicles crossed the bridge. The next year after the toll was cut to $1.25, the figure was 80,000; last year, 96,000; and the first five months of this year 120,000."

The chamber of commerce has stopped counting now. There was some question as to who owned the counter which Larry Rogers, as chamber secretary, used to stretch across the bridge approach. But the Sojourner's associate, Ralph Hilton, who has a mind for figures, says the present number of vehicles crossing is five thousand a day. That's 1,825,000 vehicles a year—and what vehicles!

They range from motorbikes and passenger cars to huge trailers and mobile monsters which look like diesel dinosaurs. Morning and evening their procession does look like evacuation or invasion. And actually it is both. Their number indicates the proportions of the problem recently pointed out by the damage to the two-lane bottleneck bridge across the creeks. It also indicates both the fabulous growth of the island and the fearful lack of housing for construction and other workers here.

By day the invasion almost swamps the island and particularly the narrow twisting roads in the developments. Cordillo Parkway may, indeed, one day look like a parkway. Today the big vehicles which relate to the construction projects along it have made it look like a passage where the Vietcong and the Yankees had recently collided and bombers above had contributed to devastation. The causeway to Calibogue Cay is clogged with motorized equipment where villas are being built as close as possible to the tide in the marshes (maybe closer). And everywhere bomb-shaped concrete mixers move like bullets under the trees.

Maybe all this movement is essential to building the best of all possible worlds. Perhaps, as Charles Fraser indicated, the area around Harbour Town will be beautiful again when the construction is done—if it ever is. The one certain thing is that there seems no prospect, late or soon, of the solution to the traffic problem which not only crowds the roads but has made parking a difficulty in the old wilderness island.

Maybe the next essential job will be designing traffic lights and parking meters which will conform to the amenities and the decor of planned paradise. But at the moment the traffic which rises like the tides at the bridge is Hilton Head's No. 1 headache. Talk of shorter routes and scenic routes is an indulgence in delusions of grandeur while the island bulges and, in effect, the bottleneck bridge shrinks. Come high water or hurricane and all our island planning may look like the design for a trap.

February 1, 1973

Eliza of the Green Thumb

Eliza Pinckney must be delighted in heaven. And all hereabouts have a right to be delighted on earth. The reason, of course, lies in the news that Pinckney Island, the south end of which we cross every time we traverse the bridge, will be preserved as a coastal wilderness, safe even from us.

One of the owners of the island, Edward Starr, Jr., has already given his half of the island to the Natural Land Trust, Inc. Now James M. Barker plans at his death to leave his four-thousand-acre share of the island to the Federal Bureau of Sports, Fisheries and Wildlife. Meantime, Sea Pines Plantation, which is Charles Fraser, will act as custodian of the Barker land and, undoubtedly, at least as adviser on the Starr tract.

This is an excellent arrangement. Freed from costs, moneylenders, and the clamor of people for condominiums, Charles Fraser could hardly be excelled as a custodian. Oddly enough, those most devoted to the areas he has created are sometimes most critical of what seem to be lapses in his dream. But all recognize him as a man sensitive and imaginative in the use of land. He has made it clear that he is no Druid in his preference for the forested wilderness above people; but on Pinckney Island, where primeval hickories and oaks now grow beside the pines, he could be an adequate keeper of the spirit of Eliza Pinckney.

Elizabeth Lucas Pinckney (1722–93) is too little remembered in this land which she touched with hard head and warm heart, a green thumb and a ready pen. No mere lady gardener, she managed plantations for profit from the time she was a girl of sixteen. She introduced the culture of indigo into the colony, and she produced at least enough silk to make some charming dresses. Pinckney Island today recalls the mansion house there of her husband, Charles Pinckney, which contained one of the best libraries in the colony. All sign of it is gone now. Some trees which are now called primeval may grow where Eliza's gardens spread.

There was something of the Druid in her. She loved both this Low Country and the English countryside in which she lived while her husband was the colonial agent for South Carolina in London. And after she returned to this country, where she was soon widowed, she wrote an anguished letter about trees to a friend in England. Her spelling now seems somewhat odd, but her preferences were always clear. She wrote, "Being a sort of anthusiaste in my Veneration for fine trees, I look upon the destroyers of Pyrford Avenue as sacrilidgious Enemies to posterity, and upon an old oak with the reverencial Esteem of a Druid."

"Pyrford Avenue" seems a little mysterious here. It was not identified even by footnote in a recent authoritative edition of Eliza Pinckney's letters (edited by Elise Pinckney—University of North Carolina Press). Obviously, however, Pyrford was a village in Surrey, near which she lived with her husband in England. Its trees and everything else have probably now been enveloped by the metropolitan sprawl of London. Other things and places she loved disappeared, too. Modern South Carolina historians writing of Pinckney Island note that "no trace remains of the plantation and the mansion house."

Loving trees as she did, she still would not have welcomed the return of the wilderness across her neatly planted fields, her carefully tended gardens, even the crumbled foundations of the Pinckney mansion. Yet she might have welcomed even less the heartless hacking which has so often moved across this land and others to make room for a sort of poisoned progress. It is quite possible—even probable—that she would have liked better the return of the plantation to nature by Mr. Barker and Mr. Starr. As both an "anthusiaste" and a practical woman, she would have every reason to approve the selection of Charles Fraser as the custodian of both Pinckney Island and the Pinckney heritage there, to which she added so much. But she'll be watching from heaven in high expectation, and the rest of us, properly denied access to the island, will be watching from the boats and the bridge.

February 8, 1973

Battle for the Book

Anybody who has been complaining about the slow movement of the mails may be able to take comfort by contemplating the pace of the United States Government Printing Office. Most of us on this quiet (except for the sound of hammer and saw) sea island have learned to adjust ourselves to something less than sudden action. Still somehow, despite recurrent petulance with the politicians, we expect more speed from a government operating on a $268 million budget.

But try to buy a book from the goverment that prints it. On September 24, 1972, this hopeful islander wrote the Government Printing Office about a book it had issued. In reply, he received in November a form and a statement that a check for $7.75 should be returned with it. He dispatched the check on November 11. The government was not exactly dilatory in taking the money. The check was cashed on November 21.

Still no book. So on December 27, not quite despairing in the Christmas season, this islander wrote another letter, this time to the superintendent of documents, stating that he really needed the book in some research he was doing. That gentleman remained an anonymous bureaucrat. His office returned the letter on January 10 with a printed card attached to it. It read: "Frankly, the present demands for Government periodicals and publications is unprecedented and we are swamped with orders." Impersonally, however, the card added "your patience is appreciated," without ever understanding that any patience which had ever existed was exhausted. "Shortly" he would receive (possibly on another printed card) "acknowledgment" of this order.

That came the first of February on another printed card carrying in large letters the heading, "SPECIAL INFORMATION REGARDING YOUR RECENT INQUIRY." Recent, hell!

Under the big type was the salutation "Dear Customer." To that affectionate greeting was added the printed message: "Every effort will be made to satisfy your claim or provide appropriate information as promptly as possible. Should you find it necessary to request additional information concerning your inquiry, please make reference to the control number shown in the block on the reverse side of this card. Thank you for your cooperation."

Now at least the islander had a number—7857, or (as printed on another card) 007857. But no book, and the government still hung on to his money. At this time, in a departure from scholarship, old 7857 was working on his income tax, and the idea occurred to him that possibly he ought to follow the example in managerial efficiency of his government.

He could tell the government how much he owed them without enclosing the check. Then when the IRS asked him for the money, he could send them back a card carrying the information that "Frankly," at this time he was "swamped" with "demands." When the IRS, as it might, made further request, he could send them another card saying that "shortly" he might get around to it, and in the meantime he could add the message "Thank you for your cooperation." He might even give the IRS a number while it stood in line waiting with the same patience for which the GPO had thanked him.

Well, a citizen surely has a right to dream. He might even indulge in the fantasy that the government was going to pay him six percent interest on the $7.75 it had kept in its treasury since November 21, 1972, without any *quid pro quo*. But dammit, he wants that book. And as a citizen he still conceives it possible for the GPO to stop wasting its time sending him anonymous and meaningless cards.

So this is a warning to the United States of America and to the head of the GPO, listed in the latest *Congressional Directory* as Public Printer A. N. Spence: Stop playing cards and get off your tail and send me that book.

Or else!

February 15, 1973

Centennial Warning

People are traveling far and fast these days and planning ahead for it. More than three years before the bicentennial of the Declaration of Independence, Charleston is planning to get ahead of the rest of the United States by celebrating the event on July 2, 1976, instead of the familiar Fourth of July. Actually, even then Charleston will be late. The Continental Congress declared the independence of the colonies on June 9, 1776, by passing a simple resolution by Richard Henry Lee: "That these colonies are, and of a right ought to be, free and independent states." The Declaration of Independence, written by Jefferson, was only the magnificent icing on the cake.

Americans celebrated enthusiastically and in various ways on the centennial of the Declaration in 1876. And free and independent travelers today may find interesting a guidebook, *How to See New York*, published then in honor of the occasion. Chuck Carpenter of Calibogue Cay has a copy inscribed "George N. Carpenter 1876." Certainly a variety of facilities were provided for the traveler then. The piers were crowded with steamers for Europe and for almost every waterside town on the eastern seaboard. Twenty-three railroads provided access to the city, many originating from the Grand Central Station and more from ferry slips to their tracks in New Jersey. Hotels ranged downward from the excellence of the marble Fifth Avenue Hotel at the juncture of Fifth Avenue, Broadway, and Twenty-third Street. Also, there were still honky-tonk refreshment stands on Fifth Avenue. Trains on elevated tracks carried dark smoke plumes above their engines. Horsecars were still in vogue. The guide advised tourists: "Strangers employing coaches will consult their own interests and convenience by making a bargain with the driver before entering the vehicle."

Travel to the metropolis was attended by luxury and also by hazard. Americans who have been warned of dangers on city streets in our time may be surprised at some of the "Advice to Strangers" given in the guide. This ran, in part:

To our friends from the country who are visiting the city, we offer a few suggestions that may assist them in their efforts to see the city to the best advantage, and the greatest economy of time and convenience.

If possible, reach the city in the day-time.

Avoid being too free with strangers.

If you are obliged to make inquiries on the street, apply to a policeman or go into a respectable place of business.

Avoid all crowds, particularly at night.

Careful attention to your own business will insure freedom from annoyance or interruption.

These may be good rules today, but it may be interesting to note that they were rules which seemed necessary when the republic was only a hundred years old, not two hundred as is in prospect now.

Note to be headed either *Power of the Press* or *All Is Forgiven.* Two days after last week's column about the struggle to buy a book from the Government Printing Office, another anonymous communication came from the GPO. It returned the $7.75 it had taken for the book in November and stated calmly that it had not been able to find the book it published, which was asked for last September.

So the reputation for honesty of the United States of America is redeemed, but even in this age of computers and printed cards the federal government still seems lost in the maze of its own printed matter.

Maybe a new declaration of independence is required of citizens wanting any prompt services from the United States. Certainly the effort to get one of the government's books from the government was a process which almost covered "the course of human events."

February 22, 1973

Far Side of Paradise

A good many of us on this island came along as a part of the society of the F. Scott Fitzgerald novels. We sometimes played roles identical to those in *This Side of Paradise*. We had grown older, Fitzgerald was dead, and Zelda had been burned to death in a fire in a hospital for the mentally ill when Arthur Mizener wrote the Fitzgerald biography, *The Far Side of Paradise*. Fortunately, as is the case with the moon, the far side is seldom seen. We did not need the assurances of astronauts to know that it was there.

We are aware, of course, of the threats to serenity which may come from a company such as BASF polluting land, water, and sky. We are wary about other industries. Now we may notice that a place as similar to ours as Boca Raton, Florida, has become aware of the danger of self-pollution. After its jump from seven thousand people in 1960 to probably forty thousand today, the city is trying by law to put a "population cap" upon the town. Building permits will be limited. The number of dwelling units—both apartments and houses—will be limited to forty thousand. The legislation may not stand up in the courts. It indicates fears that paradise, indeed, may have a dark side.

There are other signs. Some fears as well as pride went into the Boca Raton Community Hospital, built without federal or local aid. Private suites on its top floor cost $110 a day. It is, however, as Jon Nordheimer wrote in the *New York Times*, "so tony it has a French chef and gourmet menus that offer oysters Rockefeller, lobster thermidor, Chateaubriand, rock cornish hen, and pompano. (Martinis, brandy, and champagne are available to patients at extra cost.)"

Still, even in the top-floor suites, people die. And provision is made for them. Crypts at the Boca Raton Mausoleum are available from six thousand dollars to nine thousand dollars. The most expensive are those nearest the ground, not those nearest heaven. Built last year, the mausoleum's one thousand spaces were quickly grabbed up—"a record for selling mausoleum space in Florida," a salesman told Nordheimer.

A furrier who finds business good even in sunny Florida reports, "Good, honest, solid citizens like Boca to retire to because it's a place where there is still civil obedience and people can walk around the streets at night and not be molested."

But a clinical psychologist with a flourishing practice says: "Boca Raton is a splendid community, a real garden spot. The trouble is that so many of the wealthy fail to get involved with anything more than rich food, alcohol and golf. Most of the patients I see are depressed, psychosomatic, and impotent. They are flocking to doctors to escape from their loneliness. They are bored with themselves."

A novelist writing in the same years as Fitzgerald was Sinclair Lewis. One of his books was titled *It Can't Happen Here.* He was not writing about real-estate development or the quest for the ideal shore but about dictatorship and war. We have escaped both on this continent. Maybe we on this shore can escape the dangers which beset Boca Raton. There is good reason to believe that. It is remarkable here how many retired people are involved in far more things than the ominous trio mentioned by the psychologist. And, taken in proper measure, there is nothing wrong with those three. Good food, good drink, a good game are all excellent parts of the good life. The danger lies in mass flight and individual quest for escape. For many, "getting out of the rat race" may be in itself a withdrawal from life. And the dangers of that are certainly not restricted to

Boca Raton. The dreadful possibility is that on every shore men and women may pollute themselves and end their lives in stagnant pools beside the fresh and lively sea.

March 1, 1973

Ancient Swarm

This is expected to be the busiest spring Hilton Head Island has ever seen. But it certainly is not the first, maybe not the greatest, one of crowding growth. Alden Baker has loaned *The Island Packet* a rare framed copy of *The New South,* published at Port Royal in 1862. It will hang on the paper's wall until it joins other historic items in the island museum which one day will be established here. Now and later this old paper of March 3, 1862, will recall the strenuous, stirring days here at the time of its issue.

In those days the word *plush* was applied not to this island but to Beaufort. That town, "the Newport of the South," had been completely occupied by Federal troops since the landing here the fall before. And there were probably more whites on Daufuskie than ever since. They certainly missed the mobile, yellow, monster equipment now everywhere so much in evidence on Hilton Head Island. Young Yankee soldiers were busy dragging heavy guns through mud and mire with power apparently provided only by main strength and awkwardness. The soldiers could work only at night because of the proximity of rebel troops in the Savannah area.

But Hilton Head swarmed night and day with soldiers, including new black volunteers whose drilling was praised by officers. *The New South* described the war boom on this shore. "Since the 7th of November, a town has sprung up on Hilton Head, where at least a thousand civilians must be now employed, in one capacity or another—teamsters, carpenters, machinists, laborers, newspaper reporters, sutlers, postmasters and editors; and, of late, even women and children have been seen within the limits of the command. Long lines of hospitals, stables and store houses for quartermasters' and commissaries' use, bakeries, Negro quarters and other buildings have been erected, quite transforming the appearance of the spot."

And in the midst of bustle there was apparently sinister drama, too. The paper reported: "The Steamer Mississippi, from Fortress Monroe, with General Benjamin Butler aboard and a body of reinforcements for his command got aground on Frying Pan Shoals on Friday morning the 28th in sight of Cape Fear. Her anchor was immediately cast and she struck on it, knocking such a hole in her bottom as to cause a serious injury. Accordingly she put into this port on the 2nd. inst., having been obliged to keep men at her pumps constantly after the accident. She went direct to Seabrook, where the troops under General Butler were encamped. On the 11th she was so far repaired as to be got off, but ran aground again within a few hundred yards of Seabrook landing."

Then the report added ominously: "The Captain is named Fulton, and a Southerner by birth; he has been placed under arrest."

There is no information available around here as to what happened to Fulton. Maybe he was guilty of shenanigans in seagoing sabotage. But *The New South* suggested that the only evidence against him was being a Southerner. That could be a serious crime in this area in those days.

We know what happened to the possibly endangered General Butler: "General Butler with his staff and a portion of his force proceeds to their destination on the *Matanza*, loaned for that purpose by General Sherman. The *Mississippi* which has been again got off [evidently with a different captain] conveys the remainder of his original complement. Colonels Neal Dow, Dudley and Gooding are with General Butler; Mrs. Butler also accompanies the General. The health of the force was good."

General Butler's destination was New Orleans, and there he was given the bitter nickname "Beast Butler" because of his famous or infamous order: "When any female shall, by word, or gesture, or movement, insult or show contempt for any officer or soldier of the United States, she shall be regarded and held liable to be treated as a woman of the town plying her avocation."

Northerner or Southerner could be equal in crime.

Butler was accused of returning North with a lot of Southern silver spoons. Fulton's story, so far as our knowledge goes, ends with him still in jail on Hilton Head.

March 8, 1973

Sojourner's Guest

I'm an old lover of Hilton Head Island who's been away for a long time. I live now outside Brussels, near the Waterloo battleground, close by the old Forest of Soignes, which has been harvested for a thousand years. Still a delight, it proves that perfection can be preserved. I feared that the place my family and I had loved might not have been so preserved. Now, after returning for a weekend with my cousin Jonathan Daniels, what I have to report is, after all, a happy homecoming.

Six years' absence shouldn't qualify anyone to play the role of Rip Van Winkle, but having been absent these last six years from Hilton Head Island just might.

I came back prepared to bewail the bulldozing of paradise. Long ago we'd seen a map of Hilton Head's long-range development plan, which had looked to me like a Low-Country high-cost Levittown. If they really were to build all those roads and all those golf courses, it had to kill what we loved most about the place: the possibility of feeling alone, at the very edge of wilderness, yet with comfort nearby. We'd loved the great empty beaches where terns still nested in the open, the soft sandy lanes under the hanging

* Written by Peter Bagley.

mosses in the dark woods, and the very inaccessibility of so much of the island (the snakes saw to that).

None of my imaginings prepared me for the changes I found. Rip Van Winkle, awakened after twenty years, saw changes in the fortunes (and age) of his family and friends, but not in the aspect of his land. Here on Hilton Head, the fortunes seem intact after six years, and we'll all agree that we haven't aged much. But the face of the land has so changed that a return is a series of surprises. The biggest surprise of all is the discovery that there are as many pleasant changes as unpleasant ones.

The first change I noticed, driving onto the island, was pleasant. The long road from Port Royal to the circles used to run endlessly between dense woods. Now the view to the left has been opened at one point; you can see all the way to the ocean across a vast green lawn. This new golf course, the first of many new ones I saw, has turned blind scrub into parkland. I like the winding lagoons (new) with their high banks (dangerous for cocktail party returnees?) and the lovely homesites tucked in there.

Next came a sharp sense of loss. We entered Sea Pines through a new gate. We drove in—at that very place where our quiet, sandy forest lanes had been—on a smoothly paved highway through half-open, golf-course-studded country. (In fairness, let it be admitted that the highway curves gracefully and gently.) Where the dark woods had been, sand traps have replaced snakes as the hazards. A sign marks, as never before, a "wildlife preserve" which looks hardly bigger than a municipal park. (Are there paved "nature walks" in there?)

My third great surprise was Harbour Town. I know it wasn't there before; in our time you couldn't get anywhere near that corner of the island. By what magic did they conjure up a whole little Mediterranean port in six years? It's nothing like any idea I'd ever had of Hilton Head, of course, but dammit, I like it. Even the fake lighthouse. The port sits just where it should; its proportions are perfect. A quiet sunset stroll there should console anyone who deplores the "town's" proliferation (and there must be others beside Jonathan who do).

For some reason, though, they've planted a lot of houses like mushrooms on stems near the water close by. In Disneyland, such a juxtaposition of Africa and Portofino might get lost amid nearby

German castles or Matterhorns; here, it regrettably heightens an uneasy feeling of hokum, already a risk when you place a Mediterranean port in the Carolina Low Country. I thought those tree houses should have been put somewhere else.

South Beach had been our favorite spot. In those days, it was a pretty long trudge even to get to the beach, but we were usually alone there. We could even skinny-dip. After we moved away, while worrying about the fate of our island, it was a source of comfort, in the face of the long-range development plan, to have been told that here, at least, there could be no real development because of erosion and South Beach's exposure to arriving hurricanes. Where are the fears of yesteryear? They've built all over the place! Anti-erosion baffles preserve the shoreline, and perhaps there will be no more hurricanes—and our lonely beach is no more. But I have to admit that the development there looks like fun, and I wish my kids could use it.

I hope they will, before long. I'm happy to go back to Europe and report to them that our island is lovable still. It has changed. Some of its pleasures are gone, but there are many new ones to replace them. Like our Belgian forest, our beautiful Hilton Head has not been lost. I hope it never will be.

March 15, 1973

Joint Venture

Old people keep on learning on Hilton Head Island. The vocabulary expands. Those who never heard of ecology before today casually speak the whole language of environment and dangers to it. But that is only one item in the expansion of expression. There is, for instance, the new term—or maybe the old one—*joint venture*. It may be familiar to the businessmen now sheltered in security on the island. But to a sometime resident whose career was generally classified under "overhead expense," it is both new and startling.

The Sojourner, for instance, thought of joint venture as a good descriptive term for the Lewis and Clark expedition. They went out in a sort of double risk to explore the real estate which President Jefferson had purchased, sight unseen, from Napoleon. Their joint venture was eminently successful, even though the Louisiana Purchase did not contain the wonders which Jefferson's ignorance of the West had attributed to it. The results of other "joint ventures" have sometimes also been surprising. Perhaps Lewis and Clark were late in terms of joint venture. Certainly Rosencrantz and Guildenstern—whose combined endeavor was more sinister if less successful—were before them.

Probably neither history nor *Hamlet* are quite as enlightening on the subject as these times require. Charles Fraser and the Travelers Insurance people have sometimes seemed only to make the term more mystifying in the capitalistic charade which Sea Pines often seems to be. Now maybe even more confusing is the news that the Hilton Head Company, which is Fred Hack, is involved in a "joint venture" with Moore Homes of Savannah to build a total of 450 apartment units and a possible motel on a mid-island site to cost an approximate $15 million.

"The apartments," says Fred, "will be not unlike Moore Homes' Spanish Villa apartments in Savannah."

Certainly apartments promising low-cost housing will be welcomed on this island. Fred Hack, one of the joints in this joint venture, is respected as an island-loving developer who has sternly insisted upon architectural excellence in building on his lands. He had, for instance, grave doubts about *The Island Packet* building on his Pope Avenue Mall. He has admitted to pleasant surprise. Other such happy endings may be in store. But some islanders have made the long trek out Abercorn in Savannah to Saint Joseph's Hospital.

On that way they have passed the mushroom growth of pseudo-imaginative housing masses. This multiplied mediocrity for the lower middle class is not necessarily the slum for the future which it seems to promise to be. Spanish Villas has not quite the pretentiousness of some of its neighboring warrens. Normandy Towers, across the expressway, takes the prize for that with its pygmy turret-towers. Any modern equivalent of Rapunzel of the fairy tale would not need to have much gold hair to let it down for her lover to climb up upon it to her bower. The endless array of the mock mansard roofs of so-called Heritage Square are equally repellent. But Spanish Villas is bad enough—"1930 California architectural cuteness," one visitor called these apartments, which certainly do not evoke the Alhambra.

Moore Homes points the joint in this joint venture. We can hope that Fred will be insistent on his side of the joint. But on Hilton Head Island from the north to the south, joint venture has too often meant the combination of those who love the island and those who are only interested in the profits that can be squeezed out of it. In this case, we have every reason to count on Fred as first and last an island guardian. Also, we have a right to hope that low-cost housing here need not be low-level housing here. The cheap does not have to be the ugly, the pretentious, or the vulgar. Joint venture does not have to mean the partnership of those who love the island and those who do not give a damn about its quality so long as it pays off.

We have a good right to faith in Charles Fraser and Fred Hack. But we have every reason to keep our fingers crossed about those "joint venturers" who are venturing only because island dollars are more important to them than island destiny. There was a difference between the joint ventures of Lewis and Clark and Rosencrantz and Guildenstern. There are differences in joint ventures—or adventurers—here and now.

March 22, 1973

Items from Antiquity

Sometimes a scrapbook really ought to be a scrapbook. And some addicted readers of *The Island Packet* generously send in items which ought to be pasted in this one. Hilton Head Island is adequately equipped with both antiquarians and anti-despoilers among its devotees.

Bob McGowan, the erudite photographer of Marengo, Illinois, who is always hoping to see this shore through his lens, sends in an item from a book by Albert D. Richardson, published in 1865, called *The Secret Service.* In it, Richardson, a correspondent for the *New York Tribune,* included a pious or poisonous entry in his diary about the palmetto tree on April 12, 1861. That happened to be the same day on which enthusiastic Charlestonians fired on Fort Sumter. The event evidently colored Mr. Richardson's observations about this principal item in the flora of South Carolina. He wrote of the state's tree: Its flag, sword-shaped leaves branch out in flat semicircular clusters, resembling the fan palm. Its tough bulbous root was formerly cut into fine fragments by the Indians, then bruised to a pulp and thrown into the lake. It produced temporary blindness among the fishes, which brought them to the surface, where they were easily caught by hand.

"With rare fitness stands the palmetto as the device of South Carolina. Indeed, it is an excellent emblem of Slavery itself; for, neither beautiful, edible, nor useful, it blinds the short-sighted fish coming under its influence. To them it is . . . The insane root, which takes the reason prisoner."

Chuck Carpenter of Calibogue Cay, whose grandfather was a Yankee soldier from Maine, produced another scrapbook item in a piece written by Thomas Wentworth Higginson in the *Atlantic Monthly* of September 1865. Preacher, soldier, writer, and advocate of woman suffrage, temperance, and abolition, Higginson compared himself to a celebrated horse "which had never won a race, but which was prized as having gained a second place in more races than any other horse in America." In a more-than-ordinarily-mellow mood, he described a visit, as a commander of black troops, to this island and the headquarters here of General David Hunter, commander of the Department of the South. Higginson wrote: "Hilton Head, in those days, seemed always like some foreign military station in the tropics. The long, low white buildings, with piazzas and verandas on the water-side; the general impression of heat and lassitude, existence appearing to pulsate only with the seabreeze; the sandy almost impossible streets; and the firm, level beach, on which everybody walked who could get there; all these suggested Jamaica or the East Indies. The headquarters at the end of the beach, the Zouave sentinels, the successive anterooms, the lounging aides, the good-natured and easy General—easy by habit and energetic by impulse—all had an air of Southern languor, rather picturesque, but perhaps not altogether bracing."

Some of the modern guardians of Hilton Head Island would turn a scrapbook into a scrappy one. They stand appalled at the foot of the mud mountain Sea Pines is building, from the spoil of Harbour Town dredging, off the causeway to Calibogue Cay. On the other side of the road, mammoth earth-moving trucks are engaged in the commonplace activity of turning holes (soon to be called lagoons) into hills upon which more condominiums will perch. A sign announces that they will be called Briarwood Villas, though they rise from a bog once inhabited only by heron.

The trucks move the mud, concrete, and maybe dreams. Everywhere the traffic thickens, but the old image of a village tucked into a wilderness prohibits the presence of more and more traffic lights. People talk about whether Hilton Head Island should be incorporated or given some sort of rule by public service council chairman—somewhat like that of the doges of Venice. While they argue, metropolis already grows, despite developer insistence that this be advertised as a seaside sylvan dell. Its Bridge of Sighs is the one narrow crossing where more and more people squeeze into and out of the island on which, despite early Yankee condemnation, the palmetto is still cherished and semitropic languor—or a reasonable facsimile thereof—is still a commodity, certainly salable.

March 29, 1973

Of Mermaids

Practically the only item of charm not currently claimed for this shore is the existence hereabouts of mermaids. Not even the shrimpers claim to have seen them, which is strange considering how many mermaids have been seen by so many fishermen on so many seas. A writer in the *Atlantic Monthly* over a century ago provided the picture of the familiar confrontation of mermaid by seamen: "Fishermen sometimes see the Mermaid in the bright summer sun, when a thin mist hangs over the sea, sitting on the surface of the water, and combing her long, golden hair with a golden comb, or driving up her snow-white cattle to feed on the islands. [The herd, apparently, was also amphibious.] At other times she comes as a beautiful maiden, chilled and shivering with the cold of the night, to the fires the fishers have kindled, hoping by this means to entice them to her love."

Mr. Shakespeare presented the deep-sea damsel even more romantically in *A Midsummer Night's Dream:*

> . . . once I sat upon a promontory,
> And heard a mermaid on a dolphin's back

Uttering such dulcet and harmonious breath,
That the rude sea grew civil at her song,
And certain stars shot madly from their spheres
To hear the sea-maid's music.

That certainly would be a spectacle which would bring people pouring, to look and listen, from their condominiums. No such vision with music has yet been reported here, not even from such a promontory as South Beach—where transformations are the order of the day. True, the porpoises play in Calibogue Sound, but so far without dulcet-singing riders with golden hair flowing in the winds off toward Tybee Light. However, if there is a demand for them, they probably will be provided by the management, and villas like grottoes will soon be building in the sea. This would be a penultimate step in the development of Hilton Head Island—short only of centaurs in the Lawton Stables and unicorns in the wildlife preserve, both, of course, growing sleek and fat on grasses grown organically in the back stretches of Heritage Farm.

The unexpected is almost standard here. Who would be surprised if the sky-reaching village of Sealofts was followed by luxurious houseboats anchored in the margins of Calibogue Sound and Broad Creek. Skiffs to be used for access could be picked up with the keys at the new, almost-as-fabulous, open-all-night reception center by the Greenwood Gate to Sea Pines. Some shore dwellers might mutter, but there seems little doubt, considering its past vigilance, that the U.S. Corps of Engineers would be agreeable to the plan.

This time, however, the creators of wonders here might well be forewarned, particularly in relation to providing a colony of mermaids. The latest edition of the *Encyclopaedia Britannica,* in its preoccupation with such prosaic natural things as space flight and the bomb threat, has little room to give to such supernatural creatures as these ladies of the sea. The good old Eleventh Edition, published in 1910, tells more about them, and all is not reassuring. The best authorities agree that one of their chief attributes beyond their beauty is their ability to foretell the future. But it is related that these ocean ladies are sometimes as bad as they are beautiful in their relations with man. They have to be bribed or compelled to utter their prophecies. One way to compel them has been to take away their golden mirrors and to withhold them until, in dulcet tones, the mermaids begin to talk.

A few years ago, such an occurrence certainly would have been fortunate for their masters, who could have bought real estate in 1963 with sure foreknowledge of its value in 1973. Perhaps any prospects they might report now would be as rose-tinted. It is possible, however, that their prophecies now might not be as golden as their golden hair and golden combs. They might report an isle balefully altered. They might predict ill winds and truculent tides, inflation to infinity and a population knocking elbows.

Of course, it would be nice to watch from our promontories singing mermaids riding dashing dolphins through the spray along the shores. That would add to the uniqueness of this resort. Mermaid watchers would crowd here as bird watchers never did. Package rates could be provided for them. The possibilities are endless. Still, one who has muttered much mutters again. The one thing which students of this fair phenomenon have universally reported is that they should be welcomed with caution. Let the pretty creatures keep their combs. However elaborate may be the dreams of developers, it is to be hoped that they will leave mermaids to mythology. Trust a unicorn, depend upon a centaur, but leave mermaids strictly alone. They might tell us about a tomorrow we'd just as lief not see.

April 5, 1973

Mini-bottle, Maxi-price

So now we have the mini-bottle and the maxi-price.

The cost of libations on this plush island has been tentatively fixed by the nine places now legally operating in this trade at from $1.80 to $2.00 a drink. The baby bottles vary in size from 1.6 ounces for straight Scotch, bourbon, et cetera, to two ounces for manhattans, martinis, and other mixed drinks. For both, Franz Meier, beverage controller in Sea Pines, says prices in its bars "are subject to change" like landscape and everything else in this plantation. Simplifying bibulous mathematics, however, a $2.00 price for a 1.6-ounce drink means a cost to the customer of $20.00 a pint. Evidently we live in more or less expansive—or expensive—days than companions of the cup did in the past.

Our observant neighbors, Bea and Lynn Bitner, provide the evidence of that. Returning from a sea and sky safari in the West Indies, they brought back a copy of a magazine called, like our monthly periodical, *Islander*. This publication, issued on Saint Vincent, contains a remarkable piece of history in an article titled (in understatement) "Party Punches." What the article actually describes was probably the biggest and most potent mixed drink ever prepared.

419

Here's the story: "The best known Caribbean drink nowadays is rum punch, and no matter where it is drunk, whether it be in the private home or the public bar, no two taste alike. Every one has his own secret ingredient or method which has made rum punch such an institution.

"It was a popular drink with English sailors in 1599 who were at that time sailing the Caribbean Sea, and the then Commander-in-Chief of the British Navy, Sir Edward Kennel, prepared the following punch for his ship's company in a huge marble basin:

70 Casks Rum	25,000 Large Limes	5 pounds nutmeg
10 Casks Brandy	80 Pints lemon juice	
9 Casks Water	1,300 lbs. sugar	

"A platform was constructed over the marble basin to protect it from the rain. The punch was served by one of the small cabin boys who sailed the sea of punch in a small boat especially made for the occasion. To serve the 5,000 invited guests the cabin boy had to be replaced three times, because after 45 minutes the fumes had made him completely drunk.

"Punch is now popular the world over, being served hot in cold climates and iced in the tropics. It is a very good way of getting a party off its feet, especially when prepared in quantity and placed in a large bowl so that acquaintances are made whilst waiting to get to the bowl, not to mention the intoxicating effect."

"Off its feet" must have been a good term in connection with Sir Edward Kennel's party. And a party of five thousand off its feet must have been quite a spectacle even on the Spanish Main. It seems a pity that more is not known about Sir Edward. Neither new nor old editions of the *Encyclopaedia Britannica* even mention his name. Nor does it appear in Richard Hakluyt's famous collection of the narratives of the voyages of English seamen around that time. Contemporary commanders described their parties more modestly. A little earlier, one Walter Wren, writing of an adventurous voyage in the same area, only went so far as to say that his company feasted "with such cheere as God had sent us." Indeed, on this voyage Wren was shocked at the cost of drink in one port: "14 buts of wine, which cost 15 duckats, which were offered us at Santa Cruz in Tenerif for 8, 9, and 10 duckats."

However much he has been neglected by history, such a free party giver as Sir Edward Kennel would certainly have scorned the mini-bottle. Possibly he would have been shocked at the cost of 1.6 ounces, even of 2 ounces, which would hardly have made a cabin boy saucy in his time. Measures differ in bottles, jiggers, and history. Casks, in terms of which Sir Edward measured, vary in content, so there is no sure way of knowing how many ounces of hard liquor were contained in the eighty casks of it he put in his punch. The dimensions of that marble bowl he used are not available either, but it must have been something like the swimming pool being built for the new Holiday Inn or the expanded lagoon at Sea Pines Circle.

Obviously we live in mini-times when we consider the maxi-men who sailed those island seas. They must have been not only the sailors of the days of wooden ships and iron men but also the voyagers of the time of casks—and not of this time of tenth-of-a-pint pygmies.

April 12, 1973

Defense of Developers

In defense of developers:

Maybe beauty requires a mess for its production. Behind the most polished poem there is generally a clutter of blotted and crumpled paper, sheets flung aside in seeking perfection. The belle emerges from the awkward and pimpled adolescent. The now-marbled national capital of Washington, D.C., long wore an appearance which appalled foreign visitors. As the Taj Mahal rose, the earth about it must have been trampled by the working elephants. Archeologists have given more attention to the technical skill and engineering ability which was required in the erection of the Great Pyramid of Khufu than to the conditions which surrounded its construction. There is the detail reported by Herodotus, however, that it demanded the labor of one hundred thousand men over a period of twenty years. They were people with needs and faults not entirely dissimilar from our own.

So far as the archeologists have reported, the provisioners of the Egyptian builders did not wrap their food in paper, cardboard, or cellophane or put their drinks into cans. Undoubtedly, they were still able to clutter the Sahara for miles around. It is not on record that any contemporary land-moving Malphrus provided movable necessaries to meet their necessity. The necessity, while not documented, is not to be doubted. Not only the contractors' sheds but the slave shanties must have been thick about the construction job. Though Cairo was only a few miles away, the workers must have contributed both their home clutter and their work-time clutter to the sands, commuting by camel being less likely then than by Chevrolet now. The work animals had to be quartered. Those who have carefully measured the amazing dimensions of the Great Pyramid of Khufu seem to have given little or no attention to the mass of the manure piles beside it. Also, scant consideration has been given to the possible pollution of the nearby Nile or to what effect, if any, that had on the crocodiles.

This is not written to reassure or make resigned the persons on Hilton Head Island who look with wild wonder at the processes presented now by those presumably engaged in making the island more and more attractive to more and more people. Perhaps, as developers and builders seem to think, these disturbed folks fail to take the long view.

The causeway to Calibogue Cay will not be a mud rut forever, not if those condominiums emerging from the mud there are to be sold. The lumber piles which house the rats before people are housed in the Bluff Apartments at South Beach may give way to lawns smooth (to pick up a nice metaphor) as a fawn's flank. Coligny Circle will not necessarily always be a place of crowded clutter around cracked pavement. The trailers now clustered there may be only temporary ugly ducklings, which will be transformed into structures like decorative swans. Even Cordillo Parkway could be a parkway again and not merely a dirty and damaged route for mud haulers and concrete-mixing machines.

Of course, some excuse must be allowed for the present spread of mire. Anyone who has noticed the gleaming piles of big galvanized pipes near construction sites must realize that much of our beloved isle is largely an aqueous mass on which building sites need lagoons not merely for beauty but for survival. And if canals silt up, there at least may be water lilies, if not boats, at the docks.

Patience, people. You can bet your bottom dollar that developers are not messing up this place to destroy it. Their purpose is to pretty it for the very good reason that pretty sells. Where the rats run in the muck and debris of building today, happy customers will be settled tomorrow, pointing out their immaculate surroundings with pride to their guests.

The poem comes from the many discarded sheets of attempts and erasures. Washington is white and green—at least between marches on the city. Belles continue to emerge from brats, like butterflies from caterpillars. The heirs of dead Pharaohs did not permit the perpetuation of the stench and squalor around their tremendous tombs. It may be safely presumed that any old pieces of papyrus or leftover mummy rags littering the sands were carefully removed, maybe by some of the same slaves who flung them.

It can, we hope, be predicted that something of the same sort will happen here, and maybe in less time than it took to build a pyramid. But it would be pleasant if more attention were given to the amenities of the real estate while it is being transformed. Of course, nobody can expect the alteration of the earth and the multiplication of condominiums to be carried on like the delicate movements of a waltz. Some clutter is unavoidable. But it ought not to be necessary to make whole neighborhoods hideous in the process of growth. Hilton Head Island will survive its scars, but it ought not to be necessary to scare old inhabitants and possible newcomers with the ugly open wounds of development so hell-bent that it appears not to give a damn about pleasantness here and now.

Still, before we damn the builders, let us remember that they may be planting daffodils with diesel shovels. After all, there is always the bulb before the bloom.

April 19, 1973

Justice for Dogs

Of course, even a dog is entitled to justice.

That has been emphasized and reemphasized in recent years by the highest courts of the land. Indeed, sometimes the concerns of the U.S. Supreme Court for the rights of the accused has caused law enforcement officers to feel they were being fettered. Still, in a free land the rights of the individual must be protected—and that should go for dogs, too. No panic or prejudice should be permitted to prevail. The fact that some time ago the miniature poodle of the Jim Hands of Green Wing Teal was destroyed by a marauding German shepherd should not make all big dogs suspect. That point was pressed home with skill recently on the island.

William Jones, Jr., of the prestigious legal firm of Dowling, Dowling, Sanders, Duke and Johnson, recently brought the current judicial view to bear on dogs—his dog, all dogs—on Hilton Head Island, certainly in Sea Pines. The case to which Mr. Jones brought his legal learning at first appeared to be a simple one. Miss Elizabeth Hartshorn, leading her small dog on a leash, found at the end of her line a dogfight in progress involving her little dog and an English bulldog owned by Mr. Jones. In the "fracas," as Mr. Jones

425

describes the affair, Miss Hartshorn, in attempting to separate the dogs, was herself bitten. The assumption that Mr. Jones repudiates, as unproven, was that Miss Hartshorn was bitten by Mr. Jones's bulldog. Certainly, as those who have seen dogfights will understand, there could be, as the lawyers say, a reasonable doubt about which dog's teeth snagged the lady.

It is certainly possible that prejudice against the defendant bulldog may have raised its ugly head in this case, due to the fact that the bulldog was moving around unleashed in an area where that is against the rules—or the law. But certainly no minor infraction of the law can be permitted to cause a verdict of guilty for a larger crime. Also, as a sort of character witness for himself and his dog, Mr. Jones testified that this was the first time his dog had ever run loose in Sea Pines. Furthermore, one incident of malfeasance should not be allowed to sustain a finding of greater guilt. Fortunately, in this case (as the Supreme Court says should be true in every case), the bulldog was represented by counsel. As attorney for the defense, Mr. Jones confidently takes the position that "Miss Hartshorn was not attacked by the bulldog." On the basis of the old rule that an attack is the best defense, this would sharply suggest that Miss Hartshorn was bitten by her own leashed pet. But therein lies the essence of the problem of the case.

It is difficult, as students of the law have long realized, to determine with exactness the minds or the motives of men or dogs. Mr. Jones may be exactly right in his feeling that his dog, like some poor defendants in our courts, has been made the underdog. No evidence has been presented as to which dog started the dogfight. It is perfectly possible, however, that the little, leashed dog did. In a time when much emphasis is placed upon psychological factors in dealing with crime, it is certainly conceivable that the small, leashed dog resented the unleashed freedom of the other canine who was indulging in privileges which he was denied. It is widely agreed that underprivilege must be considered in dealing with crime. Certainly the little dog had nothing that the big dog needed. Why would he attack? But clearly frustration might have motivated the little dog.

Of course, this gets us into higher realms than jurisprudence. Absolute justice may be beyond the determination of the most learned men of the law—even on Hilton Head Island. But this case does suggest that, if you are an unleashed dog running around indulging in behavior which is frowned upon under the rules which all law-abiding dogs are expected to abide by, it is a good idea to have a lawyer. *Res ipsa loquitur.*

All will hope that Miss Hartshorn has healed rapidly and that neither the dogs nor Mr. Jones will suffer any traumatic effects from the episode which Mr. Jones describes as "regrettable." Still, a precedent may have been established in this case which, while not necessarily good law, makes good common sense for both dogs and lawyers: Leave the dogfights to the dogs.

April 26, 1973

Creeper's Heritage

The many creeks, islands, estuaries, and inlets which create the beauty of this Carolina Low Country give it a charm, too, to smugglers. Indeed, a good part of this land's heritage (a word now proudly used in the names of a championship golf tournament and an organic vegetable farm) goes back to smuggling—a term derived from Old English words meaning "to creep with the idea of secrecy." Certainly there seems nothing worthy of inclusion in a heritage about the numerous current instances of efforts to slip dope into the United States through waters hereabouts.

More and more narcotic agents, deputies, coastguardmen, and others are deployed in the region today. Their successes have been noted. In the last year eleven million dollars in illegal marijuana and hashish has been seized in the Beaufort County area alone. But nobody knows how many of those who "creep with the idea of secrecy" have succeeded in getting their cargoes ashore. Some losses to the law may not be too discouraging to operators who pay eight thousand dollars abroad for drugs they can push for a million dollars here (estimate by *The State* of Columbia).

Such men—playing the long chance for the incredible payoff—

should be familiar here. The Hilton Head area was once the greatest bastion ever erected against such creepers—or often bold dashers —against authority in the history of the United States. It is true that the smugglers then were romantically labeled and romantically described as daring blockade-runners. Through a vast Federal fleet, depoted here, they worked in a trade in which three-cent-a-pound cotton in the Carolinas was transformed into forty-five-cent-a-pound cotton in Liverpool. The return voyage paid off as well. Luxuries and necessities (including narcotics desperately needed then in the field hospitals of the Confederate armies) multiplied in value from their purchase in England or the West Indian islands to their delivery on the mainland side of the Federal blockade. Records show that sixty-six first-class, swift, sleek blockade-runners were built in England and Scotland. And though forty were destroyed, the payoffs for successes were incredible. Officers resigned from the British navy to take part in this lucrative, if dangerous, service.

Such men were part of a heritage, too. An authority on smuggling reports that in the centuries before "smuggling (chiefly of wine, spirits, tobacco and bullion) was so generally practiced in Britain as to become a kind of national failing." Americans had a heritage in smuggling, too, under—and through—the British trade laws which helped bring on the American Revolution. Some of the great merchants who profited from such creeping were among the most vociferous American patriots.

Not all smugglers could have regarded themselves as public benefactors. In these waters, after the importation of slaves into the United States became illegal, there were the "blackbirders." They crept from Africa into Southern estuaries with cargoes of slaves for secret auction blocks. Many other smugglers, who followed long after the blackbirders, were regarded by some on the shore as engaged in a less immoral traffic.

Writing recently from his office on Wall Street, Perry E. Moore (descendant of the gentlemen who wrote "The Night Before Christmas") told of the days when he owned Red Bluff Plantation, apparently just across New River in Jasper County and now owned by the Gale family. It did not seem a good investment. Some land pirates, not smugglers, crept in to cut his pines without permission or payment.

He wrote: "Bluffton was the only development near. Seaboard

Railroad had a stop at Levy Station, which was only a sign." He added: "After acquiring Red Bluff we found we had a problem. As it was on the Broad and New rivers and other creeks, it was a problem to run it safely. This waterway was a great asset during the Prohibition time, as the plantation was a delivery point for the rumrunners. When I would go shooting, my guide would always tell me where there was a good covey, which turned out to be a nice case of liquor."

It is not in the record that Mr. Moore, in dry indignation, resented this polite trespass on his land. There could still be guides on this shore aware of the location of larger caches of contraband, maybe even helping to hide them. And some might be double-helping both the creepers and the cops.

This country is more accessible now to federal agents and to condominium buyers. New settlers have little sympathy for dope-runners on this and other, nearby islands. But the creeks have not been entirely monopolized by the yacht owners and the sailboat enthusiasts. There are still men hereabouts who "creep with the idea of secrecy" toward the shores. Their image is disreputable today, but they fit into the American heritage, which has not always been as lofty as a long, high drive across a fairway or the remembrances of orators or the effusions of the writers of real-estate brochures.

May 3, 1973

The Beach Barlowe Saw

The first report on the Carolina coast where Englishmen hoped to make settlement—or development—sounds like a brochure about it. The report was written by Arthur Barlowe, one of the sea captains Sir Walter Raleigh sent out in 1584. He made a record of arrival which sounds like a song: ". . .we found shole water, wher we smelt so sweet, and so strong a smel, as if we had bene in the midst of some delicate garden, abounding with all kind of odoriferous flowers. . . . wee viewed the lande about us, . . . so full of grapes, as the very beating and surge of the Sea overflowed them, . . . in all the world the like abundance is not to be found."

That shore was in what is now Dare County, North Carolina. Sir Walter's colony disappeared in mystery. The Wright brothers found it an isolated area with the right winds in which to carry out their experiment in flight. That was at Kitty Hawk, where today the Atlantic is chewing the sands from under beach-front houses. To some builders there, however, erosion seems less a menace than the state, which is intervening to control rapid growth along the beaches until the county implements zoning to assure the quality of the coastal waters. With the prospects of a 91 percent increase in living units along this shore, North Carolina has invoked its right to limit sewerage permits to the capacity of the land to handle human pollution.

"Give us a chance," a reluctant county commissioner begged state authorities. "All we have is one economy, and that's tourism." Another asked that "progress not be retarded too much."

Now on old Pawleys Island, loved by generations of South Carolinians, "progress" seems threatened, too. The Georgetown County Council is considering a zoning ordinance which would permit only the construction of single-family residential dwellings on most of the island. Old and new inns would be phased out by this zoning plan, which is a prerequisite to obtaining federal flood insurance for county residents. One innkeeper with the good, ancient South Carolina name of Roberta Prioleau protests that the new rule would "make the beach totally inaccessible to anyone who cannot afford to rent a home or condominium for $500 a week."

The aristocratic Ms. Prioleau's defense of democracy in beach access may be a point well taken. American beaches—including those on Pawleys Island, Kitty Hawk, and Hilton Head—belong to all the 200 million or thereabouts citizens of the land. A great many of those citizens are headed, like lemmings, toward the sea. That can be regarded as either a people's movement or a locust horde. The poor have as much right to confront the waves as the rich do. But the possibility grows—maybe here and now—that there will be no such beach as Barlowe saw for anybody anywhere along this coast.

Man is a wonderful creature. His genus includes captains such as Sir Walter Raleigh sent out to open a new world. And on the shore they first discovered, others have put their fellows into the skies. There, too, some of the first successful experiments in radio—then called "wireless"—were made.

Now man's genius along the beaches includes the condominium, the sometimes-all-too-mobile home, the high rise—all of which make more and more places for all those Americans who Roberta Prioleau believes should not be denied cheap and easy access to the shore.

There is still the "beating and surge of the Sea." There are also still the shifts of wind and of sand. But the greatest change on the beaches is made by man, who can climb the clouds and send his song and picture through space. He still has not been able to restrain himself from slashing and soiling the shores Captain Barlowe described for the enlightenment of his patron, Sir Walter, and Sir Walter's patron, Elizabeth the Queen. Progress is too often the mark of man's greedy paw. Compared to it, the surge of the sea is only a caress.

May 10, 1973

Low-Country Gourmet

While "Low-Country cuisine" is sometimes referred to on the ornate menus of Hilton Head Island, increasingly the standard word for food served here is *gourmet*. The art of its preparation is brought hither by chefs whose foreign-pantry pedigrees are paraded for gustatory guests from Savannah, New Canaan, Peoria, and Paducah. Only Katie McElveen's comfortable Roadside Rest clings loyally to the old-fashioned home cooking of Palmetto State people.

Maybe this is as it should be on an island devoted to local ecology but demonstrating preferences for a world-wide diversity of decor. Even in architecture there seems a flight away from old-time, Low-Country architecture, though the beach houses on stilts resemble some old Southern dwellings which, rising above brick supports, left room beneath them for the chickens and the pigs and the dogs and the children to run. *Decor* and *gourmet* are our words to live by. Sometimes Dave Harrall's charming house of native design on Plantation Drive seems as alien here as the ham hock and the frying pan. Now it seems almost besieged by the multitude of condominiums behind it, growing where once the marsh hen and the mud turtle had their undisturbed habitation.

Some glistening black cooks remain—even they wearing the white mushroom caps of foreign-cuisine concocters. But Aunt Jemima has disappeared everywhere except on the frozen-waffle box at the Red & White. All this may be progress, but sometimes it seems a pity. Good cooks did not all begin as apprentices in the sculleries along the Seine and the Danube. There were artists in the craft (men and women, too) along the Cooper and Ashley rivers in South Carolina, possibly on the shores of the Savannah in Georgia. And some were kept and guarded as precious possessions on remote plantations.

In her memories of Charleston (first published in 1906), Mrs. St. Julien Ravenel wrote of two famous black maître d's in Charleston— Jones and Lee. A literate traveler wrote of the inn kept by Jones as the best in Charleston, where was served "iced claret to convert Diogenes into a gourmet." But Mrs. Ravenel added, "Both Jones and Lee were in great subjection to their wives, who were excellent cooks, and, as excellent cooks are apt to be, termagants as well."

So *gourmet* was a word used long ago and without any special gestures to European kitchens. Mrs. Ravenel wrote: "Suppers were elaborate. Boned turkeys, game, terrapin stews (only they called it 'cooter stew'), etc. The pastry-cook and her assistants had been at work for a week, making jellies, creams, custards, cakes of all kinds —all made at home. Sometimes there would be a flight of the imagination: two doves of blanc-mange in a nest of fine, gold-colored transparent shreds of candied orange peel was thought 'sweetly pretty'; and a tall iced cake in the shape of a castle, with the American flag on the tower, and the arms in coloured comfits on the walls, appealed to the patriotic. Greatest of the dishes was 'a preserve of fowle' Does anyone wish the receipt? It began, 'Take all manner of Fowle and bone them all,' the rest of the precise words are unfortunately lost, but the direction was, to begin with a small dove, into which slip a strip of bacon; put the dove into a partridge, the partridge (quail they are mistakenly called now) into a guinea hen, the guinea hen into a wild duck, the duck into a capon, the capon into a goose, the goose into a turkey (or a peacock if it please you best), each bird to be well basted and seasoned before inserted, care being taken to place white and dark meat alternately. Roast all until done through, and serve with their own very rich seasoned gravy. The carver cut down, through and across the birds, and the guests ate— and lived!"

While concoctions presented to them may not be quite so elaborate, men and women still eat some marvelous dishes in this Low
Country. And they are washed down with a greater variety of drinks
than even the landgraves knew in early South Carolina. *Gourmet,* of
course, as every restaurant patron knows, derives from Old French
words meaning "wine merchant's servant." The drink makers are
still served by the cooks. And the procession from bacchanalia to
bicarbonates still persists. Sometimes there is garlic and horserad-
ish as well as alcohol in the hangover.

Pollution of more than one sort may be resisted here by the
growing of organic foods in the plots at Heritage Farm. And there
may be something symbolic in a recent report by a writer in the
Miami Herald that the man who operates the most restaurants here
"keeps a candy jar of dried fruit (a mild laxative) on his desk." That
may mark true epicureanism on this or any other island. In the
community of the philosopher Epicurus, the general drink was water and the food, barley bread; half a pint of wine was held an ample
allowance. The philosopher himself wrote a friend, "Send me
some Cythian cheese, so that, should I choose, I may fare sumptuously."

But that, of course, was way back in B.C.—before condominiums.

May 17, 1973

Devil Fishing

It seems too bad that at this season we cannot call William Elliott (1788–1863) back from the happy hunting ground to give encouragement to the ardent participants in this year's third annual Sea Pines Annual Invitational Billfish Tournament, with its ten thousand dollars in cash prizes and silver trophies. Certainly, on this island today, all will agree with the principle Elliott taught in his famous book *Carolina Sports by Land and Water*. First published in 1859 and recently available in reprint, it held that man without recreation is like a bow always taut. That, of course, is the land salesman's line today and here. But if this grandee planter did come back to these waters he knew so well, he might be inclined to be aristocratically contemptuous, and some modern fishermen might be inclined in haste to regard Mr. Elliott as the prince of liars among piscators—which is really princely among prevaricators.

Certainly, Mr. Elliott might be suspiciously regarded by fishermen here now—and not only as to the matter of veracity. On this island, descendants of old Yankees might not care to recall the taunts he sent back north, after spending three years at Harvard, at the puny quality of Yankee sport. He may have seemed an odd

437

fisherman even in his own Low Country. He casually called fish by their Latin names. In addition to planting plantations in sea-island cotton, he wrote not only his book on sports but other books as well: *The Letters of Agricola* and a drama in verse called *Fiesco*. Politically, he even rejected the guidance of John C. Calhoun. The record of his life suggests that in the field or in a boat he must have been arrogant, enthusiastic, and austere, but with the saving graces of poetry and humor in his personality. It would be interesting to know not only what we today would think of him—but also what he would think of us.

Last year a visiting participant in the tournament here landed a 355-pound blue marlin. Island magnate Wilbert Roller, who as landowner here succeeds the landed gentry of Mr. Elliott's day, caught a wahoo of state-record dimensions. Certainly both fishermen deserved a photograph complete with dead fish and a prize. It is doubtful, however, that Mr. Elliott would have been impressed by their exploits. In his objective report of fishing for the devilfish in Skull and Broad creeks, Calibogue and Port Royal sounds, he mentioned a devilfish so big that an African slave named May jumped from the boat to the creature's back with his harpoon at the ready. Another such fish, he related, required three pairs of oxen, aided by a horse, and twenty-two men to drag it to dry land. It was estimated to weigh between four and five tons.

Also, then the exciting quest for this formidable fish could be comfortably observed by spectators on the shore of Hilton Head Island. Sometimes, watching residents provided bowls of punch for the intrepid fishermen on the water before them. On one occasion, Elliott wrote, when he and his black and white companions landed their monster on Bay Point, "a party of ladies, then on a visit there, were gratified in having an opportunity of observing this singular animal, which from size as well as peculiar structure, may well be counted as one of the wonders of the deep."

Mr. Elliott understood that there might be skepticism about his reports. He himself doubted reports that the creature—called not only *devilfish* but also *eagle ray,* even *Vampire of the Ocean*—reached a length of fifty feet on the coast of Africa. Modestly, he admitted that the largest he had seen measured only eighteen feet across the back. But he brought Rhetts, Barnwells, Jenkinses, and other planters to attest to such dimension in what became "an established diversion of the planters in the vicinity of Port Royal Sound." Though the devilfish made their summer visits here of their own accord, the sport of hunting them seems to have been imported from the West Indies—as so many Carolina things and customs were. Indeed, the solid old Eleventh Edition of the *Encyclopaedia Britannica* states as to the origin of the sport that at Jamaica the devilfish were "frequently attacked for sport's sake, but their capture is uncertain and sometimes attended with danger."

Apparently, along with other laments of ecologists, devilfish have decreased in numbers and in their presence hereabouts. But even fishers for billfish should not forget them. Perhaps the promoters of this sporting paradise should bring them back again to make Hilton Head Island not only the capital of golf and tennis, bird watching and water skiing, but of big game fishing as well. That, of course, might present some problems, but men who are making a metropolis out of what was once largely a marshland should not be deterred. Our golf courses spread; our tennis courts multiply. And once a year our billfish fishers head with hope toward the Gulf Stream. How excellent it would be to bring back the devilfish and maybe present their conflict with sports fishermen before bleachers neatly arrayed on Pinckney Island or Calibogue Cay. Devilfish fishing was obviously a spectator sport in the day when visiting ladies watched from Bay Point. Why not now? CBS or NBC might come and cover it.

Stop spoofing, Sojourner! In our times, which we do not like to regard as puny, we may be well rid of William Elliott and his devilfish, even if Abercrombie and Fitch do still publish his report of his exploits. We have much with which to be content. George Cathcart can still fix his focus on proud Wilbert Roller and his very long and very dead-looking wahoo. We can't have everything on or around this island even if Wilbert Roller seems, with little effort, to catch on the same hook the biggest wahoo, a service station, mini-bottles, construction crews, huge mechanized equipment, seaside villas, and plans for a Ramada Inn. Beside him, Charles Fraser—counting his condominiums—puts up the billfish prizes and, lacking the exercise essential to regularity, nibbles dried fruit out of a jar. Of course, it would be attractive—and attracting—here to have a few carefully chosen devilfish in lieu of the big alligators Vance Fowler sends away with regret. Still, it is always difficult to tell what bait brings in the biggest fish.

William Elliott is as dead as Wilbert Roller's wahoo. And despite all Elliott's witnesses, it may be high time to consign both him and his book to mythology. As a matter of fact, a little instant mythology may be just exactly what this island needs.

May 24, 1973

Upon What Meat—?

It may very well be like adding horses and apples to quote *The Island Packet* and William Shakespeare side by side. It could possibly be instructive, nevertheless.

Jack Bowie in *The Packet* wrote that State Senator James Waddell amended the much-revised proposed charter for the Island Council of public service districts at a meeting of the county legislative delegation. Bowie added: "Waddell, who is considering his chances for the State's Lieutenant Governor's post, struck out provisions for the democratic election of certain members of the council and said, 'Anybody can recommend anybody they want, but I am going to make up my mind who I'm going to appoint.'"

Mr. Shakespeare was not directly commenting on this point when he put into the mouth of Cassius of the lean and hungry look an exclamation which still may be pertinent in Beaufort County:

> Now, in the names of all the gods at once,
> Upon what meat doth this our Caesar feed,
> That he is grown so great? . . .

441

As far as is generally known hereabouts, Senator Waddell may only feed on hopping John, but so far as Hilton Head Island is concerned, his statement carries an imperial ring. As he states approximately correctly, under present law (and such law as he proposes), the public districts here and the suggested council of public districts are appointed at his pleasure and presumably would serve at his beck and call. The Ides of March are passed, but it should not take a soothsayer to foretell that this whole business of council on top of councils might be toppled by islanders who don't want to be taken for a bicycle ride.

Senator Waddell's assertion of authority and the proposal of the Sea Pines Public Service Commission to tax all Sea Pines property owners to build $250,000 worth of bicycle paths are apparently unrelated. Indeed, the Sea Pines Public Service Commission bases its proposal upon a declaration of democracy. A "survey" conducted by the Sea Pines Plantation Company, the commission's manager states, showed "property owners" wanted the paths and were ready to pay for them. It is not necessary to question the validity of this survey to note that it was conducted by the chief party in interest in the whole bicycle-path business, Sea Pines Plantation Company, and that the voters included many more people than the resident, qualified voters in the area. And though the Sea Pines Company is ready to make apparently generous contribution to the plan, it is avoiding its whole obligation of providing safe and adequate access by any form of transportation, presumably including bicycles, to the properties it has sold—any fine print to the contrary notwithstanding.

To say the least, governmental problems grow like condominiums here. Sea Pines, which energetically developed the whole bicycle business by its indiscriminate appeal to transients and the rental of hundreds of bicycles to them, now wants the property owners and residents, bicyclists or not, to pick up a big part of the check for the problem Sea Pines chiefly created. Similarly, while many residents on the Calibogue Canal feel that seepage of the spoil from the big Mount Unpleasant that Sea Pines has erected beside the Calibogue causeway is responsible for the silting up of the canal, the company now feels that the residents should pay for dredging to get their boats out of the mud in the "deepwater" community sold to them.

In most respects Sea Pines has done a beautiful job here. Its most restless residents love the place. The despotism of developers has generally been beneficent. And, whatever may have been his views in the BASF matter, Senator Waddell can be presumed to wish only good for this new congregation of strangers in his county. Nobody can blame James Waddell or Charles Fraser for being big. Maybe as to each of them we should go back again to Shakespeare and to Cassius:

> Why, man, he doth bestride the narrow world
> Like a Colossus; and we petty men
> Walk under his huge legs, and peep about
> To find ourselves dishonourable graves.
> Men at some time are masters of their fates:
> The fault, dear Brutus, is not in our stars,
> But in ourselves, that we are underlings.

And on such a classic note it may be best to turn to a conversation the erudite Edith Inglesby of Bluffton had with a visiting woman who happened to sit at the same table with her in a café in Savannah. The visitor said, "Hilton Head is beautiful, but they're building so many houses. You know something? I think they are putting up entirely too many of those coliseums."

May 31, 1973

Montessori-Mounted

Possibly, on this island—which was once chiefly the refuge of the elderly—there are some who warrant the accolade or the anathema attributed to the late W. C. Fields: "He can't be all bad. He doesn't like children or dogs."

At least that impression was given last week at the bicycle path set-to. Then a sort of man-and-wife joint return was filed to the general effect that those who opposed a tax levy for bicycle paths in Sea Pines Plantation spoke with a sour note, like Scrooges, when three hundred unrepresented little children, who could not read papers or sign petitions, might be left to the hazards of the highways. "Mean Hearts and Sour Spirits" was the leitmotif of this lament.

Certainly all those whose hearts as well as their arteries may be hardening recognize the perils of our cracked roads filled with the projectiles labeled as construction trucks—except the children and adults who won't use bicycle paths even when they are provided. All that is involved here is the same little issue presented when the barons met the king at Runnymede and the patriots at Philadelphia grumbled about taxation without representation.

444

Certainly there may be a comic element in this revolt of the fat cats against Sea Pines. These plush patriots could pay four mills without giving up a single bottle of Scotch. But they have a feeling, maybe an impertinent one, that the combination of the bicycle paths and the children may make a well-shined shoe toe in the door to open the way for unloading on them other obligations which properly belong to Sea Pines. If the tax can be levied for bicycle paths, why not for roads, why not for the dredging of canals? Why not, indeed? Already residents who bought in "deepwater" residential areas and have been paying annual fees for channel maintenance have been informed that they will have to pay additional capital sums for the "deep water" they were promised. Residents of Beach Lagoon Drive, who have been paying road-maintenance fees for years, have similarly been informed that if they want a passable road before their houses they will have to provide the capital for its paving.

Nobody can blame Charles Fraser for wanting to have the best of two possible worlds, the private plantation and its public maintenance. Sea Pines never was an eleemosynary institution. If Sea Pines helped create the euphoria which attended the arrival of its purchasers, it did not prohibit them from reading the small print, if any such is pertinent now. But this is a sad situation. Sea Pines has been a happy land under its insistently benevolent despot. All will hope that that will continue to be true. Boos, even when justified, make a doleful sound in paradise.

Of course we love the children, and most of us can tell a child from a red herring. But it may be well to keep children on our minds. Suddenly they popped like sugarplums into the Sojourner's head when, lying late in bed, he began this week to compose a poem. Its inspiration seems uncertain. So far as he knows, he never heard of the young George Thompson to whom it is addressed. He finished it while shaving a gray beard. No title emerged while he was brushing his teeth, but the verse, as he transposed it on his typewriter, runs like this:

> O! George Thompson, please be good!
> You're a blight on the neighborhood.
> Where you go the kittens wail;
> Not a puppy wags its tail.

Wild birds modulate their song
When they see you come along.
Shrilly shriek the little girls
Fearing fingers in their curls.
Say who clipp'd the pony's mane?
Tell who stole the blind man's cane?
Who rang the bell—ran away?
Who grabb'd the ball and wouldn't play?
O! George Thompson, mind you this,
You can't expect mama's kiss,
You don't deserve papa's pride
With so much that's bad to hide.
Go wash your hands, comb your hair.
I can't stand you sitting there
Bland, so sweet, so very mild.
You're a naughty, naughty child.
O! George Thompson, you're a brat!
Can you know in spite of that
I, who spank your hinder part,
Hold you closest to my heart?

Come to think of it, that's the way many of us feel about Sea Pines. Maybe George Thompson is just a dream stand-in for Charles Fraser, or perhaps just for any of the Montessori-Mounted on tax-sustained bikes.

June 7, 1973

Chattahoochee Poetry

Though she may bring more perceptive eyes to shore and hills, Beanie Newhall, now almost commuting between this island she has loved and served so much and the mountains far above it, is only one of our summer transients between the highlands and the sea. And her Hilton Head companions on that road are only a squad in a motorized division. Beanie's place at Tiger in Rabun County, Georgia (where you can look over into North Carolina), is almost as much a wilderness as Hilton Head Island was when she first saw it. Then maybe it was too much a wilderness for persons accustomed to the amenities of this island blessed now with plumbing as well as palmettoes. She reports by postcard: "Went to 'Big Canoe'—Charles's new resort 60 miles north of Atlanta—and fell in love with it. There will be one golf course, nine tennis courts, nature museum in the old barn, glorious wildlife trail that follows a stream, no motorboats on lakes and no motorbikes. I've a small lot, three-fourths of an acre by a stream."

There is nothing polygamous about Beanie's love affairs with both the beach and the big hills. For a long time others have shared their affection with both. There was Sidney Lanier, who is better

447

known for his poetry about the river into which the stream on Beanie's lot may flow. Others have given, and now give, their devotion to the Chattahoochee River, which begins in a crystal trickle, then dances in a tumult between rocky banks before its sluggish red waters help make the oceans.

Some of the rills of its beginning are probably in Rabun County. Lanier wrote of its sources in Hall and Habersham counties, just below Rabun. A precocious critic wrote that Lanier's "The Song of the Chattahoochee" was "a jingling poem about a Southern river with an Indian name." That Cherokee name, which means "River of the Painted Rocks," helps explain why so many today hope to protect and preserve it. Lanier made a sort of symbol poem about mountain streams which are never to be denied their access to the sea. His verses ran like the flow of water:

> Out of the hills of Habersham,
> Down the valleys of Hall,
> I hurry amain to reach the plain,
> Run the rapid and leap the fall.
>
> Split at the rock and together again,
> Accept my bed, or narrow or wide,
> And flee from folly on every side
> With a lover's pain to attain the plain
> Far from the hills of Habersham,
> Far from the valleys of Hall.

On one of his last journeys before he died, Atlanta editor Ralph McGill, who was something of a poet, too, placed the Chattahoochee's origin in Union County, a little to the west. He talked to old-timers who had known the stream before the tourists or the second-homers came—indeed, in the period of the cabin, before that of the condominium.

"Son," one told him, "don't be fooled by her beauty. She looks pretty and she is. She babbles like gossip and giggles like a girl. If you didn't care for beauty, looking at her up here, you might be callin' her a piddling river. But, son, she ain't. I've seen her come out of the mountains like a wild stallion with logs in her mane. I've seen her take grist mills and grind them up in their own stones. I've seen her tear up bridges and twist steel until it looked like bands of hogsheads."

He also answered a question about what it was like in the old days in the mountains where the Chattahoochee's tributaries begin. "It was like a lot of hard work. When you think of the mountains in the old days, don't you go thinkin' about them in terms of picnics and these little walks you call hikes. I remember the ox-carts strainin' and creakin' and complainin' along the ridges. I think of men walking a hundred and sixty miles to Augusta—walked it myself a few times—and fetching back things they needed on their backs, or maybe packin' it in on a horse. Some drove oxen there. It took a couple of months to come and go. A wheel might break or an ox might get sick or break a leg. A man's folks didn't begin to fret about him until nine or ten weeks had passed. . . . Today, I don't know. What with all the radios a-squallin' and all the useless goin' and comin' on the blacktop roads. I sometimes sit here and say to myself that maybe the oxen were the best after all. A fellow sure didn't hitch up and go someplace unless he needed to, or wanted to mighty bad."

Leisure gets more praise on that road now than labor. Travel is reduced to mere pressure on a pedal. All that is true, close to both the sky and the sea. Despite romantic memories of a leisurely old Low-Country South, Hilton Head Island was the scene of mighty labors, too. Black boatmen made lusty song as they propelled barges through the estuaries hereabouts. The same singers produced with much sweat the precious cotton·their barges carried. There are still signs on the island of little creeks shaped with much labor into navigable waterways to plantation docks. Much of the labor was done when whites had fled from the near certainty of summer fevers. And as mountain men feared the flood, islanders bowed to the hurricane. The Chattahoochee came down the hills no more fiercely than winds drove the surf high over the dunes. Sometimes tide and freshet met in the less landscaped land.

The marshes remain. So do the mountains. Conservationists are properly concerned about both. But if ecology is, as most of us have recently learned, the relationship between organisms and their environment, the organism known as man may have altered more than his supposedly much threatened environment. Not all those who come swiftly up the steep roads have Beanie Newhall's concern for her earth. Outboard motors and beer cans have both appeared on the Chattahoochee. There is more litter than labor on the beaches.

Diesels take the place of human muscle and ox power. But distances disappear. Mountain and sea are nigher neighbors. Both are closer to the Atlantas of the land. And not all Atlantans are McGills.

Maybe there is some "useless goin' and comin' on the blacktop roads" and on the new interstates as well. We hardly remember mud. But we know there are creature comforts at both ends of the line. And the possibility is that not even our most dedicated ecologists would alter this situation, though sometimes the human flow may be more damaging than high water or hurricane. Sometimes effluvium seems to move as insistently to beauty as the Chattahoochee pours to the sea. There seems no remedy for this. Perhaps none is desired. Possibly our philosophy in these enlightened years comes to preference for keeping our environment and greedily eating it, too.

June 14, 1973

Ideal Government

Certainly there has been no more noble and persistent endeavor than the quest for the ideal government of a continent or an island. The business goes back way beyond Plato, but in this area it can be precisely placed in 1669 when Sir Anthony Ashley Cooper (later the Earl of Shaftesbury) and John Locke, the philosopher, labored at Exeter House in London to draft the Fundamental Constitution for a Carolina they had never seen. The effort goes on now for Hilton Head Island in the hands of erudite gentlemen from Clemson University, who have the advantage or the disadvantage of having seen the place for which they are expected to provide a grand or at least a compatible design.

Personable Dr. Horace Fleming, now the resident designer on the island, may be a little younger than John Locke was when he helped design a government for Carolina, which certainly was then ecologically intact. Fleming is a political scientist who not long ago was a captain in Vietnam, where some problems of government remain and where he learned from multi-toasting Vietnamese officers that even conviviality may present some hazards. Locke was educated as a physician and was able to insert a gold drainage tube into

451

Shaftesbury's liver so successfully that his patron lived for twenty-four years thereafter.

Their joint design of the Fundamental Constitution for Carolina was not quite so successful an operation. The plan provided for three orders of hereditary nobility: barons, caciques, and landgraves, each with large landed estates. It projected a government "agreeable to the Monarchy under which we live" and avoiding "a numerous democracy." In his study of this enterprise, William Francis Guess described the government as "a timocracy, a state where rule and rank derive from property; not a feudality, where property and rank derive from a heaven-sent ruler." Perhaps there are some similarities to that in the situation on Hilton Head Island today. It was, said Guess, a blueprint for "a landlord's utopia" where the man with the largest acreage had "the loudest voice." Somehow the plan didn't work, just as there is some discontent with a similar situation now.

Dr. Fleming and his colleagues may face similar difficulties in a smaller area. After all, Locke was dealing at a distance with a domain which extended between the 36th and 31st parallels and swept from sea to sea. But that wilderness expanse may have seemed simplicity itself compared with a smaller, more-crowded area about which so many facts may be known that confusion is confronted. Before the new proprietors came here a little over twenty years ago, paradise seemed simple, even if briar-covered and poverty-stricken. Much law was dispensed from the praise houses without need for the intervention of the sheriff. Then Eden was created. The bridge was built. And problems worthy of the attentions of John Locke or even Plato came across it. They have multiplied almost as rapidly as people, pipes, paths, and condominiums.

No wonder it was necessary to bring in outside erudition to confront them. The certainty is that these experts will collect much information about the situation, the needs, the desires, the contentions, and the aspirations here. They will be told much by our contemporary landgraves. The caciques will be heard. The fat cats and the blacks will both have to be listened to. Possibly from all will come a harmony, not a dissonance. There are no Spaniards threatening us from the south, though there are some fears of a sort of Miami miasma. The North only threatens the island with enthusiastic newcomers. Even the blacks have much to be thankful for on an island where there are more jobs than people. This is an ideal island in so many ways that the political scientists from the college in the hills may find their task only the perfectibility of perfection.

Certainly a golden tube has been inserted into the innards of this island. As in the case of Shaftesbury and Locke, it may turn out to be a more effective instrument than any Fundamental Constitution. Still a little bile may have been produced which will require some attention by the professors. The islanders will eagerly await their ministrations, not as theorists, but as therapists.

June 21, 1973

Teeth and Travel

What's happening to this island may be best indicated by the fact that an orthodontist is opening an office here, but no periodontist has yet appeared on the scene. Braces and bicycles become our symbols instead of gums and golf.

More reports come from our travelers. Katherine Derby sent words from the isles of Greece: "Delos—such a small island with so much history. The light had a rare quality—the sea so blue with rather fierce white waves beating on the rocks—flowers everywhere. Houses slightly restored from 200 B.C., floor mosaics still beautiful. Seems back then it was the Hilton Head of these parts. People came from afar to live there. Forty thousand of them and the island is only four miles long by one mile wide! Makes Charles Fraser a piker."

If correct, that really was packing them in. Maybe that was the basis for the rule that nobody should die and nobody should be born on Delos.

In Switzerland, Hugh and Nancy Fraser found the Castle of Chillon as cold and dark and dreary as Lord Byron reported it to be nearly two centuries ago. Lake Geneva, they reported by post card, is "beautiful but so polluted, so we keep fighting for Victoria Bluff."

The Sojourner, who once lived in an apartment called *Riant Château,* or "Laughing House," just up the shore from the castle, wonders whether the swans have survived the soiling of the lovely lake. He suspects they have, because the pollution did not start last year. Begun in the ninth century, Château Chillon had toilets high up among the battlements, so constructed that, protruding from the castle walls, no flushing was needed, and Lake Geneva began to be a septic tank in the Middle Ages.

The Derby report, about the restorations on Delos as an early people-packed resort, raises the question as to what the archeologists will find on Hilton Head Island two thousand years hence. Most of our mosaics are made of vinyl. Most of our buildings are made of wood without benefit of building code. It did not take long for the structures of the Civil War city here to disappear. Little more than belt buckles and bottles remain. More of the last certainly may be found when the digging here begins two millenniums from now. Then the shell rings of the Indians may still be more tangible than relics left by Union troops or the second Yankee invasion of recent years. Still, some rusted remains of the intensive-care vehicle may lead to the supposition that no one was permitted to die or be born on Hilton Head Island in the long-past little time of its flowering today.

Possibly by then, humans, grown physically perfect, will wonder about the wires found on the teeth of small skulls. Still, the possibility is that at that future time both the diggers and the dug will be lost on a planet which began to pollute itself long before Chillon was built. But if any explorers from outer space then come poking around this dead planet, they will certainly find golf balls here which their deceased owners could not find when they were puttering about the landscaped ecology in their time. The bottle and the ball may be our artifacts, and our shell rings may be composed of a puzzling collection of cans, bereft of the labels that they once contained beer.

Being optimistic, it may be said that the human species will survive and that some pretty lady will come on a guided tour of this old place a couple of thousand years from now and send to friends the then electronic or nuclear equivalent of a post card. She may write, as Katherine didn't, "Having a wonderful time. Wish you were here." It is also to be hoped that she can report that the light has a rare quality—flowers everywhere—the sea blue, and its waves still dashing white on the shore.

June 28, 1973

Time and *The Packet*

Time, of course, is a factor in the celebration of all events. We are waiting for the two-century mark for the bicentennial of the Declaration of Independence. Some, as they wait, seem a little embarrassed as to how to celebrate revolution in a world which to some seems much too revolution-prone. No such reservations mark those who founded *The Island Packet* just three years ago in an enterprise which seemed brash, if not radical. But time is of the essence in glorious remembrance whether it be for two centuries or for three years. It does not take too long to create pride and nostalgia. Both may grow more quickly on Hilton Head Island than in the aftermath of Philadelphia. Here pride in growth is sometimes attended by pain. And any looking back across change in forest and on shore creates a sort of instant nostalgia. Here nostalgia is like Spanish moss hung in the memory with the late afternoon sun upon it.

July seems an odd time for the initiation of great events. The flies were thick and the heat intense in Philadelphia that summer when Jefferson wrote his—and our—Declaration. Certainly, though the summer folk crowded to this shore, it was hot enough in July 1970 when the first issue of *The Packet*, replete with typographical errors and wild hyphenations, was produced in an eight-by-eleven-foot room. Possibly a poor thing but our own, that first issue filled its producers' hearts with pride and was taken by other islanders to their hearts. It was nurtured by all-island affection as a new and possibly precocious member of the family. It was launched, as its sanguine crew announced quite factually, with a shoestring for a sail. There were breezes enough to fill it. The weather was only occasionally rough. The paper expanded, like the chambered nautilus, from room to room in the DeVries building. Now we're on our second alligator by our perfect lagoon.

Like the rest of the island, *The Packet* sails in growth, but what it most cherishes is the guidance of remembrance. Old people, like those who once seemed the principal migrants to Hilton Head Island, must make their good, green memories of it quickly. Three years may not be long in the history of a republic. It is a good span in the story of people who came here in hope of making their last years their best ones. And they are the ones most apt to be startled by the advance of mastodon machines and the howl of hammers where once only bird song filled the woods. The shattered image makes the one remembered most important. And though it may seem a paradox, the memory of the past may provide the best patttern for the future.

At the outset, the crew of *The Island Packet* took boldly as its anthem a verse by Edward Lear, who added a talent for nonsense verse to great ability as a painter of birds. It ran like this:

> They went to sea in a sieve, they did;
>   In a sieve they went to sea. . . .
> And when the sieve turned round and round,
> And everyone cried, "You'll all be drowned!"
> They called aloud, "Our sieve ain't big;
> But we don't care a button; we don't care a fig—
>   In a sieve we'll go to sea!"

Miraculously, perhaps, there have been no leaks. And miraculously, perhaps, the island *The Packet* was launched to serve remains beautiful and beloved. The prospect of wreck has been forever present, but the shore has remained a haven. It needs now only the cherished nostalgia for the shore first seen to be the shore, despite all things, still preserved for delight. *The Packet* still has no other mission than to make homesickness for the past the design for the home of the heart in the future. And that goes for both the island and the republic.

After three years *The Island Packet*'s flags are flying. The wind is fresh and strong. The sea is blue and hearts are high. Sail on!

July 5, 1973

Index

Index

THE GENTLEMANLY SERPENT *and Other Columns from a Newspaperman in Paradise*

Manufactured by Kingsport Press, Inc., Kingsport, Tennessee.

Composed in VideoComp Baskerville with selected lines of display in Monotype Bulmer. Printed by offset lithography on Warren's University Text, an acid-free paper, watermarked with the University of South Carolina Press colophon. Bound in Elephant Hide paper.

Designed by Robert L. Nance.